The Way to Make Wine

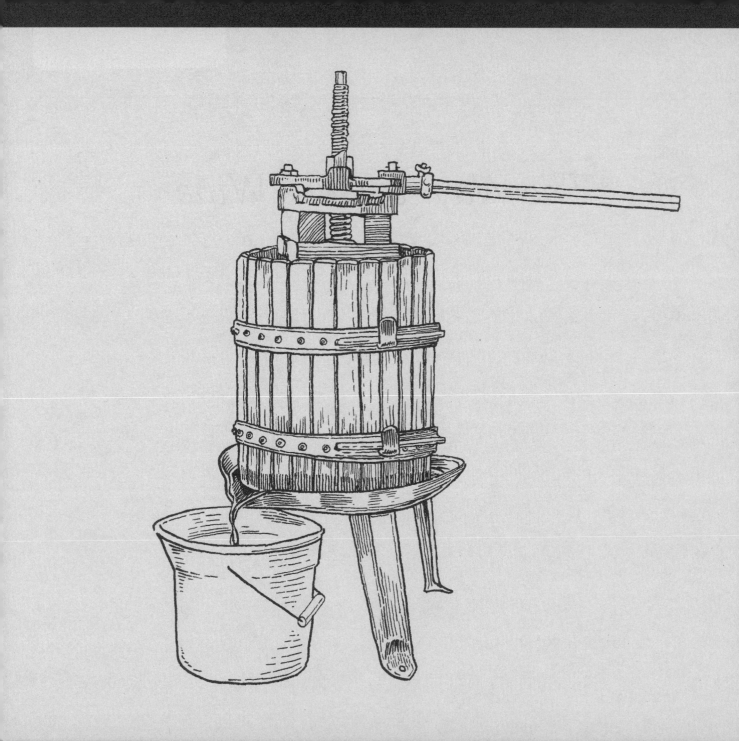

The Way to Make Wine

HOW TO CRAFT SUPERB TABLE WINES AT HOME

Sheridan Warrick

To Carol —
Sheridan Warrick

UNIVERSITY OF CALIFORNIA PRESS

Berkeley   Los Angeles   London

University of California Press, one of the most distinguished university presses in the United States, enriches lives around the world by advancing scholarship in the humanities, social sciences, and natural sciences. Its activities are supported by the UC Press Foundation and by philanthropic contributions from individuals and institutions. For more information, visit www.ucpress.edu.

All illustrations by Mary Sievert, Sievert Illustration & Design.

University of California Press
Berkeley and Los Angeles, California

University of California Press, Ltd.
London, England

Library of Congress Cataloging-in-Publication Data
Warrick, Sheridan F.
    The way to make wine : how to craft superb table wines at home / Sheridan Warrick.
      p. cm.
    Includes bibliographical references and index.
    ISBN-13 978-0-520-23869-5 (cloth : alk. paper), ISBN-10 0-520-23869-9 (cloth : alk. paper)
    ISBN-13 978-0-520-24719-2 (pbk. : alk. paper), ISBN-10 0-520-24719-1 (pbk. : alk. paper)
    1. Wine and wine making—Amateurs' manuals.   I. Title.
    TP548.2.W366   2006
    641.8'72—dc22   2005016914

Manufactured in Canada
15 14 13 12 11 10 09 08 07 06
10 9 8 7 6 5 4 3 2 1

dedicated to karen

with karen knows what

and karen knows why

The sun, with all those planets revolving around it and dependent on it, can still ripen a bunch of grapes as if it had nothing else in the universe to do.

GALILEO GALILEI

I can no more think of my own life without thinking of wine and wines and where they grew for me and why I drank them when I did and why I picked the grapes and where I opened the oldest procurable bottles, and all that, than I can remember living before I breathed.

M. F. K. FISHER, *The Book of California Wine*

When wine takes hold of a person, it tends to sink its claws in pretty deep.

JANCIS ROBINSON, *Tasting Pleasure: Confessions of a Wine Lover*

Contents

Part Two. MAKING EVEN BETTER WINE

Tables

Acknowledgments

MY WIFE, KAREN, AND I MADE OUR FIRST WINE from grapes we picked ourselves, starting in the vineyard just past dawn so the bunches would still hold the autumn night's chill. I remember the vines' scraggly bark, the brick-colored earth, and the spicy taste of the grapes—Merlot berries so sweet we couldn't resist biting off mouthfuls. We both chewed the tough skins for a long time, trying to imagine what sort of wine the fruit would make. Something dark and rich, I remember wishing. And when a week later that's what flowed from our press, we were hooked. Now, a quarter-century later, we still are. For our happy condition we're deeply in debt to Si Foote and his late wife, June, whom we met through my wise and thoughtful parents, Betsey and Sherry Warrick. From the Footes' hillside vineyard on Napa's Silverado Trail came splendid Merlot and Cabernet grapes. From their hand-built home and home winery came wine-country lore, enological insights, and great companionship. For our instant welcome into the winemaking fraternity, I'm likewise indebted to their friends Gordon and Marion Davies of St. Helena, who were unselfish with their time and their crusher-stemmer, and to Angie Christmann of Santa Cruz, who didn't bat an eye when a couple of greenhorns arrived to drive off with her floor corker.

Many other people helped shape this book, although any lapses of interpretation or fact are mine alone. Mike and Anne Dashe, of Dashe Cellars in Oakland, bravely hired me as an intern for their 2001 crush—I was the slowpoke at tank shoveling—and generously rewarded me in dollars, wine, and insider knowledge. Later, Mike offered many helpful comments on the manuscript. Matt Smith, assistant winemaker at Dashe and proprietor of his own Black-smith Cellars, tutored me sagely in barrel care, sulfite science, and lab techniques. Meanwhile, I turned regularly to Peter Brehm of Brehm Vineyards for his great grapes and calm counsel. And I learned much from Rhone Ranger Steve Edmunds during days at his acclaimed Berke-ley winery, Edmunds St. John.

Jay Smith, a treasured friend and rising home vintner, contributed more to the book than he knows; I cannot thank him enough. Thanks, too, to his wife, Andrea Paulos, and their daughter, Mabel, for their engagement and forbearance during many hours of wine work. Once and present winemakers Dave Coder, Heath Curdts, David Darlington, Ken Winchester, David Lansford, Carlo Calabi, and Elmer and Pam Grossman all shared their knowledge of enology, and the book's much better for it. Larry Meinert, professor of geology at Smith College and a master home vintner, greatly improved the manuscript with his detailed critique. Mickey Butts, Val Cipollone, Ed Dolnick, Bob Doyle, Connie Hale, Melissa Houtte, Peter Jaret, Tony Schmitz, and David Stanford offered their support, friendship, and wisdom on the making of books. Bernie Rooney and Homer Smith of Oak Barrel Winecraft in Berkeley supplied me with sound advice and good gear, while Graeme Blackmore and Michael Butler of Kermit Lynch Wine Merchant, Peter Eastlake and Steve Graf of Vintage Berkeley, and Greg Estes of Vino! kept my palate in tune. I'm grateful, too, to Sunshine Cowgill, Nicole Haller-Wilson, and Lisa Van de Water of the Wine Lab in Napa; Nancy Freire of Vino Fino Consulting; Rebecca Staffel of the Doe Coover Agency; Dick and Mary Hafner of Hafner Vineyard—and especially Gene Holtan and Bill Prochnow for our terrific wine labels. To those who've helped tend the wine over the years—Rob Bosworth, Nancy Lewis, and Marty Jara—may the hinges of our friend-ship never grow rusty nor our wines musty. And toasts, too, to Blake Edgar and Laura Harger of UC Press for their astute editing, to Bob Holmes for his stellar photography, and to Mary Sievert for her stylish and informative illustrations.

Introduction

REAL WINE, REAL ENJOYMENT

ONE WARM SUMMER EVENING, with smoke from the grill drifting by, I poured a glass of Syrah for a guest. She took a sip. "You made this?" she said, with her eyebrows arched. "That's very nice wine."

The glow I felt just then was surely from my own swallow of Syrah—or maybe not. My wife and I bottled our first wine more than 20 years ago: a Napa Valley Merlot, deep purple and crystal clear with a clean, pleasing aroma and a soft, fruity flavor. We poured it for friends at dinner parties, gave it as gifts to family members, traded bottles to other winemakers, and generally served it and enjoyed it the way we would any good wine. Over the years, as I've pulled corks and refilled glasses, I've heard those words and seen that astonished look many times.

We've all soaked up so many images—of Depression-era rotgut brewed in bathtubs and outlandish grape mashings à la *I Love Lucy*. I've met more than one person whose grandfather made his own in a dank basement smelling of mold and vinegar. And I've had to smile and comment on murky stuff that—how to say it nicely?—was interesting and unusual.

"Real" wine versus homemade. Home winemaking does have a bit of a sour reputation,

but I'll let you in on a secret: there's nothing magical about top-quality winemaking, never mind what the world's wine experts would have you believe. I've made wine in lots as small as 10 gallons, and I've worked in wineries that produced thousands of gallons. At Dashe Cellars, a premium winery in Northern California, I've put bunches by the ton through a crusher, pumped over, punched down, shoveled out tanks waist deep in grape skins, topped up barrels, run lab tests, made sulfite additions, tasted, blended, bottled, and labeled. It's true: the pros know a lot of tricks and own loads of equipment. But actually, apart from the size of the tanks, there's not a whole lot that's different. Most of what the world's top vintners do you can now do at home.

A new view of quality. Consider yourself blessed to be living at the height of winemaking's golden age. In wineries around the world, enologists are perfecting the details of what it takes to make delicious wine. And while they forge ahead—running lab tests, conducting tastings—you and I get to ferment our wine with special yeasts they have bred, keep it clear and clean with smart methods they have refined, and bottle it with simple tools they have devised. That means we really can produce homemade wines with the superb flavors we've come to expect of wines from the store—reds with bold, berryish flavors that linger in your mouth; whites with fruity or flowery aromas and tastes that are smooth and delicate or pleasantly piercing.

ANSWERS TO SIX FREQUENTLY ASKED QUESTIONS

Can't I make wine with grapes from the supermarket? Sure, but you'll eventually wish you'd taken up skydiving, decoy carving, or some other hobby. Industrial-scale wineries regularly use ordinary grapes to make bland white wines that they blend with more flavorful whites or flavor and mix into coolers and other drinks. That's fine, but nothing you can find in the market will deliver the distinctive flavors of the classic grapes whose names you see on better wine bottles—Cabernet, Chardonnay, Merlot, Syrah, and Zinfandel, to name a few.

Won't I need a lot of expensive equipment? No, although it's easy to shell out for a garage-ful of gizmos. Depending on the time you devote to bargain hunting and the amount of wine you make, you could invest as little as you'd spend on a case of inexpensive wine. It's more likely that in the first year you'll run up a gear and supplies bill equal to what you might pay for a few cases of notable wine. Renting some key pieces of equipment may nudge the cost up a notch. But if you make wine a second year—and why wouldn't you?—your outlay falls to a fraction of that initial one. You'll need some fresh supplies, and you'll run the same rental fees, but otherwise you're set. (For a rundown on essential gear, see chapter 2.)

Which is easier to start with, red wine or white? Many winemakers feel that reds are easier to make and more forgiving than whites. Red grapes' pigments and tannins help protect the wine from spoilage, and the bolder flavors can help make flaws seem minor. White wines, on the other hand, are generally deemed fussier and more demanding. All fermenting wines tend to warm up as they ferment. But ask any vintner: white wines taste better—fruitier and more lively—when they're fermented at fairly low temperatures. For you, that can mean extra bother and expense (for some type of cooling setup). What's more, with fewer pigments and tannins and often less alcohol, white wines can be more vulnerable to spoilage and oxidation. If you're not careful, that brilliant, pale gold wine you're hoping to make will instead come out hazy and brown.

Isn't the best way to crush grapes to stomp them with my feet? For thousands of years, villagers in France and Italy and Spain climbed into vats and stood shoulder to shoulder, stepping in time to music on whole bunches of slippery grapes. The idea is to break open every berry, or most of them, anyhow, before bucketing out the sticky skins and juice and starting over. It's hard, messy work, especially if you decide, as do most vintners these days, that you want the grapes to end up in the fermenter without the stems, which can contribute a green, or "vegetal" flavor. Whatever glory you feel while tramping out the vintage will quickly be dimmed by the task of dredging out the stems by hand. Most home winemakers take the easy route and rent a crusher-stemmer. Whole grape clusters go into the hopper on top, while crushed grapes and bare stems drop separately into tubs below. (For more on crushing and destemming, see chapter 3.)

Won't I have to wait years to drink my wine? Not necessarily. When it comes to Zinfandel, Syrah, and today's other fruit-forward wines, drink up and don't look back. It's true that vintners need a bit of patience that beer brewers do without. But if you've ever planned ahead for a vacation, you have all the patience you need. Suppose you follow the classic schedule: fermentation in fall, cellar work in winter and spring, bottling in summer—say, June. When can you start pulling corks? Right away! Once the wine has aged a few months or a year, it will almost certainly taste better—more rounded out and polished. But don't wait for magic to happen. Most of the world's wines are drunk young because they're best then. You'll of course want to lay away some wine from each vintage to see how it changes year to year, particularly if it's red. (For more on aging wines, see pages 88 and 214.)

Every wine I buy says "contains sulfites" on the label. Can I make mine without them? Possibly, if you're fanatical about cleanliness, bottle the wine as soon as it's made, and then guzzle it down as if there's no tomorrow, which there really isn't for wines finished without sulfites. Otherwise, to make clear, clean-tasting, long-lived wine you'll want to do as virtually all professional winemakers do and add tiny amounts at several stages along the way. Used as these pros use it, in precisely measured parts per million, sulfite is a flavorless, odorless, harmless additive that protects crushed grapes and finished wine from all kinds of problems, including bacterial spoilage, browning, and oxidation. (For details on how sulfites protect wines, see chapter 14, page 189.)

FIVE GOOD REASONS TO MAKE YOUR OWN

But why not take the easiest route and just go buy your wines already made? I've pondered that question myself, usually while standing in soggy shoes on a concrete floor and staring at the next 20 cases of empty bottles waiting to be filled and corked. And the verdict? I'd never let a couple of cold feet put me off winemaking's pleasures.

The friendship factor. As hobbies go, winemaking is among the most classy and companionable. At several stages—crushing, pressing, fermenting, blending, and bottling—my wife and I often invite friends over. The old saying's really true: many hands make light work. But more to the point, working together makes pouring the wine at a dinner later an even bigger pleasure.

A world of wisdom. There's a deeper side. You may have some flush and bibulous pals who've tasted their way through the great wines of France, Italy, Spain, and Germany. That's of course the traditional way to become a world-class expert. But once you're actually a winemaker, once you've turned messy grapes into smooth wine, your own knowledge becomes intense and intimate. The meaning of a wine's legs, the clues to quality in its aroma, the importance of its color and clarity—these are things you'll know by heart. And you'll never be bamboozled by a wine snob again.

The pull of the past. At some point, when you're up to your elbows in fermenting grapes and waiting for the action to wind down, it'll dawn on you that you're acting as midwife at one of the true miracles of life. You'll realize the steps you're taking and the sensations you're feeling are hardly different from those of, say, a Mediterranean winemaker born at the time of Jesus. And if a 2,000-year-old craft seems notable, consider that for some 3,000 years before the birth of Jesus grape wine had been made in places such as Persia and Crete. You're joining one of the oldest fellowships on earth.

The bank account boon. Psychic payoffs are all well and good, but the fact is that making your own is also a fine way to get wine at a good price. If you're really a wine lover—and why bother to make it if you're not?—your passion probably costs you at least several hundred dollars a year. For less than that you can equip your winery and buy enough grapes to turn out several cases of noteworthy wine. The following year, with your gear already bought, your cost falls by half.

The dining dimension. Of course, there's the pleasure of the tasting itself. You won't turn out a sumptuous Châteauneuf-du-Pape or a silky Pouilly-Fuissé in your first or even fifth vintage. But so what? You can make really delicious American wines: deep, flavorful reds perfect to enjoy with tomatoey pastas and grilled meats; crisp, fruity whites to go with salmon and roast chicken.

LEGAL? IT'S AN AMERICAN TRADITION

You may have heard that President Thomas Jefferson hoped to build a winery at his Virginia plantation and that he once said, "Good wine is a necessity of life for me." But did you know that home winemaking has been practiced from the nation's founding to the present? Even during Prohibition, 1919 to 1933, when you could go to jail for making or selling alcoholic beverages, it was deemed legitimate for each head of household to produce up to 200 gallons a year of "nonintoxicating cider and fruit juices," as the law then put it. "Although too much wine can obviously prove intoxicating," writes Paul Lukacs in his book *American Vintage,* "the Internal Revenue Service, which was in charge of enforcement, had no intention of pursuing home winemakers. The statute read 'nonintoxicating,' not 'nonalcoholic,' and what happened in private homes was private business."

Today's rules—and this is a direct quote from current federal law—permit any adult to make "(1) 200 gallons per calendar year if there are two or more adults residing in the household, or (2) 100 gallons per calendar year if there is only one adult residing in the household." The law goes on to say that the wine "may be removed from the premises where made for personal or family use including use at organized affairs, exhibitions or competitions, such as homemaker's contests, tastings or judging." In practice, the only thing you can't legally do with your wine is sell it.

HOW TO USE THIS BOOK

I've made just one big assumption, and that's that you're already a wine lover. I don't necessarily assume you're a globe-trotting oenophile or a major hoarder of fancy bottles. I figure simply that you're someone like me—someone who regularly drinks wine with dinner and enjoys getting to know more about it.

Where to begin. You can dive into the pages wherever you like, of course, but if you're just getting started, I suggest reading all of part one, "Success with Reds and Whites" (chapters 1 through 10). If you've already made wine at least once and have stocked up on the basic equipment and supplies, there's no reason you shouldn't skip ahead to chapter 3, "When Red Means Go." Just remember that you may want to go back and scan the first two chapters for tips. And if you've been at it long enough to have several vintages in your cellar—that is, you're up on the basics—you'll nonetheless find useful methods and insights in part two, "Making Even Better Wine."

About wine kits. This book focuses on the steps you can take to make dry table wines from virtually any kind of fresh or frozen wine grapes—information that will also serve you well if you plan to make wine from a kit. The latest kits, available at most beer- and winemaking supply shops, come with complete instructions and typically include a foil bag of

Winemaking at a Glance—a Checklist and Calendar

Making wine isn't hard, but it does require bits of work year-round. What are the main tasks at each stage? Here's an overview to help you plan. Of course, with today's supplies you can make wine anytime. But the stages flow most naturally when you follow the ancient cycle and gear up in summer for what vintners call "the crush." As you'll see, one year's cycle overlaps the next.

JUNE TO AUGUST: *Get Ready*

1. Order grapes or grape juice.
2. Find and wash the fermenter and tools.
3. Stock up on yeast and supplies.
4. Arrange to rent or borrow a crusher and press.

AUGUST TO OCTOBER: *The Crush*

1. Bring in and crush the grapes.
2. Test and correct the sugar and acid, if needed.
3. Start the fermentation.
4. Punch down twice a day for about a week.
5. Press the wine.

OCTOBER TO FEBRUARY: *Cellar Work*

1. Finish the secondary fermentation.

(continued)

pasteurized concentrated grape juice with the sugar and acid levels adjusted into the ideal range. They also contain yeasts, yeast nutrients, fining agents, preservatives, stabilizers, and, sometimes, oak chips. However, different makers include different components, which is why you won't find details on making kit wines in this book. Instead, the book can fill you in on the whole winemaking process. You'll at least find out what tasks you've dodged. And you might find yourself inspired to get more involved and make better wine.

About fruit wines. Since I'm assuming you're devoted to good wines, I'm also assuming that the ones you love most are table wines made from classic European wine grapes—not from blackberries, say, or pears. You can of course make delicious fermented drinks from many kinds of fruit or honey, and people have been doing so for centuries, especially in places such as England where wine grapes have trouble ripening. But fruit wines are often assertively sweet and may lack the subtle and complex flavors that make grape wines especially good with food. What's more, fermenting other fruits requires techniques that are beyond the scope of this book.

About winemaking words and terms. Fining, racking, pumping over, punching down, topping up, barreling down, cellaring—every pursuit, from tennis to fly-fishing, has its own jargon, and winemaking is no exception. What's the term for the act of breaking up the cap of grape skins that rises to the top of your fermenting wine? It's fourth in the list above. Suffice it to say that I've kept the language simple but couldn't help introducing a handful of special words for which there's no everyday equivalent.

About measurements. I've used the standard—if awkward—mix of American and metric units of measure. You'll find that for volumes I've used mostly gallons and for weights mostly grams. I say "mostly" because there's no way around sometimes scrambling the systems. The big glass jugs used in home winemaking, called carboys, hold an even 5 gallons, while ordinary wine bottles hold 750 milliliters. Grapes are often priced by the pound or ton, while yeast is sold in 5-gram packets. In a perfect world, our measures would be like our money—divisible by 10, mostly—but for now we're stuck with conversions such as 3.785 liters to the gallon, and 28.3 grams to the ounce.

2. Rack (transfer) the wine to a clean container.
3. Wait for it to settle and clarify.
4. Rack again and start oak aging, if desired.

MARCH TO APRIL: *Following Through*

1. Taste and test the finished wine.
2. Round up corks and bottles.
3. Arrange to rent or borrow a corker.

MAY TO AUGUST: *Bottling and Aging*

1. Rack and bottle.
2. Make up a label.
3. Store the filled bottles in a cool place.

Part One

SUCCESS WITH REDS AND WHITES

What's the single most important thing to know about winemaking? That you can use the same principles and practices to make most kinds of wine. That's why in this book you won't find separate recipes keyed to different grape varieties. Instead, you'll find universal methods that will help you make almost any type of dry table wine. Do you plan to make red or white? Once you've made that choice, the steps are largely the same whether you make, say, Zinfandel or Syrah or go instead toward Sauvignon Blanc or Pinot Gris. There are of course options and exceptions and refinements—but not to the basics. The goal in both cases is to capture the true flavors of the fruit at harvest.

1

GRAPES AND OTHER INGREDIENTS

THERE'S MORE THAN ONE WAY to get started in winemaking. Consider my friend who, on a picnic outing with pals in the Napa Valley, pulled up beside a tractor hauling a trailer full of grapes. He poked his head out the window. "Got any for us?" he yelled. The tractor driver waved an arm. "Still some out in that vineyard," he said. "If you want 'em, help yourself." The surprised picnickers laughed, but in minutes they were on their knees beside the dusty vines, hacking with pocketknives at the clusters of grapes. Hours later, with a few hundred pounds of fruit in the trunk, they sobered up. "We didn't have the slightest idea what to do with it all," my friend says. He called the owner of a beer-brewing shop and begged for a rundown.

That was 30 years ago. He now owns a vineyard in Washington State and runs a business selling grapes to home winemakers around the country. He has since made many remarkable wines but swears the Zinfandel from those first grapes—which they crushed themselves that night—could hold its own against any of them.

The moment of truth: Wine is ready to pour—and enjoy—as soon as it's in the bottle. Of course, age can improve wines that are carefully stored.

In other words, making good wine your first time out, or your seventh, is not such a difficult trick. The key thing is to find good grapes. That doesn't mean you have to haunt the Napa Valley hoping you'll bump into a generous grower. It does mean that before you start rearranging your garage or investing in equipment, you'll want to know what grapes you'll begin with. Put aside for now the choice between Zinfandel and Cabernet, Chardonnay and Sauvignon Blanc. Here's a rundown on some more basic options.

About two and a half pounds of grapes— that can be as many as a dozen bunches— go into each standard-size bottle of wine.

Fresh fruit. Grapes right off the vine are the gold standard of winemaking. The most desirable varieties are in the species *Vitis vinifera,* the European wine grape. Unlike other grapes and virtually all other fruit, vinifera grapes ripen to have an ideal mix of sugar, acid, and flavor compounds. What you get, after fermentation, is wonderfully balanced wine with enough alcohol to stay fresh-tasting and stable for months and even years. What's more, the many varieties of European wine grapes have for centuries been bred and selected to differ in remarkable ways—some ripening earlier, some later; some producing wines with exceptionally deep color, or extra acid, or stronger fruity or floral aromas. Cabernet Sauvignon, for instance—a king among wine grapes—is known to be a centuries-old hybrid of two venerable Europeans: Cabernet Franc, a full-flavored red, and Sauvignon Blanc, a grape that makes brisk, fruity white wines. Whether the grapes spontaneously crossed in the vineyard or were deliberately mated is not known. But clearly someone tasted the fruit of the union and chose to propagate it. Cabernet Sauvignon is now among the most widely planted wine grapes in the world.

Luckily, you don't have go to Europe to find great grapes. Wine grapes in the vinifera species—as well as hybrids between that and native American species—are now grown in most of the 50 United States. Check first with the staff at a brew shop in your area to see if they offer fresh grapes during the fall harvest season. (Start asking in June or July.) Ideally, the fruit would be trucked from a vineyard within a day's drive—any farther than that and the grapes can spoil in transit. Ask the price per pound, and expect to hear that the grapes cost quite a lot more than the ones at the supermarket. Find out what services the shop offers. If you're hoping to make red wine, will the shop crush the grapes for you, or rent you a crusher? If you're making white wine, will they also press the crushed grapes so you can take home just the juice, ready to ferment? Or will you need to rent a crusher and a press? How much will it all cost? (For details on procuring fresh wine grapes, including hybrids of American grape species, see chapter 11, page 137.)

Frozen grapes. Many brew shops now sell high-quality crushed red grapes and white grape juices (in making white wines, the skins are always excluded). They come frozen solid in small tubs and large drums. More than a dozen different wine grape varieties are offered. Here's a partial list of the red and white grapes that have been offered by a supplier that delivers them, frozen, to home vintners all over North America: Barbera, Cabernet Franc, Cabernet Sauvignon, Carignan, Chardonnay, Gewürztraminer, Grenache, Merlot, Mourvèdre, Muscat, Nebbiolo, Petite Sirah, Pinot Noir, Riesling, Sangiovese, Sauvignon Blanc, Syrah, and Zinfandel. If you, like many wine lovers, prefer your Cabernet softened with a dose of Merlot, you may be able to order a blend. Once the containers thaw, you simply add yeast and carry on as if you'd done all the crushing and pressing yourself.

> *The juice of most wine grapes is nearly colorless. The deep color of red wines comes from pigments in the skins.*

TABLE 1 *How Much Wine Do You Want to Make?*

As a general rule, 50 pounds of grapes is about the smallest amount that's practical to make into wine. That may sound like a lot, but keep in mind that it fits into a single 6.5-gallon plastic pail. Actually, 400 to 500 pounds is a convenient amount—it fits nicely into a 55-gallon drum. When making white wines, it's necessary first to extract the grape juice from the skins and stems, which make up about a fifth of the weight. (These are discarded.) Alternatively, you can purchase already extracted wine-grape juice, fresh or frozen, in which case you'll most likely order your juice by the gallon instead of by the pound.

RED WINES				
Weight of Whole Grapes	Volume of Crushed Grapes	Minimum Fermenter Volume	Volume of Finished Wine	Quantity of Bottles Needed
50 pounds	5 gallons	6.5 gallons	3.5–4 gallons	1.5 cases
100 pounds	10 gallons	20 gallons	7–8 gallons	3+ cases
200 pounds	20 gallons	32 gallons	15–16 gallons	6–7 cases
400 pounds	40 gallons	55 gallons	30–32 gallons	12–14 cases

WHITE WINES					
Weight of Whole Grapes	Volume of Extracted Juice	Weight of Juice	Minimum Fermenter Volume	Volume of Finished Wine	Quantity of Bottles Needed
65 pounds	5 gallons	50 pounds	10 gallons	4.5+ gallons	2 cases
100 pounds	8 gallons	80 pounds	10 gallons	7+ gallons	3 cases
200 pounds	16 gallons	160 pounds	20 gallons	15+ gallons	6 cases
500 pounds	40 gallons	400 pounds	55 gallons	39 gallons	16.5 cases

So far frozen grapes and juice are available in only a few shops nationwide, but you can also order them online or by phone (see page 233). One winemaker I met—a Californian born and raised in Italy, where as a boy he watched his father turn newly harvested grapes into wine—had made his first batch from frozen crushed Barbera grapes. With no further knowledge than his own faint memory of the way things were done back home, he had made a remarkably clean and well-balanced wine. He seemed amazed that anyone found it drinkable.

THE YEASTS WITHIN

For all but a half-century of the 6,000 years in which people have been turning grapes into wine, vintners simply crushed ripe fruit and waited. Nature, or God, would do the rest—and almost always did. It took Louis Pasteur, the nineteenth-century French scientist, to figure out that the *agents provocateurs* were living yeasts, sugar-happy single-celled microbes present on grapes and in every batch of fermenting wine.

With no encouragement, native yeasts at large in the winery or transported from the vineyard often spontaneously set to work on a vat of crushed grapes, starting a full-on "natural" fermentation. It sounds ideal—why should anyone interfere?—and in fact some modern vintners make their wines exactly that way. But those free-range yeasts can be unpredictable, sometimes generating off flavors and odors, sometimes giving out before all the sugar is gone. Most modern vintners—and you should count yourself among them—hedge their bets and add cultured yeasts with specific traits, such as the ability to thrive in the presence of alcohol.

It's amazing to consider what the tiny creatures pull off. Just a few tablespoons of yeast cells added to 500 pounds of

Stems make up about 3 percent of the weight of whole grape clusters, skins and seeds up to 22 percent. One gallon of destemmed crushed grapes weighs about 10 pounds.

crushed ripe grapes will double in hours, doubling again and again over the next several days in a classic out-of-control population boom. When the yeasts are raging, a single milliliter of wine—a quarter-teaspoon—may hold as many as 100 million cells. By the time the mayhem ends when the yeasts run out of food, they will have consumed virtually all the sugar,

In pursuit of rich flavors, grape growers these days sometimes let their fruit get so ripe that it's wise to reduce the sweetness a bit by adding some water—ideally chlorine-free springwater from the supermarket. But if you add only water, you'll dilute the acid level of the finished wine, possibly leaving it with a flat or flabby taste. The solution is to add acid as well, bringing the grape juice back up to the acidity it had originally, a step often called acidulating. The right choice is tartaric acid, which occurs naturally in grapes. (Stay away from acid blends sold in brew shops.) Buy 4 ounces or more when you're assembling your ingredients and equipment, and be happy if you don't need to use it—it's cheap insurance. If, on the other hand, your hydrometer shows that your grapes contain a less than ideal amount of sugar, you'll need to add ordinary table sugar. (For details on adjusting oversweet grapes or on adding sugar to underripe grapes, see pages 42 and 169.)

generating almost 40 pounds of carbon dioxide gas and more than 5 gallons of alcohol. Just a day after you launch your fermentation, you'll be up to your elbows in punch-drunk yeasts, and it won't be long before a faint aroma of toasted bread follows you everywhere—your secret badge of honor.

Brew shops typically stock several varieties of wine yeast, usually in flat packets (5 grams each) similar to those for baking yeast sold in supermarkets. Don't get hung up on the differences. For most red wines you simply want a strong, heat- and alcohol-tolerant yeast such as Pasteur Red. For white wines, you want a kind that ferments more slowly and prospers at cool temperatures, such as Premier Cuvée. Don't believe that if you use, say, Champagne yeast to make Zinfandel, it will somehow end up tasting like Moët & Chandon. Other things—the grapes themselves and the length and temperature of the fermentation—have far more to do with your wine's flavor. You may someday want to experiment with specialized yeast strains (see page 177). But keep in mind that many wineries use basic yeasts and stick with them year after year.

THE OTHER BUGS

Yeasts aren't the only organisms happy to make a home in crushed grapes. Vintners have long known that by the time the ravenous yeasts finish up, special benign bacteria are usually in there launching a secondary fermentation. Unlike yeasts, who love sugar, these "malolactic bugs" gobble a harsh kind of grape acid (malic) and turn it into a gentle one (lactic). Miraculously, it seems, the wine's flavor softens. (For more on this process, see chapters 4, 9, 10, and 13.)

In the past, winemakers simply hoped that bacteria around the winery would hop in and do the job—and often they would. But *often* isn't *always*. So enologists singled out and bred the finicky microbes, and now anyone can snip open a packet or screw open a jar and just add them, greatly upping the chance of turning out pleasing, food-friendly red or full-bodied white wines. (Light, fruity white wines don't usually undergo malolactic fermentation.) When you go shopping for wine yeasts and other items, ask also about cultured malolactic bacteria, available in liquid form or freeze-dried in slim foil packets that hold about 1.5 grams of "inoculant"—that is, many millions of dormant bacteria. The packets will be stored in a freezer at the shop. You should keep them refrigerated, too, until you're ready to use them.

THE WINEMAKER'S UNDERCOVER AGENT

Although grapes and yeast are winemaking's only absolute essentials, there is in fact another key ingredient. For centuries, vintners protected their wine from spoilage by burning pure sulfur inside empty barrels and casks. Without understanding the chemistry—but appreciating the outcome—they were actually adding minor amounts of a compound known as sulfur dioxide. Today it's added in precise doses not only to wines but also to a wide range of foods, including dried peaches and apricots, fresh greens in salad bars, and specialty vinegars.

Although it sounds like something no one would want to eat or drink, sulfur dioxide is completely flavorless and odorless when used as it is in virtually all wines these days. The compound plays a role at nearly every stage of winemaking, inhibiting spoilage bacteria, suppressing rogue yeasts, preventing discoloration, and helping dispose of off odors. What's more, it is amazingly safe. A small number of people have a condition that makes them exceptionally sensitive to the compound, which can irritate their respiratory passages. But many millions of people worldwide have for hundreds of years drunk wines treated with sulfur dioxide with no short- or long-term effect of any kind. Most winemakers now add it as a white powder called potassium metabisulfite, or simply sulfite, available at brew shops.

Although you can make wine without sulfite, it's extremely difficult to make good wine without it. In professional tastings of commercial wines with and without the additive, those made with sulfite are consistently rated cleaner tasting and with better color. It doesn't take much. To protect 5 gallons of red wine that is being racked (transferred away from any sediment) for the first time, all that's required is about a half teaspoon of powdered potassium metabisulfite.

That's an overly general guideline. For one thing, everyday measuring spoons are far from exact. The teaspoon in your kitchen drawer may hold as much as 20 percent more or less than your neighbor's—and there's no way to eyeball which is more accurate. What's more, the dose of sulfite your wine needs at each stage isn't always the same. White wines may need more than reds. Grapes picked in wet weather—that is, grapes on the verge of turning moldy—may need a bit extra at crushing. Likewise, grapes that start out low in acid may need more protection. (For full details on sulfite and sulfur dioxide, see chapter 14.)

Because you want to add just enough sulfite, you'll want an exact means of measuring it. Most winemakers prefer to buy sulfite as a loose powder, in bags or jars, and then weigh it out on a gram scale, a light-duty weighing device calibrated not in ounces but in grams, the metric system's basic unit of weight. The ideal scale for winemaking—a triple-beam balance—allows measurements from zero to 600 grams (around 1.3 pounds), with each gram between zero and 10 marked off in tenths. (A tenth of a gram is what a big pinch of salt weighs.) But a scale that precise isn't absolutely necessary, and you can do just fine with a less expensive version from a brew shop. Most of your measurements—and you'll make many—will range from 0.1 gram (a small dose of sulfite for a gallon of wine) up to about 100 (perhaps to make a sulfite solution; see page 197). In a bind, a reasonably accurate kitchen scale can save the day.

If spooning out loose powders seems bothersome, you do have options. Many brew shops carry premeasured doses of sulfite called Campden tablets. Most of them contain exactly 0.44 gram of sulfite—a scant quarter-teaspoon—although other sizes are available (usually 0.55 gram). As a general rule, two 0.44-gram tablets crushed and dissolved in water are enough to protect 5 gallons of healthy wine at racking. (For more on the exact sulfite doses needed to preserve your wine, see pages 190–196.) But don't think the tablets free you from fussing with powders. It's pointless to drop the tablets in whole—they often need to be chopped into pieces so you can mete out precise amounts, and they should then be crushed and dissolved in a bit of water so the ingredient will disperse.

To help you skip the crushing and dissolving, some brew shops carry special effervescent sulfite tablets. They're made with a flavorless fizzing agent that helps mix the compound into the wine—a neat trick except that the tablets are expensive compared to powdered sulfite and they're sized for the convenience of commercial winemakers, who typically add them to 60-gallon barrels. You'll often need to do some arithmetic, and then carefully break the tablets into pieces, to get the sulfite doses you want. As the leftover fragments pile up, you'll find yourself longing for a gram scale.

No matter which kind of sulfite you use, bear in mind that all sulfite loses potency over time, so it's important to buy a fresh supply every year. Don't throw the leftovers out! Save them to make a solution for sanitizing your siphon and other tools (see page 33).

2

THE INS AND OUTS OF A HOME WINERY

WE'VE ALL SEEN PHOTOS OF DANK CELLARS in France, the rows of barrels lighted by bare bulbs dangling from arches of moldy stone. It's a charming image—and in part a true one—but it sends a misleading message to anyone thinking about making wine at home. Wine doesn't have to be fermented in a chilly cellar. In fact, red wines made in small amounts usually need a bit of warmth. And even if you're making white wines, which are best when fermented slowly at cool temperatures, the ideal winery is not truly frigid. (Once bottled, wine should be stored in a cool place; for details, see page 99.)

Over the years I've made wine in a bedroom, a laundry room, a garden shed, a basement workshop, a portion of a crowded garage, and on a back porch. The porch seemed fine at the time—we could lug up the tubs of crushed grapes without traipsing through the house or worrying about staining the wall-to-wall. But it quickly proved troublesome. Chilly winds swirled around the wine at night, threatening to stop the fermentation. Raccoons and opos-

---

Home winemaking's basic tools: a food-grade plastic pail, 5-gallon glass carboy, siphon tube, plastic wine thief, hydrometer and test cylinder, wine funnel, fermentation lock, and floating thermometer.

sums, attracted by yeasty smells, scratched at the fermenter and even succeeded in knocking the top off. I can't say I slept well that year, but the wine, a Napa Valley Cabernet, came out fine despite it all.

Actually, the most comfortable and functional winery of all has been the garage, with its big door that opens onto a concrete slab—but that's in California. Winemakers in regions where the cool fall harvest season gives way to icy winter may need either to retreat indoors and set up shop in the basement, or to insulate and heat the garage.

A quiet corner. Most important, your winery should be out of the way of your everyday life. The space doesn't need to be huge. Eight feet by eight feet is ample unless you're starting with more than several hundred pounds of grapes. For most people, that rules out the kitchen. Besides, garlic odors, dog and cat fur, kids' dirty hands, and nosy guests don't mix with winemaking. Still, the kitchen's always a tempting choice because of its big, versatile sink.

A vintner at a high-end California winery was once asked what he considered the key to creating great wines. "Winemaking is dishwashing," he said. "You wash your equipment, use it, wash it, use it, wash it. If you can't stand getting wet, forget it. You'll never make fine wine." He exaggerates, perhaps, but water is winemaking's phantom ingredient. Very little goes in the wine, but a lot of it runs everywhere else and at virtually every stage. The most crucial matter in picking the place for your winery is access to water—either an outdoor faucet or a big indoor sink, or both. Best of all is being able to blast both cold and hot water from a hose.

CONTAINERS, OPEN AND SHUT

A lot of home winemaking gear isn't especially modern. Medieval tapestries show winemakers squeezing grapes with a hand-cranked press, and then filling barrels with funnels and tubes. Imagine a vintner from the fifteenth century dropped into a present-day brew shop.

He'd gawk at all the plastic and stainless steel—unknown in his time—but he'd know just what to do with the tubs, jugs, siphons, stoppers, wine thiefs, and the like. He'd walk out a happy guy, and with his arms full.

The issue modern winemakers face is deciding what *not* to bring home from the winemaking shop. Shopkeepers are almost universally helpful and encouraging, but they're also eager to sell you that one extra gadget that will of course make your winemaking easier. Wise home vintners start with the bare essentials and add tools bit by bit.

The big drum. To ferment red wine in modest amounts—about 5 to 40 gallons—the best primary fermenter is a new plastic drum or garbage can rated "food-grade," meaning it's designed to hold foods in bulk. The rating will be embossed in the plastic on both the barrel and the lid, and you definitely want to look for it. Food-grade polyethylene plastics, which are often milky-white and quite rigid, are free of the "plasticizers" that give vinyl and other plastics their springiness and strong smell—which is to say that unless you want chemical flavors in your wine, don't buy an ordinary hardware-store garbage can for a fermenter. And pass up used plastic containers. A drum filled just once with olives will forever bear an oily, briny residue. The big white pails that held pickles or mayonnaise or detergent will always carry—and give off—the scent and flavor of their original contents.

It's also best to avoid the beige pottery crocks, which for decades were standard equipment for home brewers and winemakers—likewise a used oak barrel with an end knocked out. Both can harbor spoilage microbes that before long will make you wish you'd spent a little more for a food-grade drum. Choose the smallest fermenter necessary for the amount of wine you plan to make—but make sure there's about 20 to 30 percent extra space for the rising layer of foam and skins.

Clear is beautiful. Makers of white wines can gloat that because they ferment just the juice and discard the grape skins, they have no need for a big open-topped fermenter. But they do join the makers of red wines in needing a stockpile of the 5-gallon water bottles known as carboys. Plastic versions of these big jugs are everywhere now that they're the vessel of choice for delivering springwater to homes and offices, and food-grade plastic is fine for the drums and pails that do short-term duty during fermentation. But for the subsequent stages, when the wine spends weeks or months in containers, glass has many surpassing virtues.

Home winemaking's most useful fact: 1 gallon equals 3.785 liters. A standard 5-gallon carboy holds just under 19 liters and weighs 42 pounds when full.

Unlike the ones made of plastic, glass carboys are completely impervious to air—a requirement for any container that will hold wine for months. And unlike the special carboys made of a nonporous plastic called PET (polyethylene terephthalate), they can be cleaned easily and repeatedly without scuffing up the surface; so they stay crystal-clear for years, making it easy to see what the wine is doing. Though heavier than plastic ones, glass carboys are light enough to carry when full. Some shops sell 7-gallon carboys and various large-capacity demijohns (encased in molded plastic). These can come in handy when you've made too much wine for one regular carboy and not enough for two; but they are heavy when full and prone to breaking. For ease and flexibility, smaller carboys—you'll see both 2.8- and 3-gallon versions—are a safer choice.

Even carboys that once served as miniature greenhouses can be emptied, scrubbed, and made virtually new with judicious use of strong cleansers (see below). That's because glass is essentially inert, and very few chemicals—even extremely harsh ones—can degrade it. In fact, any used glassware that's free of cracks, stains, and deep scratches can be cleaned up enough to produce good wine for years.

How many carboys do you need? At a minimum, one extra. That is, if you're making

TABLE 2 *Your Home Winemaking Shopping List*

Here's everything you'll need to buy to make a top-quality red or white—except the bottles and corks (see page 93). The list looks long, but most of the items are inexpensive, and many fermentation supply shops offer discounts on ready-to-go tool kits that include the essential items. Copy this checklist and take it with you to the shop.

SUPPLIES

_____ 1. Wine grapes, minimum of 50 pounds (5 gallons); if fresh, order in July or August

_____ 2. Wine yeasts, one 5-gram packet for each 50 pounds of grapes

_____ 3. Malolactic bacteria (optional), one 1.5-gram packet for up to 600 pounds of grapes

_____ 4. Potassium metabisulfite, powdered, 4 ounces or 100 grams minimum

_____ 5. Tartaric acid, 4 ounces or 100 grams minimum

_____ 6. Citric acid, 8 ounces or 200 grams minimum

EQUIPMENT

_____ 1. Drum or garbage can, food-grade, with lid

_____ 2. Carboys, glass, 5-, 3-, or 2.8-gallon capacity

_____ 3. Pail, food-grade plastic

_____ 4. Funnel, carboy-size

_____ 5. Siphon tube, clear vinyl, 4 to 6 feet, with nylon clamp

_____ 6. Racking wand with cap

_____ 7. Wine thief, plastic

_____ 8. Fermentation locks, as many as carboys and jugs

_____ 9. Stoppers, drilled, nos. 7 and $6\frac{1}{2}$, as many as locks

_____ 10. Hydrometer and test cylinder

_____ 11. Thermometer, floating

_____ 12. Gram scale, in 0.5-gram increments or smaller

_____ 13. Acid test kit (optional)

_____ 14. Carboy brush

5 gallons of wine, you'll want at least two carboys so you can move the wine from one to the other and leave any yeasty sediment behind. For larger amounts, the one-extra rule still applies—that is, if you don't mind rinsing the just-emptied carboys one by one as you go. The ultimate convenience is to have two carboys for every 5 gallons of wine, so you can transfer the wine all at once, and then wash the empties when you're done.

Beyond that, you'll want to collect several 1-gallon glass jugs, or perhaps a 3-gallon carboy and a jug or two, for those times when you end up with a gallon total not divisible by 5.

Glass is fragile, naturally, which makes used beer kegs a good option. Small breweries and beer distributors often sell stainless steel kegs that have been dented or slightly damaged but are still sound. They come in 7.5- and 15-gallon sizes. Cleaned thoroughly (see below), they make excellent storage vessels, although you can't see inside them, as you can with glass carboys, and they're brutally heavy when full.

MOVING YOUR WINE AROUND

Of course, you have to get your wine from the fermenter to the press and from the press to the carboys. For that you can always use a stockpot or other large pot borrowed from the kitchen, but only after washing and rinsing it until it's free of both grease and detergent residue. A smarter idea is to buy a food-grade plastic pail—light, durable, easy to clean, and best of all inexpensive. Add to this a carboy-size funnel, with both a wide throat to let the wine pass quickly and a high rim to catch any splashes.

Let gravity do it. One beauty of small-scale winemaking is that you don't need an electric pump to move the liquid from one carboy to another. All that's required is a simple siphon tube. Granted, you have to lift full carboys so they sit above the ones to be filled, and you'll use a bit of lung power to start the flow. But after that, the force of gravity does the work for you.

Winemaking shops stock spools of clear vinyl tubing, usually in diameters of three-eighths and five-eighths of an inch. The tubing is sold by the foot; most winemakers buy 4 to 6 feet. But because it comes wound on a spool, the tubing retains a perpetual curl that can make it hard to control when threaded into a carboy. That means it's easy to suck up sediment along with your beautifully clear wine, which defeats the purpose of racking. A device called a racking wand—basically, a short piece of rigid plastic or stainless steel tubing—solves the problem. It fits into the end of your vinyl hose and comes with a special cap or spacer that holds the tube about an inch off the bottom, where the sediment lies. Your siphoning kit is completed with a nylon or steel hose clamp that stops the flow with a pinch.

Disposable plastic pipettes make handy, inexpensive tools for taking samples of wine from carboys. Otherwise, a plastic or glass wine thief is essential.

What if you want to taste your new wine but don't feel like lifting a carboy and starting a siphon? The perfect tool is a wine thief, a thick, tapered tube with a handle and small holes at both ends. You dip it into the wine, cover the dry end with your thumb, and lift out a sample. A plastic version, which can be pulled apart for cleaning, is a wiser choice than one made of glass, which is pricey and fragile and requires scrupulous care. An alternative is a disposable pipette (10 milliliters or larger). *Disposable* simply means inexpensive; kept clean, it will serve for years.

FERM LOCKS AND STOPPERS AND BUNGS

New red wine poured into a carboy or keg is still fermenting—that is, still pumping out carbon dioxide gas—so you can't just plug the container with a cork and expect the stopper to stay put. Vintners long ago found that glass tubing bent into an S, filled with water, and poked through a cork into a wine jug would let gas escape but keep air and spoilage microbes out. Fermentation locks, or ferm locks, as these gadgets are often called, have become standard tools for winemakers making anything from a few to many thousands of gallons. (Commercial wineries place them on barrels full of wine that's still fermenting.)

A plastic version of the original model has two little water chambers molded onto an S-shaped stem—no moving parts. Another type is a three-piece affair with a cylindrical reservoir, a simple valve, and a cap. Both do the job, provided that they're kept full of water and are set in a drilled stopper, or perforated rubber cork, that fits snugly into the mouth of the container.

These one-hole plugs come in a range of sizes, graded by number, from little ones that fit a standard wine bottle (no. 1) to big 3-inchers for use on barrels (no. 12). The grade numbers are usually molded onto the stoppers. Most carboys take no. 7s, though you'll need some no. 6½s for any gallon jugs you've acquired and for the odd carboy with a narrow neck. You can also find rubber sleeves that fit like stocking caps over a carboy's mouth and neck. These hold ferm locks fairly well but may not seal perfectly and can hide the wine's top surface from view—a crucial flaw. You want to be able to see through the glass to that surface, since that's where some spoilage problems can appear.

Is it also necessary to invest in solid stoppers (which if they're barrel-size are called bungs) for when the wine stops fermenting? Maybe. Wine expands when it warms—when, for instance, it sits in a garage on a sultry day. In a carboy with a ferm lock, the expanding wine can rise up into the stem or perhaps even overflow—not an ideal scenario but not a disaster, either. A solid stopper, on the other hand, may pop free and go bouncing away, leaving the wine open to the air until you stop by. But if the carboys are left someplace with a steady temperature, such as a basement or air-conditioned room, solid stoppers are fine. They're indisputably better at keeping air out—when they stay put. My advice: Use ferm locks year-round, but keep them filled with water treated with a pinch of sulfite to stop microbe growth.

CRUCIAL MEASURES AND TESTS

Carboys, tubs, funnels, stoppers, fermentation locks—isn't that enough to get started in wine-making? Yes and no. A few other basic tools will help keep you and your grapes on the right track.

How sweet it is. Wine grapes ready for the fermenter are among the world's sweetest fruits—almost 25 percent sugar by weight. But no matter how devoted the grape farmer or how scrupulous the brew-shop owner, the grapes you bring home may possibly contain more or less sugar than you want. You can correct the sweetness—it's easy and perfectly legit—but only if you know exactly what you're starting with. Despite a highfalutin name, a hydrometer and its companion test cylinder make it almost mindlessly easy to check the sugar level, not only at the outset but also as it falls day by day during fermentation.

A hydrometer looks like a little glass torpedo 8 to 10 inches long. One end is fat, with a metal weight inside; the other end is pencil-thick with tick marks and numbers. To take a measurement, you pour some juice into the tall cylinder, float the hydrometer in it, give it a gentle spin, and find a number between 25 and zero that lines up with the surface of the liquid. That's the sugar percentage, or Brix. As the fermentation proceeds and the yeasts turn the sugar into alcohol, the hydrometer sinks farther and farther into the juice, giving ever lower readings. When they eventually stop falling, your juice is officially wine. (For more on using a hydrometer, see chapters 4 and 12.)

Taking your wine's temperature. Knowing the sugar percentage is important—it's what determines the amount of alcohol—but it's just as crucial to keep an eye on the temperature in the fermenter while the yeasts go through their heat-generating boom. That warmth can be both a blessing and a curse, and it's in your interest to watch it closely and control it. Red wines turn out best when they're allowed to warm up during fermentation. White wines, on the other hand, are best when fermented cool. Yet yeasts are particular. They slow down and give up whenever their environment gets too hot or too cold. The temperatures at which they're most happy and productive range between 50°F and 90°F.

The Brix scale, commonly used to note the sugar percentage in grape juice for wines, is named for its inventor, German scientist Adolf Brix, born in 1798.

If you're frugal beyond reason, you can wash an old-fashioned wall thermometer and stick that in your fermenting grape juice or use an instant-read food thermometer from the kitchen drawer. But you'll be happiest if you buy a floating thermometer, which is simply an ordinary midsize thermometer encased in a sausage-shaped bubble of glass. Even when buried in the thickest, stickiest mass of crushed grapes, it will work its way to the surface. And it will never plunge to the bottom of a carboy full of wine.

KEEPING THINGS CLEAN

If, as the saying goes, cleanliness is next to godliness, then the best winemakers are veritable saints. But even these swirling dervishes know there's no hope of getting their carboys and other pieces of equipment so clean that they're completely devoid of microbes. Nothing in any winery is ever sterile—so forget the word *sterilize*. Your goal is simply to keep your gear sanitary and absolutely free of residues. For that, your first and perhaps most important need is a carboy brush, which has its bristles at an angle to the handle so you can scrub your carboys' inner shoulders, where deposits often cling. Never wash your gear with household detergents or soaps, which can leave foul-tasting residues. Instead, use the cleansers listed below.

Sodium percarbonate, or oxygen bleach, is a chlorine-free powder with the power to loosen or dissolve bits of grape juice, spent yeast, and other detritus that can harbor spoilage microbes. Brand names include, among others, Proxy Clean, Proxy Carb, B-Brite, OxyClean, and Barrel Clean. It's basically a strong alkali (like soda ash or old-fashioned washing soda) that also incorporates a dry form of hydrogen peroxide, which when moistened gives off oxygen and helps the product work as a sanitizer and stain remover. It's approved by the government for use on food-prep equipment. Fill a gallon jug halfway with warm water, measure 1 tablespoon sodium percarbonate into the jug, shake it until the powder dissolves, and then fill it to the top with warm water. After washing, rinse the equipment thoroughly (until it no longer feels slippery) and dispose of the used cleanser.

Citric acid and sulfite. Water, of course, is the cleanup common denominator, to be sprayed and splashed liberally. (It's said commercial wineries use up to 10 gallons of water for every gallon of wine they make.) However, for before-and-after treatment of carboys, buckets, funnels, and siphon tubes, a dilute mix of citric acid and metabisulfite can help deny microbes a toehold. The citric acid neutralizes any traces of alkali from the other cleansers and liberates antiseptic sulfur dioxide. To a clean gallon jug, add 1 teaspoon or 2 grams of citric acid and 2 teaspoons or 4 grams of potassium metabisulfite (left over from a previous vintage). Add 1 gallon of clean tap water, stopper

For an all-purpose cleaner, add 1 tablespoon of sodium percarbonate to a gallon jug half filled with warm water, shake to dissolve the powder, and top up with warm water.

the jug, and shake until the powders dissolve. Label the jug "Citric-sulfur for cleaning." The mixture can be poured from one vessel into another—avoid breathing the fumes—and reused until it looks murky or stops giving off its characteristic burned-matches smell, at which point it should be poured out. Finally, always rinse your equipment with cold water and let it air-dry. Rinse again before use.

To remove a red wine stain, University of California enologists say, drench it with a one-to-one mixture of standard (3 percent) hydrogen peroxide and Dawn liquid soap, and then launder as usual.

Chlorine or household bleach (sodium hypochlorite) is too caustic for standard use. Reserve it for hard-core sanitizing of glass equipment you have reason to suspect—for instance, carboys bought at a garage sale. Make sure you use the unscented, normal-strength variety. Measure 1 teaspoon into a gallon jug and fill it with water. Keep in mind that chlorine can be a wine contaminant in its own right, possibly contributing to a "corked" or musty smell in otherwise fine wine. Rinse, rinse, and rinse again, preferably with very hot water, until you can't smell even a hint of the chemical, and then rinse with the citric-sulfur solution. Never use any type of chlorine cleaning agent on stainless steel; it may react with and pit the metal and eventually cause leaks.

GEAR YOU'LL WANT BUT SHOULDN'T BUY—YET

Once you start stocking your winery, you'll feel the pangs of a syndrome that afflicts everyone with a new avocation: equipment lust. For each task—from grape crushing to bottle washing to corking—there's an ingenious device that promises to make the operation just that much simpler and tidier. I've seen home wineries jammed with motorized crusher-stemmers, variable-capacity stainless steel tanks, hydraulic-ram basket presses, electric wine pumps, cartridge and pad filters, and much more. Yet to equip a home winery to complete every possible job in the most efficient way could mean an outlay of several thousand dollars. Your saving grace is that the truly essential gadgets can be rented for a modest fee.

If you plan to start your vintage with whole fresh grapes, as opposed to getting them already crushed or pressed into juice, you'll need to rent a crusher-stemmer and a basket press from a brew shop. Likewise, when it comes time to bottle your wine, see about renting a floor corker, a nifty tool that in one smooth motion compresses a cork and pokes it to exactly the right depth in a bottle's neck. There are other types of corkers, the most common being a two-lever version that looks like an exercise gadget. The levers swing down and activate jaws that grip the bottle while a plunger drives the cork home. Floor corkers are easier to use, however, which is why it's best to rent one for your first vintage. (For details on corks and bottles, see chapter 8.)

Alternatively, join with some other winemakers to share equipment. (Ask at the place where you get supplies if there are any winemakers' groups in your area.) The priciest winemaking tools—the crusher-stemmer and press—are used for just a few hours over a few weeks each year and then put away for months until the next vintage. What's more, you can probably arrange for a discount on bottles, corks, and other supplies by merging your orders and buying in bulk. Naturally, you'll end up trading bits of know-how and bottles of wine—sharing's own reward.

But for now, put off buying an oak barrel. True, the subtle vanilla flavor of well-selected oak adds complexity to most red wines and some whites, but that flavor is a finishing touch, not an essential ingredient. Instead, try one of the several low-cost products (page 89) that can give you some of the benefits of barrel-aging without the expense. Save the money you're tempted to spend on a barrel and put it instead toward the best grapes you can find.

3

WHEN RED MEANS GO

IT'S NO WONDER MEDITERRANEAN POTTERY and other ancient artworks were so often decorated with pictures of grapevines and grapes. Just stroll through a modern vineyard. The leafy vines, twined along wires, may have been trimmed into a top-heavy hedge—a vertical curtain, vintners call it—with shoots curling up toward the sky and bunches of ripening grapes dangling below in the sunshine. Draped just so, as if on display, the purple bunches look radiant and practically magical against the green foliage and dark earth. But their magnificence is destined to fade once they're snipped from the vines. Heaped in a harvest bin, bruised and exposed to the hovering fruit flies, the grapes are now headed the way of all produce left out too long—unless a winemaker hustles to their rescue.

Crushing Cabernet Sauvignon grapes in a hand-cranked crusher-stemmer placed atop a 50-gallon food-grade plastic drum that will serve for the next week or so as the primary fermenter.

CRUSHING YOUR GRAPES

Vintners call the hectic harvest season "the crush." It's an apt term that describes both the mashing of the whole grapes to release their juice and the staggering load of work required to deal with tons of ripe grapes on the verge of going bad. The point of the crush is to break every grape without smashing the seeds inside, which contain enough tannin to impart an unpleasantly bitter and astringent taste to the finished wine. Winemakers in antiquity discovered perfect grape crushers out at the ends of their legs, and in fact, the human foot does a fine job. It's broad enough to squash several grapes at a time, and it's gentle by comparison to, say, a horse's hoof or a log or other pounding tool. It's built for repetitive work, and it comes with its own power source.

Nonetheless, it's hard for all of us in the appliance-crazed twenty-first century to grasp how much work it is to crush a large lot of grapes by foot. What a small mechanical crusher-stemmer can do in several minutes might take an inexperienced grape stomper hours. What's more, early winemakers often crushed their grapes in specially made stone or barrel-wood basins. What would you use? Not a galvanized steel washtub, which could taint your grapes with metallic residue. Maybe an old claw-foot bathtub? Or a hard plastic wading pool? Or a sawed-off wine barrel or plastic garbage can? Possibly, but you'll need to scrub out the dirt from earlier uses, and unless you want to bruise your feet, you'll do your legwork in a pair of knee-high rubber boots.

Don't forget that there's another step involved in crushing by foot: removing the stems. Like grape seeds, grape stems—about 3 percent of the weight of just-picked grapes—are filled with bitter tannins. It's okay to end up with a small portion of the original stems still in the crushed grapes: some amount of tannin is good in wines, at least in reds (more on this later).

But that means removing 90 percent to 95 percent of the stems using your hands or a tool, such as a rake, or perhaps by forcing the sticky, clingy mess through a coarse sieve made of chicken wire stretched on a wooden frame. Crushing grapes by foot may be picturesque and fun—for a while—but it's easily the messiest and most time-consuming task you'll take on as a winemaker.

Running a rented crusher-stemmer. By contrast, it's easy to push the button on a power crusher-stemmer, dump in your grape bunches, and watch your future wine plop out while the denuded stems pile up a few feet away. But although the process is efficient, it's not fuss-free. The machines are big, heavy, and unwieldy to move and run. The actual crushing may take just minutes, but hosing and brushing the bits of grape skin and pulp out of the device's nooks and crannies can take many times that long.

Crusher-stemmers have three key parts: a hopper into which you dump the grapes, toothed rollers that lightly mash each grape bunch as it passes through from the hopper, and a horizontal shaft equipped with paddles to knock the crushed grapes one way and the stems another. If you're starting with more than 100 pounds of grapes—that is, if you're using a large fermenter with a mouth that's at least 24 inches across—you can simply place the crusher-stemmer on top and crush the grapes right into it. If you're making less, however, you'll need to set the machine so it securely straddles a gap, perhaps between two tables or chairs, with a wide tub or basin placed below. In either case, it's wise to place a second tub next to the main one and a large clean sheet of construction plastic below both of them to catch the many crushed grapes that go astray.

Most brew shops rent crusher-stemmers, although some stock plain crushers—rollers only, no paddles for the stems. You'll also see machines designed especially for crushing apples for cider. Try to rent an actual wine-grape crusher-stemmer. The hand-cranked versions work best with a team: two people to steady the machine and a third to turn the crank. Ones powered by an electric motor are easier to use but pricier to rent. Shops often let you reserve ahead, a smart practice during the busy harvest season. Some charge by the hour, others by the half-day, but don't neglect that final spray-and-scrub or you could end up also paying a cleaning fee.

A DOSE OF PREVENTION

First-time vintners, accustomed to everyday cleanliness, are often amazed to learn that dusty wine grapes go straight from the vineyard to the crusher without washing. (Water could be picked up by the grapes and dilute the sugar that the vineyard manager has worked so hard to achieve.) Into the hopper with the fruit go ants, spiders, bees, bits of dirt, and even occasional bird droppings. It all ends up in the fermenter—which is to say that newly crushed grapes are anything but pristine. That's not a problem. The guiding principle at this stage is to be fussy later. Since it's impossible to start with immaculate grapes, the goal is to let the wine clean itself by degrees. Most detritus stays with the skins when the wine is pressed; more eventually settles out. And as for any microbes in the juice, they're likely to be overwhelmed by the booming yeast population. But even though the hard-charging yeasts are in many ways a wine's best defenders, wise winemakers prefer not to gamble and keep their equipment scrupulously clean to eliminate any bugs that might be lurking in cracks and corners.

Achieve cleanliness in steps. Once crushed, wine grapes are a virtual time bomb. If the weather is warm and if rogue yeasts were at large on the grapes, crusher, or fermenter, your precious haul could start becoming wine all by itself. You want to buy some time and stay in control—no spontaneous fermentations, please—which means adding a smidgen of sulfite to the grapes as they're crushed. The easiest method is to measure the right dose into a cup or two of water, and sprinkle the solution onto the crushed grapes a bit at a time as they fall into the bin. (If you've bought precrushed grapes, find out whether the supplier added sulfite and if so, how much. If none was added, you can simply dissolve a dose in a small amount of water and stir it in.)

How much sulfite is enough? If your grapes arrived clean—that is, completely free of rot or mold and with no hint of a vinegar aroma—you can add the advisable minimum, 1.0 to 1.5 grams of sulfite for each 50 pounds of grapes, for 30 to 45 parts per million of sulfur dioxide. If the grapes are less than perfect—some berries are turning brown or show a fuzzy white growth—then you'll want to add 3 grams for each 50 pounds of grapes, for up to 90 parts per million of sulfur dioxide. You'll get a sharp whiff of burned matches when you sprinkle in the sulfite-water mixture; that's the protective sulfur dioxide gas, freed by the action of the grape acids, escaping from the compound. Don't worry; that odor will entirely vanish when the juice is stirred. And although this minimal treatment is remarkably effective at fending off browning (oxidation), spoilage bacteria, and vagabond yeasts, the domesticated yeasts you'll add have been bred to thrive in spite of it. Your wine gets several benefits including cleaner flavors, better color, and a longer life in the bottle. And you're far less likely to suffer fermentation heartaches in the days ahead.

One caution: adding sulfite to crushed grapes is like adding salt to soup. A little bit works wonders, but a lot can be disastrous. An overdose of sulfite can harm the color, flavor, and aroma of the finished wine or even impede the fermentation itself. Make your measurements carefully and double-check the appropriate dose before you add it.

TIME OUT!

You've crushed your grapes; then, suddenly, you're back from returning the machine to the brew shop and your fingers are worrying the edge of a packet of wine yeasts. Hold that thought—the yeasts' time will come. But before you tear the foil, it's important to run the same tests performed by professional winemakers.

Speaking of the pros, you'll want to use the word they do for the mass of juice and skins in your fermenter. *Must* is the standard term for that grape soup before and during fermentation. Once that fizzy stage is over and the sugar's all gone—then what you have is *wine*. Meanwhile, don't worry that your must will spoil while you run the tests. The dose of sulfite you added will keep it safe for a day or two.

The word must, *meaning a soupy mass of crushed but as yet unfermented fruit, has been in steady use for several hundred years.*

Why mess with the tests? Musts with too much sugar turn into superalcoholic monsters that may never finish fermenting. Ones with too little sugar make thin, unstable wines. Likewise, overly acidic grapes become harsh, sour wines, while acid-poor grapes turn into wines that taste flat and are prone to spoilage. Ideally, the grapes you buy will have been picked at the exact stage when sugar and acid are in perfect balance. In fact, grape growers strive for that ideal mix—for example, fussing over their vines and cutting away leaves so extra sunlight hits the grapes.

Checking the sugar. First, find your hydrometer and test jar and set them somewhere nearby. Now line up a couple of clean measuring cups and, if you have one, a strainer. With one cup, scoop out a portion of sweet juice and skins, and strain the juice into the second cup. It's important to get pure juice—no skins or seeds. (Take a taste while you're at it.) Let the juice stand for several minutes, so the heaviest bits of pulp can settle and any bubbles can pop, and then carefully pour some into your test jar, filling it about three-fourths full. Set the jar on a flat surface.

Grasp the hydrometer by its skinny stem and gently lower it into the jar. It will sink past the bulb so that only the stem shows above the liquid. Give the hydrometer a gentle spin to be sure it's not stuck to the jar, and find the tick marks from zero to 30 or 35 labeled "Brix." Look for the number that lines up with the surface of the juice, most likely between 20 and 27. That's the percentage of dissolved sugar.

If the vineyardist who raised and harvested your grapes did his job well, the Brix reading of your must will fall between 22.5 and 24.5—maybe as high as 25 or as low as 22. Write down the number, the date and time, and the temperature of the must. These notes will become the first of a series of entries you make as you track the drop in sugar and rise in temperature.

Angles on acidity. After the sugar percentage, the most important thing to know about your grapes is how much acid they contain. A wine's tartness is a key aspect of its flavor, and the acid content of the crushed grapes governs the new wine's vulnerability to spoilage and whether the beneficial malolactic bacteria will promptly do their job. Your grape supplier probably ran an acidity test at the time of harvest. Make sure that

It's not necessary to refer to "degrees Brix" or to use the degree symbol (°). Brix is an accepted unit of measure, like feet or inches.

you receive the reading. The total acidity, or TA, of your must should fall between 6.0 and 8.0 grams of acid per liter of juice—or, to put it a more common way, between 0.60 and 0.80 gram per 100 milliliters. If it's in or near that range—it probably is—and your sugar's also fine, your grapes are ready to ferment.

FIXES FOR FLAWS

Most suppliers bend over backward to offer ex-cellent grapes that will make first-rate wine. So if your grapes are in fine shape and everything's okay, you can move straight ahead to adding yeast to start the fermentation—chapter 4—which is the most likely scenario. But what if your grapes' sugar and acid readings come out high or low, or you never learned the acid level?

Don't fret. Ripeness guidelines are just guidelines, not absolute rules. Your wine is unlikely to taste terrible because you decided to ferment a must with a sugar level slightly outside the usual range. It will probably be perfectly likable, in fact. That said, even commercial wine-makers sometimes find it necessary to bring their musts into balance before fermenting, and there's no shame in doing so. (For more on grape ripeness and must adjustments, see chapters 11 and 13, pages 137 and 169.)

TABLE 3 *Gallons of Water to Add to Dilute a High-Sugar Must to 24.5 Brix**

STARTING BRIX	STARTING GALLONS OF MUST				
	10	20	30	40	50
29	1.5	2.9	4.4	5.9	7.3
28	1.1	2.3	3.4	4.6	5.7
27	0.8	1.6	2.4	3.3	4.1
26	0.5	1.0	1.5	2.0	2.4

* For details on how these addition quantities were calculated, see page 171.

High-sugar grapes. Diluting an overly sweet batch of grape must is an easy two-step process. First, you need to make sure you know how many gallons you have. If you're reckoning in pounds and gallons (as opposed to kilograms and liters), the weight-to-volume ratio of crushed grapes is approximately 10 to 1, so each 100 pounds of must has a volume of 10 gallons or so. Once you know your starting volume in gallons, and the must's Brix, or sugar percentage, you can use table 3 to determine the amount of water to add to bring the Brix down to 24.5.

Why dilute to 24.5 Brix instead of something else? It's best to avoid greatly diluting the many other components that give the wine its character. Musts at 24.5 Brix readily ferment to completion and make wines with deep color, substantial body, and long lives—better wines, in other words. It's safest to add the water in stages. Mix in about two-thirds of the calculated water and test the Brix of the diluted must with your hydrometer. If the reading is still high, stir in some of the remaining water and test again. Ultimately, you may need to add a little less or a little more than the formula suggests. Trust your hydrometer—and make note of exactly how much water you end up adding.

Replacing the acid. Since you've now diluted the must, you need to follow through with the crucial second step and bring the acid back up to its original level. It's actually easiest to make this addition if you do some simple math and shift back and forth between gallons and liters. That's because grape acid levels are noted in grams per liter (or, as noted above, in tenths of a gram per 100 milliliters), but you're most likely thinking in gallons.

Ideal acid levels for red grapes are 6.0 to 8.0 grams per liter. (For more details on acid levels, see chapter 13, page 169.) That means that for each added liter of water you want to put back about 7 grams of tartaric acid. Or, since a gallon equals 3.785 liters, you should add 7 × 3.785, or 26.5, grams of tartaric acid for each added *gallon* of water. Dissolve the powder in a small amount of water, pour it into the must, and stir it in thoroughly. You're now ready to ferment—unless you have reason to believe the grapes' acid level is still low.

Low-acid grapes. Grapes that are extra-sweet at harvest may sometimes benefit from a modest acid boost. That's because as a ripening grape's sugar goes up its acid tends to go down. To raise the total acidity of your must by 0.10 gram per 100 milliliters, add 1.0 gram of tartaric acid per liter of must. There are 3.785 liters in a gallon. So to raise 1 gallon's TA by 0.10, add 3.8 grams of tartaric acid to each gallon. Suppose you have 10 gallons with a total acidity of 0.55, and you want to raise it to 0.65. In this case, you'd add 10 × 3.8, or 38, grams of tartaric acid.

Remember, the general target for red grapes is a total acidity of 0.60 to 0.80 gram per

> *The key rules to remember when adjusting musts: Take it easy. Go slow. And when in doubt—don't add anything.*

100 milliliters and a sugar reading of 22.5 to 24.5 Brix. (There are different ripeness targets for white grapes; see chapter 9.) Once your must is in that range—or close—it really is ready to ferment. Since calling a time-out on your just-crushed grapes, you've been through a lot of testing and figuring, weighing and mixing. It's time for some action.

4

THEN A MIRACLE HAPPENS

RIPE GRAPES WANT TO BECOME WINE, as vintners love to say, and any winemaker's job is simply to help them do what comes naturally. It's no stretch to regard the grapes' metamorphosis as an actual miracle. At some point in every vintage I stop next to a drum of fermenting fruit and eavesdrop on the yeasts' bacchanalian babbling—a cheery buzzing like the sound from a hive of bees. Mesmerized, I pull off the lid and poke my nose in, only to be knocked back by a gust of heady alcohol and choking carbonation. Right then it's easy to imagine a winemaker in the days of Homer or Ovid tipping hastily away from his own vat, blinking and wondering.

Even though this so-called primary fermentation is winemaking's busiest stage, you really won't have much to do. All the same, you should plan to spend about 15 minutes twice a day every day for a week or a little more. You've scheduled a weekend away? Think twice. Slack off for a couple of days, and you'll end up with stuff you won't want to drink. Of course, you can pull a Tom Sawyer and enlist a friend to tend your wine while you're gone. There's no real risk—the duty's not difficult—but you'll regret skipping out on such a wondrous event.

Preparing to punch down the thick cap of skins and seeds floating on a
400-pound batch of actively fermenting red grape must—a task to be
carried out at least twice a day.

Besides, as every professional vintner knows, the steps you take now have much to do with the character of your future wine—whether it's light and fruity or dark and tannic.

Bringing your yeasts to life. Find your thermometer and your packets of wine yeasts—one 5-gram packet per 50 pounds of grapes. Don't do anything with the yeasts just yet; and most important, don't get itchy and add the dry yeast directly to the must. The yeast cells need to be rehydrated in warm water, or they'll get off to a feeble start. For each 5 grams of yeast, you'll need a half cup of water warmed to not less than 95°F and not more than 104°F. A Pyrex quart measuring cup works well—but don't snip open those packets just yet. Place your thermometer in the measuring cup and add hot and cold water from the tap, adjusting the temperature to the right range. (Don't use distilled or deionized water, which will deprive the yeasts of dissolved minerals they need as they revive.) Or, if you like, measure out the water, and then warm the whole amount in the microwave—removing the thermometer first! Check the temperature every few seconds until it's perfect. Believe it or not, these steps really matter. If the yeasts aren't treated gently at this stage, they can die in droves.

At the height of fermentation, a single milliliter of must—a quarter-teaspoon— may hold as many as 100 million yeast cells.

Got your water just right? *Now* cut open your yeast packets. Sprinkle the yeasts onto the surface of the warm water and wait five minutes. With a clean spoon, gently stir the yeasts into the water. Break up any big lumps that form, but take it easy; you're not whipping cream. Let the mixture stand for up to half an hour—but no longer. Meanwhile, check the temperature of the crushed grapes. If it's 60°F or less, you should help the rehydrated yeasts avoid cold shock in their new home. Using a cup and sieve, take out enough grape juice to match the volume of the yeast-water mixture. Over the course of a minute, slowly mix the juice with the rehydrated yeasts.

START YOUR FERMENTER!

This is the big moment, the launching of the fermentation. Step one: Lift the lid on your fermenter and pour in the rehydrated yeasts—with or without some added juice. Step two: Close the lid, wash the measuring cup, and go do something else. If you wish, you can gently stir the warm yeast slurry into the cool must. But many winemakers prefer to let the yeasts acclimate for several hours before mixing them in. (If you add your yeasts in the evening, come back the next morning. If you add them earlier, check in around dinnertime.) Either way, the next step is the same.

Roll up one sleeve, thoroughly rinse your hand and arm (skip the soap), and stir up the must as best you can. It'll feel stiff and thick, like split pea soup. Nothing will happen right then, since the yeasts need time to get busy. Go rinse the juice off your arm and wipe up any drips so roving ants won't find them and come back with their friends.

Before you close the fermenter, find your thermometer. If it's the floating kind, simply drop it into the must. Otherwise, lay it someplace handy but safe. Loosely cover the open top of the fermenter with its own lid or with a clean sheet of construction plastic tied on with string. At this point I always find myself hanging around, peering in at the grapes and fretting, "What if the yeasts don't *do* anything?" But you know that saying about a watched pot? If you're wise, you'll get busy with some other job for the rest of the day.

The meaning of foam. When you come back, the yeasts will have sprung to life in the fermenter. You'll know because there will be pale pinkish foam in a ring around the tub or in patches on the must's surface. Don't panic if you don't see any. Chances are your must is merely cold. Check the temperature with your thermometer. If it's between 50°F and 65°F, simply wait a day. If it's under 50°F, you'll probably want to move your fermenter to a warmer place or, possibly, wrap it temporarily from head to toe in an electric blanket.

Remember, the grapes want to become wine. The chances of the fermentation failing are extremely slim—assuming, that is, that you added real wine yeasts (see page 177). When you do start seeing significant foam, mix up the must as you did before, put the lid back on (loosely!), and go drink a toast to the health of your yeasts. They're off and running, gorging on sugar and multiplying like crazy.

To find your wine's potential alcohol percentage (by volume), multiply the Brix of the unfermented must by 0.59.

The cap also rises. As the yeasts feast, they do three amazing things. They generate heat, which helps free extra flavor and color from the grapes. They turn the sugar into alcohol, which not only makes the wine wine but helps it last for years. And they burp out carbon dioxide, which wards off spoilage bacteria that could ruin everything. Meanwhile, those little bubbles of gas, like the ones in soda and beer, are lighter than the liquid around them, so they pop right up—or they would if their way weren't blocked by crushed grapes. Instead, they drag the grapes up with them, forming a thick floating layer of skins, pulp, and trapped bubbles called the cap.

PUNCHING DOWN

Here's the main reason for your twice-daily duty in the winery: breaking up the cap and mixing it into the must, a pleasant job known as punching down that loads up the juice with color and flavor from the skins. Your yeasts won't mind when you go off to work for the day or turn in for the night, but they will suffer if you neglect them. There's one hard-and-fast rule: *punch down the cap at least twice every 24 hours*, perhaps even four or five times if you're aiming for a full-flavored red. Like most living things, yeasts need air—oxygen, actually—and that dense mass of skins can suffocate them. What's more, mixing up the must ensures that the skins don't dry out, get too warm, or become contaminated with bad bugs that can turn the wine to vinegar.

Of course, you already punched down once when you stirred in the yeasts with your hand. But now that the cap is forming, the must will feel different: you'll notice as the days pass that the cap clearly separates from a layer of juice below, and that the cap is much warmer. Push your hand through the cap and if necessary use your whole arm to give the layers a good mixing—your hand will tell you when the warmth has been distributed.

Taking the wine's temperature. Another nonnegotiable job, which you should do right after you punch down each time, is to record the must's temperature. Once you know the number, remember to write it down along with the date and time. These readings tell you how the yeasts are doing—whether they're thriving or struggling. They give you a timetable, since the temperature climbs and falls predictably. And they help you make especially flavorful wine.

At some point during fermentation, the must's temperature should climb to between 80°F and 90°F. It doesn't need to stay there. Can you picture what number-crunchers call a bell curve—a camel's hump of data points with just one or two at the peak? That's what the temperature-versus-time graph of an ideal fermentation looks like.

For good color and flavor in red wines, try to ensure that the temperature of the must rises to between 80°F and 90°F during fermentation.

Unfortunately, small batches of wine don't always warm right up. There are lots of wrinkles: the ripeness and variety of the grapes, the kind of yeast, the temperature of the room, and—maybe most important—the quantity of must. Modest volumes of liquid cool off rapidly. So unless you're making a really big batch (more than 40 gallons), you may want to take steps to make sure your fermenter's cozy. Many wine-

Do I Have to Check the Sugar Every Day?

Many winemakers insist that along with taking the wine's temperature twice a day you should measure the amount of sugar. Don't feel bad if for simplicity's sake you decide to skip that step every other time. (It's messy and slow compared with taking a thermometer reading.) Of course, you get the fullest picture when you track the rising warmth *and* the falling sweetness as the yeasts do their work. But unless you sense that something's wrong—the heat doesn't climb or the must barely bubbles—you'll be fine. Besides, punching down with your hand lets you feel the sticky sugar, which serves as a fine gauge until the stickiness vanishes. At that point it's crucial to see exactly how much sugar's left so you can decide when it's time to pull your wine off the spent grapes (see chapter 6). What does warmth now have to do with the wine's taste later? The heat of fermentation acts on the soaking grape skins, helping extract a bunch of flavorful compounds and colorful pigments. These, more than the juice itself, give red wine its rich taste and dark purple hue.

makers move the tub or drum off the cool floor onto a pad or board and insulate it with an old sleeping bag or even warm it gently with a spare electric blanket. It works—but check that thermometer religiously (and see "Not so fast!" below, page 56).

FOLLOWING THROUGH

In the old days—in fact, until recently—that was about all anyone did during home winemaking's first phase: punch down, watch the temperature and sugar, and wait for the yeasts to finish. But modern vintners have discovered that it pays to do a little more.

Feed your yeasts. You might assume that with all that sweet juice around, your wine yeasts would be as happy as pigs in slop. They are, up to a point. Yeasts are actually microscopic plants, and like other plants they sometimes need a little extra nourishment. You *can* make wine without adding special yeast food. But consider this: Yeasts, during their growth spurt, sometimes give off a natural but nasty gas called hydrogen sulfide. Vintners call it "sulfide stink"; most people know it as rotten-egg smell. Left untreated, it can permanently taint an otherwise nice wine with an oniony or rubbery scent. What's more, yeasts in the middle of a fermentation sometimes use up all the nitrogen and other nutrients they need to survive; and if the shortfall is severe enough, the fermentation can slow or even stop. You're better off trying to dodge the problem up front than to cure it later. Giving food to your yeasts, in the right doses at the right times, can often do the trick.

What is yeast food, exactly? You'll find several versions out there, but most contain some form of nitrogen, a nutrient as essential for yeasts as it is for roses and corn, along with blends of vitamins and minerals, like your own once-a-day supplements, and some exotic items like yeast hulls. (For more details, see page 180.)

Yeast food typically comes as a pale, clingy powder that you add in stages to the fermenting must. (It won't spoil the flavor of your wine.) You don't want to toss it in all at once, however. The danger is in setting off a burst of rampant growth that could overheat the yeasts. Here's an easy feeding schedule, adapted from directions for Superfood, a blend developed by the Wine Lab (Gusmer Enterprises) in Napa, California. (It's best to weigh out the powder, but if you don't own a scale, add a half teaspoon per 1 gram of yeast food called for.)

Day 1 (yeast starter added): 5 grams food per 5 gallons must

Day 3 (lots of bubbles; Brix about 18): 2 grams food per 5 gallons must

Day 5 (still bubbling; Brix not lower than 10): 1 gram food per 5 gallons must

Simply dissolve the yeast food in water, sprinkle it right on the must before punching down, and take pleasure in helping your tiny wine workers run a healthy, stink-free fermentation.

BRING ON THE BUGS

As the fermentation proceeds, you'll want to think about adding your malolactic bacteria (see page 183), which will take the wine through its secondary fermentation, softening its flavor. (A caution: If your grapes started out low in acid, you may want to skip this step.) With the cultured bacteria varieties available now, you shouldn't have to do anything more than sprinkle them in before punching down. There *is* a little twist, however. Experts haven't yet settled on the one perfect time to add the bugs. That's in part because different labs breed strains with their own special needs. Studies on one kind (*Viniflora oenos,* produced by the biological supply company Chr. Hansen) suggest the microbes grow best when they're added as soon as the yeasts are raging—that is, around the third day. Your safest bet? Follow the directions for whichever kind you buy. And remember that not all wines benefit from malolactic fermentation (see page 184).

Not so fast! By about the third day, your fermenter will be gurgling happily and your punching-down hand looking a little purple. You've already added some yeast food and maybe malolactic bacteria. Perhaps you've sipped some juice and noticed it turning less sticky and sweet.

And now the temperature's higher each time you check it. That's great—if you don't let it get out of hand. Apart from failing to punch down, letting the must grow too hot is the only big mistake you can make right now. Overheated yeasts will eventually swoon and die, leaving you with half-finished wine. (A "stuck fermentation" is what vintners call it; for a remedy, see page 76.) And even if the yeasts do pull through, high heat can brand your wine with odd, unpleasant flavors.

How hot is too hot? A thermometer reading above 90°F, taken after punching down, means you should promptly cool the must. (Chances are you won't need to perform this maneuver.)

Remove any sleeping bag or electric blanket you might have wrapped around the fermenter to keep it warm. Drop ice cubes from your freezer into a sturdy plastic bag, place that bag in another plastic bag, and then, so they won't leak, cinch both bags shut with rubber bands. Sink the ice bag in the fermenter and wait half an hour. Remove the ice bag, thoroughly mix the must, and check the temperature. Since yeasts, like Goldilocks, prefer their porridge just right, keep at it until the thermometer falls to about 80°F. Some wise winemakers fill a couple of plastic milk jugs with water and tuck them in the freezer ahead of time, just in case. (The pros have cooling units built right into their tanks and, yes, they use them.)

One 1.5-gram packet of freeze-dried cultured malolactic bacteria is enough to inoculate 60 gallons of must. Don't worry about adding too much inoculant.

A TARGET TO SHOOT FOR

So that's it. Your fermentation's rolling, and the week's ticking away. By about the fifth or sixth day, you may notice that the thermometer's falling, not rising, and things aren't so sticky anymore. In fact, the grape skins, which were once plump with juice and pulp, are now going limp, like tiny deflated balloons. When you stir up the must you can hear loose seeds rattle on the bottom of the tub. It's getting near the time to press—that is, to strain the spent skins and seeds out of the wine. And that means it's time to pay less heed to the temperature and more to the remaining sugar. This is when you really need your hydrometer. Winemaking's most enjoyable job is coming up.

5

A PRESSING ENGAGEMENT

It's hard to know whether to cheer or sigh as the primary fermentation bubbles to an end. At this stage, the only things between the stuff in your fermenter and actual wine are some grape seeds and skins. That's a heartening thought. But at the same time it's now truly autumn, and suddenly, as the cheery rhythm of the yeasts' life slows, your days aren't as eventful—no more punching down, no more purple arm, no more heady aromas filling the room. By the way, take note of a key wording change. You initially *crushed* the fresh grapes to let the yeasts at the juice inside; now you're about to *press* the fermented grapes to squeeze out the wine.

HOW TO TELL WHEN IT'S TIME

Each day you've watched your hydrometer sink lower and lower into the test jar—to 8, then 4, then 2. And then, surprisingly, it sinks below 1. What gives? The fermenter's still bubbling

Pulling on the ratchet-powered crank handle of an Italian-made no. 35 basket press to free the new red wine held by the grape skins. Most of the rig has sunk into the basket.

faintly and the cap is still rising, though not with the same force. Those are clear signs of life. But isn't the fermentation over when the hydrometer reads zero?

In a word, no. The juice in your fermenter—call it wine—is now about 13 percent alcohol. If yeasts consumed sugar and left only water, the hydrometer at the end of fermentation would read exactly zero. But yeasts make alcohol, and alcohol is so much less dense than water that it skews the readings lower and lower as it builds up. In fact, the exact timing of the pressing isn't crucial. Once the Brix is down to 2 or 3, you can press your wine and let it finish up—go dry, in vintners' lingo—in the carboys rather than in the fermenter. Or you can extend the time the grape skins stay in contact with the wine.

Because, like many aspects of winemaking, the decision on pressing is a matter of judgment, you'll hear a range of conflicting opinions. Press before the wine goes dry, some say, to dodge any possibility that spoilage bugs will infect the wine when it's no longer protected by a thick layer of carbon dioxide. Wait as long as you dare, others say, so that the flavor and color compounds in the grape skins have more time to diffuse into the wine. There's no single rule. The safest, easiest approach is to press when your hydrometer reading is in the range of zero—perhaps a few degrees higher, perhaps a few lower. If you hold off on adding sulfite and don't let the new wine get chilled, the last bit of sugar in the wine will ferment out in the carboys.

SQUEEZE AND SQUEEZE AGAIN

Your job now—a pleasant one—is to separate the grape skins and seeds from the wine. In theory, you could just pour the whole mess through a big sieve, keeping the wine and throwing out the rest. But those wet skins hold a lot of good wine—wine you worked hard to make. My advice is to rent a basket press from a brew shop for several hours. You've probably seen a picture of one in use. The device, seemingly a throwback, looks dark and musty, with staves of stained wood bound by metal hoops into a circular picket fence—the so-called basket.

Basket presses not much different from those used today by home winemakers have been employed since the Middle Ages. At some modern boutique wineries, they're now back in favor.

Basket presses, though antiquated, are the tools of choice for home winemakers. They come in a range of sizes from very small ones able to handle just a few gallons of grape skins to others that in one shot can press the skins from up to 100 gallons of must. Most are the hand-cranked type, with a stout screw through the center of the basket and a wooden plunger forced down by an iron lever-and-ratchet device at the top. They are graded by number in increasing size, commonly 25, 30, 35, 40, 45, and 50 liters. It's best, as a rule, to pick a press that seems small for your batch of wine, because you're likely to get more wine from the grapes if you press them in two or three little batches rather than one huge one. Also, you might want to keep an eye out for presses with baskets of perforated stainless steel. They're easier to clean and so are less likely to harbor spoilage bugs. Other types squeeze the grapes by means of a rubber bladder inflated via a hose hooked up to your home's water system or by a powerful hydraulic plunger driven by an electric motor; however, these versions aren't as commonly available for rent.

Homespun solutions.   There are options other than renting. For my first vintage, I studied pictures of basket presses and figured I could build my own. I cut oak staves with a power saw and hired a metal shop to make steel hoops. I made a press table out of oak and plywood, and bolted onto it two tall rods and a steel crossbar, with room beneath for the basket. Under the bar I placed the power of the press—a car jack from a flea market—and for years this setup served perfectly. Of course, there's no reason you should go to such lengths, especially if you're making a small amount of wine. Some brew shops sell a light-duty press made from a perforated plastic bucket rigged with a metal plate and screw. Or you can build a simple paddle press by hinging together two stiff pieces of wood, each 8 or 9 inches wide and perhaps 18 inches long. Scoop some wet grape skins into a clean cloth bag or a pouch made of cheesecloth, hang it above a tub or other wide-mouthed container, and then place your paddle press around the bag and squeeze as hard as you can.

If you do rent a basket press, be sure you get all the parts, including the crank handle, the plunger plates, wood blocks to stack between the plates and the ratchet, and especially the pawls—pointy little chunks of steel that are the ratchet's teeth, enabling it to drive down the plunger with each push or pull of the handle. Without the pawls, the whole rig is useless.

Fuss-free pressing.   Besides the press, you'll need a clean pail to catch the wine, a backup pail, some kind of big scoop—perhaps a 1-quart measuring cup or saucepan—and a carboy-size funnel. (For more on these items, see chapter 2.) Of course, you'll want clean, freshly rinsed carboys and gallon jugs standing by. I like to set up the whole business outside, even if that means dragging out the heavy fermenter, because the weather's usually fine and the pressing can get messy, especially if wine-laden grapes burst in the basket and spew magenta wine out between the staves. Also fetch a glass, so you can taste the new vintage, and perhaps put out a lawn chair or two, so friends who drop by can settle in and toast your success.

In other words, take your time—that's the single rule for easy pressing. Grape skins surrender the full measure of their wine only bit by bit. Don't resort to brute force, straining against the press handle with your teeth clenched. Go easy from the start, slowly scooping juice and skins into the basket and letting the wine drain gently into your pail. Stir the skins a bit, and then add more—stirring, scooping, stirring, scooping—until the press is quite full and no more wine is draining. Empty the first few buckets of drained wine into a carboy or jug, and ponder the one decision you have to make at this juncture: whether to keep the wine you just poured, the so-called free run, separate from the wine you press.

Tannins and pigments in the new wine may react with the iron in the handle on a basket press to stain your hands. Use fresh lemon juice or citric acid dissolved in water as a cleanser.

Free-run versus press wine. One of winemaking's age-old wisdoms is that free-run wine is softer and less tannic than press wine. It makes sense: The skins and seeds are in fact where the tannins reside, and giving them a squeeze must certainly liberate more bitterness. But does it really? Experts differ. Small basket presses, compared to the heavy-duty pneumatic ones used in commercial wineries, don't exert all that much pressure. But most home winemakers repeatedly break up and press the same batch of skins, bearing down hardest in the last pressing. What it comes down to is that the choice is yours. I like wines with bold flavors, and I don't like keeping track of extra lots, so I usually blend the press and free-run wines right then and there. But taste both as you go and decide for yourself.

You'll have plenty of time. Once the basket is full, place the half-moon plunger plates on top of the skins and push down gently with your hands. When you feel significant resistance, start stacking the blocks on top; they're needed to keep the ratchet from sinking uselessly into the basket. Build a tall log cabin of blocks—two this way, two more the other way—and then by hand wind the ratchet mechanism down the screw until it rests on the uppermost blocks. Things get tricky at this stage because any movement of the ratchet disturbs the blocks, disrupting the whole stack. There's nothing to do except fiddle with it—the technology is centuries old, after all—until there's enough friction to hold everything in place. Then crank the handle and watch the wine run. Take your time here, too, and give the grapes a break between squeezings.

The second pressing. Eventually, after many pushes and pulls, you'll feel the handle offering more and more resistance. Don't kill yourself trying to wring out those last few drops—you'll get them in a minute. Reverse the pawls so the ratchet winds up instead of down. Crank the whole works loose, lift out the blocks, and remove the basket and the plungers. Packed around the screw will be a dark cake of skins and seeds. Let it be for a moment. You're about to break up the cake, reassemble the basket, and press a second time, so you need to choose a clean place to drop the skins—possibly into your just-emptied fermenter or onto a clean garbage bag or sheet of construction plastic.

Grape seeds contribute most of the tannin in wines. To keep your wine from becoming overly tannic, take care during pressing not to crush or overpress the seeds.

When you do pull apart the cake, the skins will still feel heavy and wet. Don't blame the press. Winemakers have done the press-again two-step for centuries, and in fact the same thing goes on in commercial wineries, except that they have big pneumatic presses with computer controls that repeatedly ease the pressure, loosen the skins, and automatically start the press cycle over. Patience has its reward, which in this case is a lot more wine. Crumble the loosened skins back into the basket—it'll take more of them now—and then press a second time, and even a third if you won't feel let down by the diminishing returns on your investment. Try to end up with a bit of extra wine—a standard wine bottle or even a gallon—to use for topping up (replacing the wine the carboys lose to sampling) when the fermentation is finally done.

INTO THE CARBOYS

As you pour the new wine from the buckets into the carboys or jugs, fill them nearly but not quite full, which is to say up past the shoulders but not into the neck. You want a couple of empty inches there so the still-fermenting wine has room to bubble and foam without overflowing. It's okay to let the bottles stand around open while you finish pressing, but if there are fruit flies or other bugs around, wad up some clean paper towels and temporarily stopper each jug until you have time to fetch the fermentation locks.

Of course, you'd be smart to have some ferm locks and drilled stoppers already washed and at hand. Either way, before you get started on the task of cleaning the press, buckets, and fermenter (see page 66), gently lift each carboy or jug as if it were your firstborn child and move it indoors to a quiet place where it can stay for the next few weeks. Place a stopper in each jug and a ferm lock in each stopper, and then fill the locks with water and take a deep breath. Hard to believe, but your wine is nearly made. That's not to say there's nothing to do—or that nothing else will happen—only that you've passed a milestone and from now on, really, it's all small stuff.

THE IMPORTANCE OF BEING EARNEST

The mortal enemies of wine are air and spoilage microbes. Sometimes they go hand in hand, which is to say that some bad bacteria grow only in the presence of air—or oxygen, rather, which makes up about 20 percent of the air we breathe. But oxygen alone can ruin wine; and some microbes thrive in wine protected from air. So there are really two kinds of winemaking hygiene: one to prevent unwanted oxidation, the other to keep spoilage bugs at bay. You don't have to become a fanatic, but it does pay to be devout.

- *Wash after, rinse before.* A cardinal rule of winemaking: never let just-used presses, pails, funnels, siphons, and empty carboys stand around dirty. Wash them as soon as you can—ideally, within the hour. It's far easier to clean equipment before spent yeasts and residual pulp have dried into a tough crust. A related caution: Don't assume that a seemingly clean piece of equipment is really clean unless you washed it and stored it properly yourself. If you have done so, all it will need before its next use is a thorough rinsing with water. (For details on cleaning agents, see page 33.)

- *Store it dry.* Molds and bacteria love moisture and humidity, especially around wine residue and yeast dregs. After that final rinsing of your empty fermenters and carboys, drain them well and set them aside unstoppered so the last traces of water can evaporate. I've found that clean paper towels, crumpled loosely, make good porous but dust-blocking plugs for the necks of empty carboys. However, there are worse sins than leaving carboys standing open but dry. Whatever's floating in the air where you make wine is likely to be less troublesome than what can grow in the damp. Likewise, drain and dry your hoses and racking wands by hanging them from hooks. And don't put wet stoppers or ferm locks in plastic bags; they'll turn moldy in days. Instead, drop them still wet into clean paper bags and fold the bags closed; everything will dry promptly.

- *Trust your nose.* It's an exquisitely sensitive detector. If any container smells funky—like dirt, mold, vinegar, rotten eggs, sulfite, or chlorine—keep washing and rinsing until it smells perfectly fresh and sweet. Of course, your nose can't sniff out every possible contaminant—spoilage microbes can be odorless—but no matter what, you want to get rid of everything that *does* smell.

- *Top up now.* If Bacchus claimed a glass of wine from every vintner who muttered, "Got to top up soon" and then didn't, the old god would be tipsy around the clock. Topping up—that is, adding back to carboys and barrels the wine lost to sampling and evaporation—is winemaking's easiest task and the easiest to let slide. Yet it's the best way to keep air and bacteria from causing trouble. Once a week is not too often. A couple of tips: When you can, add wine of the same vintage set aside in bottles for that purpose—perhaps some of the reserved press wine. Or use a mid-priced commercial wine akin to your own, preferably from a large, well-established maker likely to sterile-filter its wine. Don't forget to replenish the water in the ferm locks.

- *Remember to write!* Keeping a few notes, like pouring a little wine every week, is crucial and easy. It's the only way to keep track of what the grapes' sugar and acid were, how hot or cold the fermentation got and how many days it took, how much sulfite you've added, how many rackings you've done, and many other details you'll want to know later.

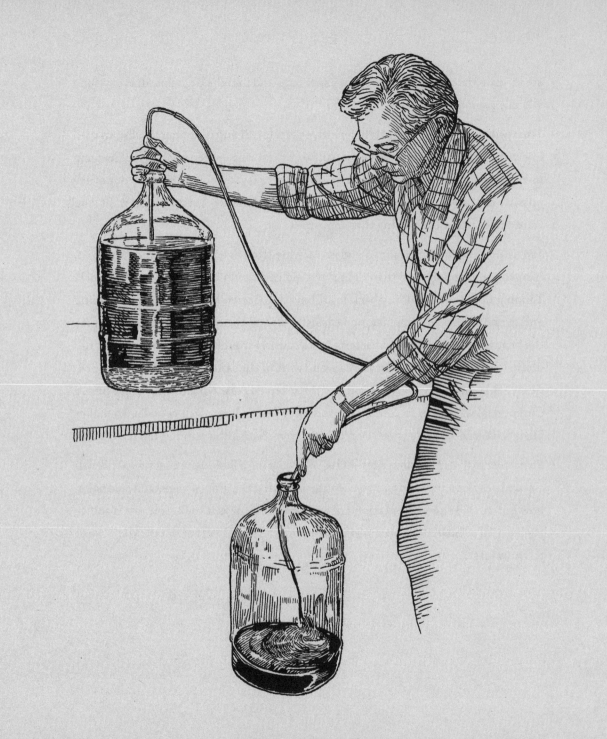

6

THE QUIET STAGE

WANDER THROUGH A SMALL COMMERCIAL WINERY in early winter, after the hubbub of the fall crush and the doggedness of the fermenting and pressing, and the place will seem almost sleepy. Perhaps an electric pump is humming as it sucks new wine from one steel tank and pipes it to another, leaving behind some muddy sediment. Or maybe a winery worker is rinsing empty oak barrels to ready them for the new vintage. There might be someone tugging a hose between rows of barrels, filling one after another with young wine, while a vintner, clutching a wineglass, ambles around taking samples—first swirling the glass and sniffing, then brusquely tasting and spitting. No one looks to be in a hurry.

In fact, what all wines need at this stage is an abiding calm. Straight out of the press, new wine is cloudy and almost thick with spent yeasts. If you swirl some in a wineglass and then wait a few seconds, you'll see the legs, or tears, crawling up and down in the glass above the liquid, proof that the wine is graced with a respectable amount of alcohol. Nonetheless, it

---

Racking—that is, siphoning—the newly made wine away from the gross lees (spent yeasts and pulp) that have settled in a thick layer at the bottom of the carboy.

hardly even smells like the wines you're used to and maybe tastes both sour and sweet. It's wine, all right, but barely. Right now, the yeasts need time to polish off the last smidgen of sugar, while the special bacteria you added will be at work turning tart malic acid into mild lactic acid. The dead and inactive yeasts will slowly settle out. Your job is mainly to watch and wait as the wine improves itself.

The purple and pink. The first thing you'll notice—soon after pressing, in fact—is that the wine is already "falling clear," or beginning to clarify with a little help from the force of gravity. Vast numbers of yeasts, which as microbes go are virtual elephants, have already joined the grape pulp and detritus at the bottom of your carboys, leaving a large amount of deep purple wine standing atop a pink layer of sediment, known to winemakers as the lees. Resist the temptation to hurry things along by, say, pouring the wine off the lees. Unless there's a problem (see "Signs of Trouble, and Remedies," below), the lees are actually helpful for a while, supplying nutrients to the malolactic bacteria, adding flavor complexity to the wine, and even capturing some of the compounds that can generate off odors.

KEEPING YOUR BUGS HAPPY

The one action you definitely want to take is to keep the carboys at a middling temperature— that is, between 65°F and 70°F. Malolactic bacteria are finicky creatures who give up when they get too cold or too hot. If you can arrange to keep the room temperature steady around the clock, great. If not, you may want to wrap the carboys loosely in an electric blanket or perhaps place them in a closet or large box alongside a heating pad. (Never set a carboy directly on a heating pad or electric blanket—the heat can be too intense.) Dial the device's temperature to the lowest possible setting, wait a few hours, and then with your thermometer check the temperature of the wine itself—and keep checking it regularly. Don't let the wine get much warmer than 70°F. Remember, you haven't added any protective sulfite since pressing, and warm temperatures can favor the growth of spoilage microbes.

Tiny bubbles. Soon after the lees first settle in the carboys, you'll see bubbles rising through the wine and at times hear the ferm locks burping, indicating that carbon dioxide is still being made. You may not see *a lot* of bubbles. The evident activity can vary enormously depending on how much sugar was left when you pressed, how warm the wine is, and how far the malolactic bugs have already come in their low-key fermentation. You do want some bubbles, however, even ones so tiny that they appear as a nearly invisible mist inching up the shoulders of the carboys. If you're a worrywart, as I am, you'll sometimes find yourself on your knees, searching with a flashlight for signs of life in your dark, diminutive universe.

Malolactic fermentation can last a long time—weeks or even months—and it can take a while to get rolling as the bacteria slowly multiply. Don't worry if soon after pressing your wine goes still. Chances are good—especially if you added freeze-dried malolactic bacteria—that during the primary fermentation the bugs finished their job alongside the yeasts. If after a couple of weeks despite your ministrations with the blanket and thermometer, all remains quiet in the carboys, you should check to see if the secondary fermentation is indeed over.

Start by running your own seat-of-the-pants assessment. Suppose your newly pressed wine started out quite tart, with a faint flavor of green apple (from the malic acid). In the carboys, it bubbled lightly but continuously for two weeks before slowly falling still. Sampled now, the wine tastes markedly less acidic and the green apple flavor is gone, replaced by one that's more grapey. Another approach is to stopper tightly and refrigerate a small bottle of the just-pressed wine, and then weeks later warm it to room temperature and taste it side by side with the wine on the lees. If the wine from the carboy tastes and smells less tart and appley, you can assume—though not with absolute confidence—that it has gone through malolactic, as vintners say.

Only checking the actual malic and lactic acid levels can tell you beyond doubt whether the secondary fermentation is over. To run a check at home, you'll need a malolactic test kit, available at a brew shop for the price of a couple of bottles of wine. (For details on running and interpreting malolactic tests, see page 161.) Or send a sample to be tested by a professional lab (see page 233).

READY TO RACK?

Two weeks have gone by and your wine is now quiet. At the bottom of each carboy is a thick layer of pink lees. Your assessment—from either a sensory or a chemical test—is that the malolactic bugs have done all they're going to do. It's time to start clearing up the wine and getting it ready for bottling. The process is called racking. It's an ancient term for the venerable step of removing the wine from the lees. Although the first racking comes on no set schedule, you don't want to put it off for too long. The lees may not be evidently active, but in fact the dead yeasts are slowly beginning to break down, like fallen leaves in a forest, possibly adding funky flavors to your wine. And the wine needs a small dose of sulfite to keep it healthy.

For easier racking, place a wide wedge of wood under one edge of the carboy so the jug remains tipped at a slight angle.

You've tasted wine vinegar, right? The root of the word *vinegar* is French: *vin aigre,* "sour wine." In fact, it wouldn't take much to turn your nice new wine that way—just a bit of air and some bacteria of a kind that are only too happy to change the alcohol the yeasts made into sharp acetic acid. These microbes, a kind known as *Acetobacter,* get around on the feet of fruit flies. One way to stop these bad bacteria from having their way with your wine is to add a touch of sulfite while racking.

Lift each full carboy up onto a table or a stack of crates or boxes, taking care not to tilt the bottles and disturb the lees, and then pull off and set aside each stopper and ferm lock. (You'll want to clean them thoroughly before putting them back on.) Line up a variety of clean, empty carboys and jugs. (You'll lose some wine in the racking, so give yourself some size options.) Set a freshly rinsed carboy on the floor—its neck should sit a couple of inches below the bottom of the full carboys—and locate and rinse your racking wand and siphon hose. For convenience, park them in the empty carboy while you follow through with the next step.

Keep in mind that sulfite—the powder you add—is less than two-thirds sulfur dioxide and only a part of that is active. The doses that you're adding are tiny.

Measuring out the sulfite. You've already added sulfite once—when crushing the grapes—but most of that initial dose is now gone. Some of it dissipated as sulfur dioxide gas during the heat of fermentation, while another portion, absorbed by the grape skins themselves, vanished at pressing. The small dose you add now will not only help keep bacteria at bay but also preserve your wine's color and flavor. It's best to add about 45 parts per million of sulfur dioxide—an amount well below what your nose and taste buds can detect. A perfectly respectable rule of thumb is to add 1.5 grams of sulfite (or three-quarters of a teaspoon) to each 5-gallon carboy at the first racking. (There are times when you'll want to add less or more. See "Signs of Trouble, and Remedies," below, and chapter 14, page 189.)

I find it easiest to weigh out each dose of dry sulfite, dissolve it in a bit of water, and pour the mixture into each empty carboy, swirling it into the first few inches of wine to be sure it disperses fully before I fill the container. Others favor preparing a stock solution of sulfite and water, which they then measure out with a pipette. (For a formula, see page 197.)

Letting gravity do it. With your new sulfite dose ready and waiting, remove the racking wand and siphon tube from the empty carboy and add the sulfite. Place the wand in the full carboy—but *don't let its tip plunge into the sediment on the bottom*. Holding the tube several inches into the wine, lower your head near the carboy to be filled, exhale deeply, and start the siphon by sucking on the tube's free end until wine flows continuously. Stop the flow with your thumb, and shift that end of the tube to the empty carboy. It's a good idea to splash and swirl the wine gently as it fills the carboy. The agitation stirs in the sulfite, gets rid of some unpleasant aromas built up during fermentation, and adds a dose of oxygen, which helps the wine's flavor begin to soften.

While the carboy drains, swing the end of the racking wand over to the near side so you can see it through the glass. Keep pushing the wand down while tipping the bottle slightly, taking care to avoid breaking the suction or letting the wand pick up sediment. Close to the bottom, use the hose clamp to slow and then stop the flow. With the clamp pinched shut, lift out the siphon and quickly place both ends in the liquid in the newly filled carboy so wine remains trapped in the tube. This step isn't necessary—you can just let the wine run out—but keeping the siphon full is a neat trick that lets you carry on with the next carboy without having to restart the suction.

Before doing so, rinse the lees from the just-emptied carboy and pour a sulfite dose into the next empty carboy. As you proceed, you'll realize that losing the lees means the fresh containers won't fill as full. In fact, depending on how much pulp and yeast made it into the carboys and how careful you were with the siphon, you may end up as much as 10 percent to 20 percent short of the original volume. Don't shed any tears—you certainly didn't want the yeasty goop you got rid of. Instead, divide the purified wine among smaller containers, or combine it in larger ones, so that each one is full right up into the neck. A bit of oxygen was fine at racking, but now air is your wine's sworn enemy. Put clean stoppers and ferm locks in the mouths of the containers, place them in a quiet spot, and dust your hands. Your wine is made.

SIGNS OF TROUBLE, AND REMEDIES

Although most fermentations run through to completion without problems, sometimes things can and do go wrong—and not always because of actions you did or didn't take. If you're an observant vintner, watching, tasting, and sniffing at every stage, you can catch your wine's maladies while they're just getting started and take steps to cure them.

Stinky! The must during active fermentation should smell clearly grapey and pleasantly yeasty, and in fact it's wise to give the fermenter a pointed sniffing each time you punch down. If you begin to notice a strong dirty-socks or rotten-egg odor, think about taking action. What you're detecting is hydrogen sulfide gas, which yeasts sometimes make from sulfur in the must. As often as not it simply fades away, or "blows off," in vintners' lingo, which is to say that a faint funky aroma is not cause for alarm. But if enough of the gas builds up, it can permanently taint the finished wine's aroma and flavor with secondary sulfur compounds called mercaptans. Enologists quibble over the causes of sulfide stink. Some point to vineyard practices, others to the nutrient needs of particular yeast strains. No matter what, good evidence suggests that adding yeast food early in the fermentation can in many cases fend off the problem. Start your treatment immediately by mixing 2 grams of yeast food into every 50 pounds (5 gallons) of must. Don't add more! Instead, wait a day or two and add another 1 gram per 5 gallons, and the same dose two days later as the fermentation reaches its midpoint. After that, don't add any more yeast food.

Adding yeast food early in a fermentation can often stop the formation of pungent hydrogen sulfide gas. Use your senses from the start, and make any additions cautiously.

If after pressing your wine still smells of hydrogen sulfide, sit tight while the wine rests on the lees and finishes its malolactic fermentation. Then, at the first racking, vigorously aerate the wine. Fill carboys half full and shake them hard for several minutes to free the dissolved gas—you'll smell it blowing off—and then pour together two half-full carboys. Or repeatedly pour the just-racked wine through a funnel from one carboy into another. Be sure to mix in a dose of potassium metabisulfite as usual, at least 1 gram per 5 gallons of wine, or about 30 parts per million of sulfur dioxide (see page 191). It's counterintuitive, but the sulfur dioxide reacts with the hydrogen sulfide, cleaning up the aroma. Repeat the aeration in successive rackings and with luck your wine will come out smelling like a rose.

Still sweet. A less-common wine malady is known as a stuck fermentation. Ordinarily, the yeasts are happy to consume every last bit of sugar in the must, and vintners hoping to make wine with a small amount of residual sugar often have go out of their way to preserve it. Occasionally, however, a red wine fermentation will greatly slow or even stop before the hydrometer reading hits zero or even 2 or 4.

There's no single cause of stuck fermentations. Sometimes the fermentation has simply been started in a must that was overly sweet—28 or perhaps 30 Brix—and the yeasts can't polish off the sugar before being overwhelmed by the rising alcohol (about 17 percent). In other cases, a must with a normal sugar percentage gets too hot or too cold. If the temperature during fermentation rises to 100°F, the yeasts may be killed outright. If it falls below 50°F, the yeasts may so sluggishly attack the sugar that they might as well be dead. Other causes may be less obvious—nutrient shortfalls in the grapes, for instance, microbial infections, or an overdose of sulfite.

Not surprisingly, different causes call for different remedies. If the fermentation is simply sluggish—that is, there's a weak cap of skins—but the temperature of the must is below 55°F, take steps to warm it to about 70°F, perhaps by wrapping the fermenter in an electric blanket or moving it to a warm room. At the same time, add a small dose of yeast food (about 1 gram per 50 pounds or 5 gallons) and there's a good chance your must will spring to life. If during fermentation the must got quite hot—above 90°F after punching down—and has now gone completely quiet with several degrees of sugar left, take the two steps above plus an additional one. Make an active yeast starter by inoculating a half-gallon or gallon of crushed wine grapes or unfiltered, organic grape juice with a 5-gram package of wine yeast, carefully rehydrated (see page 50). (Pour the juice into a pail before adding the yeast.) Wait to add it to the fermenter until the partly fermented must has warmed to at least 65°F, and punch down this time with some extra vigor, deliberately mixing some air into the must.

If the fermentation fails to kick off again, try this somewhat laborious method. While keeping the must warm (at least 65°F), hydrate a fresh batch of yeast and use it to start a wholly new active fermentation in a modest batch of crushed wine grapes or unfiltered organic grape juice. Check the Brix religiously. When the Brix of the newly active must has fallen by about half, pour the fermenting must into a separate fermenter large enough to hold it *and* the entire amount of stuck must. Next, mix in enough of the stuck must to double the new must's volume; the merged musts should remain active. Measure the sugar. When the Brix in the active fermenter falls by half, double its volume again with more of the stuck must. Keep up this doubling and waiting until you've transferred all of the stuck must into the active fermenter. With luck, the fermentation will gurgle to completion within several days.

If that doesn't work, your wine may have some other issues, so to speak. In fact, fermentations that can't be restarted with these steps may never finish. Don't give up and do something drastic like pour the wine down the drain. Simply reset your expectations. In spite of your anxious labor at this stage, your slightly sweet wine may come out quite delicious. Blessedly, stuck fermentations are rare—and they're especially unlikely when the must's sugar and acid start out in balance and you launch the fermentation with genuine wine yeasts.

Barely any bubbles. Malolactic fermentations can also stick, after a fashion, which is to say that the benign bacteria get off to a slow start in their job of transforming malic acid into lactic and never pick up steam. They creep along for weeks or months, putting out barely enough carbon dioxide to make a ferm lock burp. Sometimes what causes the bacteria to falter is an oversight on the vintner's part—racking the wine off the lees too soon or adding too much sulfite—and there's little to do in such cases. Most commonly, though, the winemaker simply allows the wine to get too cold, perhaps storing it after pressing in a chilly garage or shed.

The remedy is to warm the wine in the carboys to about 70°F—measured with a thermometer in the wine itself—and maintain it at that temperature. (More warmth is *not* better— you could be rolling out the red carpet for spoilage bugs.) You can also try reinoculating the wine with a fresh dose of cultured malolactic bacteria, although some varieties prefer to take hold in wine that's actively fermenting. If mild, steady warmth and new bugs don't do the trick and eventually the wine goes completely still—some wines "wake up" in springtime warm weather—consider it finished, malic acid or none. Keep in mind that some of the most food-friendly red wines have relatively high acid levels. And besides, there are other methods of lowering a wine's acidity, if absolutely necessary (see chapter 13, page 169).

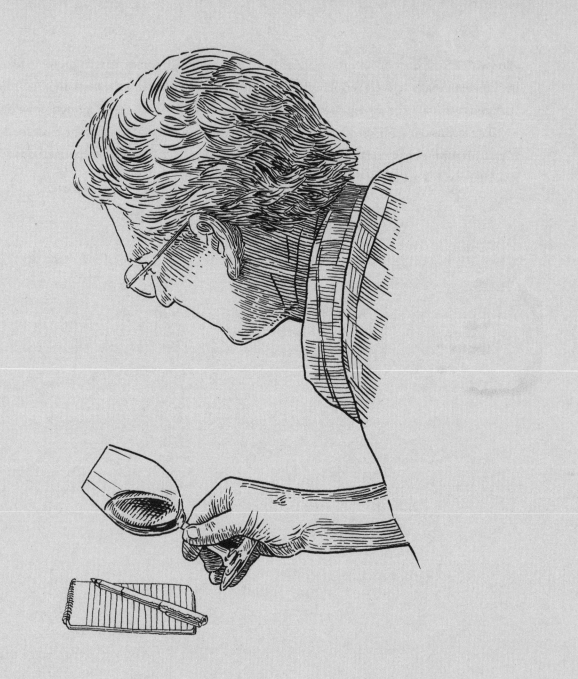

7

WATCHFUL WAITING

AMATEUR BREWERS LOVE TO TEASE HOME WINEMAKERS. Wine takes so long to make, they say. Our brew is ready in days—well, okay, weeks. But you have to wait, what, years? Of course, their taunts hold a grain of truth. It's now way past harvesttime and well into winter, and you still have months to go before you bottle the vintage. Ideally your new wine is resting in a cool, quiet spot, and the weeks are ticking by.

In the first racking, after the end of the fermentations, you siphoned the new wine away from the "gross lees," the thick layer of grape pulp and spent yeast that settled out after the wine went still. Now, after the racking, a new, much thinner layer of sediment is forming on the bottom. (This is one reason to choose carboys initially over stainless steel kegs: you can see what's happening through the glass.) Yet what's in the carboys is indisputably wine—flavorful and drinkable. It's like a college senior on the verge of graduation, a fully formed personality

Looking through a sample of young wine at a sharply defined background to check for cloudiness, browning, or effervescence—the first step in a full sensory analysis.

that's perhaps a little rough-hewn and tentative. Patience is the best policy at this stage. Now's the time to give the wine a thoughtful tasting.

SWIRLING AND SNIFFING

We've all seen caricatures of the snooty wine snob, reverentially holding a glass up to the light and swirling the wine before burying his nose in the glass and sniffing at length—an earnest, doglike sniff that gives way to a sucking, slurping taste with pursed lips and furrowed brow. It's a pompous display, and anyone caught dramatizing a commonplace like enjoying a sip of wine deserves a shot of ridicule. Or an elbow in the ribs.

But winemakers (and wine professionals) get a special dispensation. They can swirl and slurp and snuffle all they want—only down in the cellar, out in the garage, or far away in the yard. (When dining with family or friends, they should sip without fanfare, no matter how remarkable the bottle.) Ridiculous though it looks, the whole swirl-and-sniff ritual is a vintner's duty. When it comes to analyzing—and sometimes correcting—your newly made wine, your own senses are the cheapest and best tool you'll ever have.

Your tasting assistants. You can enjoy wine from juice glasses, tumblers, or even mason jars, as some friends of mine do, but the best glasses for wine analysis are the standard ones with stems, perhaps a bit larger and lighter than the ones they might use at your local spaghetti joint. Forget the fancy "tulip" glasses with straight sides that bulge at the bottom, the squat goblets broad enough for a Saint Bernard, and the pricey crystal specially designed to showcase the flavors of Cabernet or Burgundy. When it comes to stemware, like so many things, simple is best. You want tall wineglasses that are smooth and clear so you can easily judge the contents; with a long stem to hold so your hand doesn't block the view; with a tapered, moderately deep bowl so there's room for vapors to collect; and with a narrow mouth so aromas are funneled toward your nose. The glass should be completely clean, which in particular means free of any soap smell.

To do a legitimate sensory check of your wine, first give your senses some elbow room: Turn off the cell phone, put the dog out, and close the door. Set out a piece of paper and a pen, and then with a wine thief or pipette, dip into a carboy and withdraw some wine—about 2 ounces, or enough to fill your wineglass to a depth of about an inch. Don't swirl just yet.

When it comes to analyzing your newly made wine, your own senses are the cheapest and best tool that you'll ever have.

Look both ways. In bright light, tilt the glass so the liquid spreads up the side; then against a white background take a hard look at the sample. Actually, look *through* it, preferably at the sharp edge of some object against the pale background—a knife blade, a ruler, or some text on a page. (I often use the face of my wristwatch, which is white with silver hands and is always with me.) If you see any cloudiness, write down whether you consider it slight, moderate, or pronounced. Make a note, too, if you see any minute bubbles dispersed in the wine.

Now tilt the glass again and check the wine's color, focusing especially on the zone near the wine's edge. Is it dark and nearly opaque or light and quite transparent? Is it grape purple, cherry red, or cordovan brown? Write down everything you see, but don't expect any *aha!* moments. Right now, you're mainly establishing benchmarks, recording the wine's early state so you can watch it evolve.

One detail that doesn't warrant much scrutiny is the wine's legs, or tears—those long, mostly clear droplets that shimmy up and down inside the wineglass. Although you may have heard that a wine's legs are a sign of its quality, they simply tell you that the wine's endowed with a respectable amount of alcohol. It's fine to admire your wine's legs—they can be mesmerizing—but you'll learn much more from its other attributes.

The droplets that dance up inside wineglasses, which are called legs or tears, say nothing about quality. They mean only that your wine is well endowed with alcohol.

The nose knows. Don't taste the wine just yet. Set your wineglass on a smooth counter or tabletop, and holding the stem with one hand give it a quick, level swirl so the wine rises up the sides of the glass, circling around like water draining from a sink. Now lift the glass to your nose—put your nostrils down inside—and sniff a few times. Exhale, then swirl and sniff again.

Try to sort out the different scents. Does the wine have any off aromas—things like rotten eggs or wet dog? Describe what you sensed—just jot down whatever words come to mind—and say whether the aroma seemed mild, moderate, or strong. Swirl and sniff again. Beyond possible funky odors, do you smell grapes, blackberries, cherries, or other fruit? Can you detect what vintners call a vegetal aroma like that of newly mowed grass or green bell peppers? Is there a strong or mild alcohol smell? Maybe a suggestion of nail polish remover? Write everything down, and don't worry if you later read something like "Nice aroma of cherries, maybe raspberries. Slight grassiness." It's all legitimate and, eventually, helpful.

At long last, a taste. Pick up the glass and take a generous sip—good health!—but don't swallow it just yet. Swish the wine around in your mouth, making sure some of it passes between your teeth and your cheeks. Hold it on your tongue for a few seconds, letting it warm a bit. Finally, go ahead and swallow, then immediately exhale through your nose. Take note of any and all sensations. Does the wine feel hot or slightly fizzy? Does it provoke a puckery or drying sensation on your gums (what vintners call astringency)? How would you describe the wine's texture or body? Does it feel thin and watery or comparatively thick and viscous? (Think of nonfat versus whole milk.) Was the wine sweet or tart? What, if any, new scents did you pick up from that postswallow exhalation? Again, write it all down in whatever language makes sense to you.

THE SECOND RACKING

You now have a full sensory, or organoleptic, analysis of your new wine. Like an expert wine taster, you've noted aspects of its clarity, gas content, color, aroma profile, astringency, viscosity, and acidity. But what to make of it all? What should you do with the information? In theory, your observations help you decide what to do as you head toward the second racking. If, for instance, you see or feel pinprick bubbles in the sample, it's a safe guess that the wine is releasing carbon dioxide gas, which is to say that it may still be finishing its secondary, or malolactic, fermentation. The best step then is to let the wine stand for a few weeks, ignoring any sediment, while it ferments to completion.

Likewise, conspicuous cloudiness is your cue to sit tight. Every red wine should be clear by the time it's bottled—colorful, yes, but also brilliantly clear. New wines usually aren't. That's not necessarily because the winemaker made a mistake (although it can be). It most often means that the wine simply needs more time to get rid of whatever's still suspended in it. Most early cloudiness comes from particles that are fairly big and heavy, such as spent yeast cells, which after a week or two in the carboys give in to the force of gravity and fall to the bottom. But others are much smaller and settle more slowly. So if your wine looks hazy after its first racking, just wait and watch for a few weeks while the particles sink. In other words, there's no set schedule for the next racking (except that you don't want to wait forever). A good rule of thumb: Do the second racking about a month after the first. To each empty carboy add 1 gram of sulfite dissolved in a little water, fill the carboy up into the neck, put on a ferm lock, and set it in a cool place.

A handy rule of thumb: Adding 1 gram of potassium metabisulfite to a 5-gallon carboy yields 30 parts per million of sulfur dioxide in the wine.

About that funky smell. There's one crucial exception, however. If your tasting after the first racking turned up some strong or moderately strong off odors or flavors, you should rack again promptly, perhaps within a day or two. Don't worry if you noticed some mild to middling odors that might be described as raw or yeasty; those fermentation aromas will fade with time and additional rackings. But strong, unpleasant odors—especially a rotten egg smell—are cause for concern. That's because in many cases such off odors are from dissolved gases, typically hydrogen sulfide, which over time react with other compounds to form foul-smelling mercaptans, which can be hard to get rid of. To help disperse the gas, actively aerate the wine during racking. Partially fill clean carboys, and then stop the flow and give each jug a vigorous two-minute shake. Or pour the wine back and forth from one carboy to another. Before you finally top up the carboys, mix in at least 2 grams of potassium metabisulfite per 5 gallons of wine, for about

60 parts per million of sulfur dioxide. The compound will interact with the hydrogen sulfide, helping to neutralize the smell.

As for all the other qualities you noted in your tasting—color, body, astringency, tartness—they're important to know but tricky to change. A wine's color can't be easily shifted after fermentation except by blending (see page 217). Nor can you adjust its viscosity, sometimes described as body or mouthfeel, which comes mainly from the alcohol. Astringency, from tannins in the grape skins and seeds, actually *can* be softened, as can the tartness, or acid level. However, performing those adjustments requires some special know-how; for details, see chapter 15. You're best off at this stage striving to make a wine that's clean, clear, and free of sediment.

Crystals in the carboys. As you watch the last yeasts and bacteria pile up, you may begin to see a different kind of deposit in the carboys. The culprit is a compound called potassium bitartrate—tartrate, for short—a mildly acidic crystal that's chemically identical to the cream of tartar used in the kitchen to help baked goods rise. It forms spontaneously when tartaric acid from the grapes (or added by the winemaker) combines with potassium compounds in the wine, creating crystals that may settle into a crust on the bottom, cling to the carboys' sides, or perhaps even drift freely in the wine. You may have seen tartrates when you pulled the cork from a bottle of commercial wine. It's all perfectly natural, but because the crystals can be bothersome—that last sip from a wineglass can leave you with a mouthful of grit—winemakers take steps to get rid of them before bottling.

Some winemakers encourage tartrates to form by first chilling their wine, and then seeding it with rinsed tartrate crystals reserved from an earlier vintage.

Tartrate crystals form most readily at cold temperatures, so some vintners chill, or "cold stabilize," their wines before bottling so the crystals won't show up later in the bottles. The downside is that the chilling can lighten the color and detract from mouthfeel of big reds such as Cabernet and Syrah. At home, simply keep the carboys as cool as possible for several weeks and don't worry if you never see any crystals. Because of the unpredictable chemistry involved, some wines never produce tartrates, even when chilled.

THE THIRD RACKING

After cooling each carboy, rack immediately, while the wine is still cold, to leave any tartrate crystals and other sediment behind. Don't let the carboys warm up to room temperature before racking or a portion of the crystals may go right back where they came from—into solution in the wine. If you're thinking, *I never chill red wine before drinking it, so why should I care?* keep in mind that cooling helps in another way, too. Coaxing out some tartrate slightly lowers the wine's acidity, softening its flavor.

You can use your judgment about whether to add a touch of sulfite at this racking. If you've added it religiously up to now, you're planning to bottle fairly soon, and the wine is quite cold and clean-smelling, you can reasonably skip the sulfite dose. If, however, you skimped earlier on sulfite or the room is sometimes warmer than 65°F or the wine still has any kind of off odor, then a fresh sulfite addition's a must. As before, add 1 gram per 5 gallons and mix it in thoroughly.

A touch of oak? The third racking is also a good time to think about whether you want to expose your wine to oak, a step commonly called barrel-aging. It's standard practice at respected wineries, but a touchy one. If you want a stark example of what it means to be ambivalent, get a winemaker talking on the subject of oak. He or she will sing the praises of imported French barrels, made from oak harvested in hundred-year-old groves, which when air-dried and toasted impart an exquisite depth to a rich Cabernet or Syrah. Then the same vintner will turn around and complain bitterly about the barrels' breathtaking cost, their tendency to leak and lose flavor in a few seasons, and their propensity to lose wine through evaporation and to harbor spoilage microbes, so that they require perpetual refilling and fanatical care.

Says Randall Grahm of California's Bonny Doon Vineyards: "The people who consider oak a fundamental taste of wine are the same people who consider ketchup a vegetable."

That said, oak barrels do two notable things (apart from looking classy in a cellar). They admit small amounts of oxygen, which interacts slowly with the wine, giving it a softer feel and flavor. Meanwhile, the oak adds a gentle vanilla taste and aroma to the wine—more when a barrel is new, less and less with each year of use. The tough bind for home vintners is that in the world of barrels, sweet deals are hard to find. New oak barrels—even small ones—cost hundreds of dollars each, raising the cost of each bottle. And used barrels are a devil's bargain. You may be able to find one at a good price, but it's hard to know whether it's being banished for a reason: it sat empty too long and smells of vinegar, or it has leaked ever since it was new, or it's old and mostly flavorless, or, quite possibly, it's contaminated with invisible bacteria (often *Brettanomyces*) that taint any wine aged in it with a funky, earthy aroma.

Happily, some benefits of barrel-aging can be achieved in other ways. Oxygen seeps into the wine at each racking, reducing the need for further oxidation. And as for oak flavor, products available at brew shops have turned things upside down. Instead of putting the wine in wood, as is conventional, it's now possible to put wood in the wine, in the form of specially processed oak chips, cubes, or staves.

Made from the several types of oak commonly used for wine barrels, these products come in a range of styles. Often they've been toasted (lightly scorched by a flame), as is commonly done to the insides of quality oak barrels, and then sterilized with steam. The chips—coarse oak fragments—are the crudest and least costly. Cubes, sometimes labeled "beans" or "marbles," are small, square-sided pieces of toasted American and French oak. You can also find various types of oak staves—narrow planks—more suitable for use in an old, flavor-depleted barrel or stainless steel keg than in a narrow-mouthed carboy. Vintners at boutique wineries like to scoff at these products as ersatz and downscale—the enological equivalent of liquid smoke—but for home winemakers they're a cheap way to add a bit of complexity.

They're easy to use. You simply drop them into the carboys with the wine, tasting periodically as they steep for several weeks. Then, when enough oak flavor has diffused into the wine, rack again, setting aside the wood for possible use in the future. The caveat is to check the flavor and aroma early and often so you don't end up with wine that tastes like a newly sawed plank. It helps to hold out at least a small amount of untreated wine so you can sample the before and after side by side. Rack when you can just barely detect the oak.

The "no wood" option. Of course, many superb wines, especially crisp, light-bodied whites such as Sauvignon Blanc, Pinot Gris, and Riesling, are traditionally bottled with no oak aging at all. That's because the wood's flavor can overwhelm the clean and fruity taste of the grapes. What's less obvious, because barrels have become an icon of quality winemaking, is that red wines can also do without. Barrel-aging is a winemaking choice. The best wine my wife and I ever made is a Napa Valley Cabernet that fell beautifully clear at a time when we were between barrels. We bottled it anyway, and no one who has ever tasted it—including some ardent oenophiles—has missed the added flavor. In fact, what they've often said is, "This is a really excellent Cab. Where in Napa did you say the grapes are from?"

8

BOTTLING AND BEYOND

According to decades-old handwritten notes, my wife and I bottled our first wine barely four months after the harvest date. Using a new siphon and a floor corker we borrowed from friends, we started filling bottles and driving corks in mid January. Our wine had "aged" in a brand-new 15-gallon French oak barrel for all of three weeks—ample oakiness by then—receiving a fourth and final racking before bottling. As it turned out, we jumped the gun. My notes say the bottles soon began showing a thin layer of sediment (yeast, I assume), and just-poured glasses had what I described as a "bit of spritz." We poured the wine freely anyway—loved it, actually—but we've long since become more patient. And more observant.

Wine is ready to bottle when it's clear, clean-tasting, balanced, and stable. The swirl-and-sniff and racking techniques explored in chapter 7 helped you move your wine along to the clear-and-clean stage. And now, after just a few rackings, your wine is well on its way to stability—future stability, that is. A stable wine is one that won't someday act up

Bottling the finished wine, using an Italian-made floor corker, while bottles are filled from a recently racked carboy set on a stack of several cases of empty bottles.

in the bottle, either by dropping loads of sediment or by spoiling through the action of microbes or oxygen.

THE FOURTH AND FINAL RACKING

The third racking, right after you chilled or cooled your wine, got rid of any tartrate crystals that settled out. Now the weeks are rolling by, and the wine's just sitting there, apparently doing nothing. As a rule, red wines tend to keep getting clearer as more minute particles settle into a light new layer of sediment. Check the clarity once a week—you eventually want to see no haze whatsoever—and then rack for the fourth time after a month or two, or at least before the weather warms up in May or June.

It's essential to add a dose of sulfite at this final stage. The wine is facing possible years in the bottle, but much of the sulfite you added earlier is no longer helping. Some of it stayed with the fermented skins and yeast lees, now long gone, while the bits added in the intermediate rackings have by now lost much of their protective oomph. To prevent oxidation and spoilage in the bottle, weigh out 1 gram of sulfite per 5-gallon carboy and add it during racking.

A professional vintner wouldn't only check the clarity and add sulfite at this prebottling stage. He or she would also send a sample of the wine to a lab for wide-ranging analyses that might include precise readings of the total acidity, pH, sulfur dioxide content, malic acid levels, residual sugar, alcohol, volatile acidity—perhaps as many as 25 different tests in all. But tests take time and cost money, and besides, there's no use fussing over technical details you can't do anything about. You checked the sugar and acid before fermenting? Got rid of any off odors during racking? Let the wine fall completely clear? Added a last dose of sulfite? That means you're ready to bottle.

BOTTLES AND BOTTLING

There's a happy finality to bottling your wine, and on one level the job couldn't be easier. You simply siphon the wine into clean bottles, drive a cork into each one, and call your work done. But the road to bottling has a few twists and turns—and some shortcuts as well—that make it worth your while to think things through before the fateful day. At the very least, you'll need to make some decisions about which kinds of bottles and stoppers to use, what sizes, how much money or energy you want to spend getting them, and whether to buy or rent a corker.

Where the green glass grows. Having made a batch of nice table wine, you'll of course want to show it to best advantage. You have a range of options. I've met winemakers who started out with beer and so had on hand a supply of sturdy sparkling-wine bottles. These bottles' virtues are strength—to bear the pressure of the carbon dioxide gas—and a special stout lip designed to accept a bottle (crown) cap, used temporarily at a stage in the making of many sparkling wines. Bottle your wine with beer caps? Sure, if you're already set up to do it that way.

But let's face it. Standard wine bottles are classier. It's not ridiculous to think of them as coming in just two styles and two colors—either straight-sided or sloped, and green or clear. In fact, though, wine bottles come in a maddening variety, and even within "green" you have a choice of perhaps 20 different shades, from a pale yellow-green to bluish to grayish to a forest green so dark it's almost black.

One way to avoid having to make a choice is to save or scavenge empty wine bottles and just take whatever you end up with. It's a fine way to get free bottles—well, they're free if you overlook the considerable labor of soaking and scraping off the labels and sanitizing the bottles. But the easiest option is to buy cases of new empties. (I actually buy recycled bottles from a company that runs them through a huge dishwasher to blast off the labels and sterilize the glass.)

Buying new (or sterile recycled) bottles has one huge advantage: you just fill them up—no washing or rinsing needed. Shouldn't anything that holds wine be cleaned? In this case, no. At commercial wineries, new bottles go straight onto a conveyor that takes them to the filler and corker—no wash water in sight. And those bottles hold wines destined to age for decades.

The elements of style. The other advantage of buying new glass is that you get to choose your bottles—traditionally deep green for red wines, yellow-green or clear for whites. Cabernet Sauvignon, Merlot, Zinfandel, Sauvignon Blanc, and Pinot Gris (or Grigio) usually take straight-sided Bordeaux-style bottles, while Pinot Noir, Syrah, and Chardonnay end up in the slope-shouldered Burgundy- or Rhône-style ones. Whatever the style and color, don't feel that you have to buy bottles with punts (bottom indentations). Plain, flat-bottomed bottles hold wine every bit as well, and they're often cheaper.

Before you take the easy route and buy your bottles at a brew shop, check the phone book and the Web to find some of the many glassmakers and distributors in cities around the country. They'll almost certainly offer better prices. A full case (12 bottles) runs from about $3 to $10, depending on, among other things, how many cases you buy. (To figure out how many cases you need, divide the total gallons of wine you plan to bottle by 2.4—the number of gallons a case holds.) If you bump up against a minimum order—say, ten cases when you need just five—see if you can find another winemaker in need or, perhaps even better, stockpile your extras for the next vintage. Think, too, about bottling a portion of your vintage in 1.5-liter magnums; one magnum does the job of two 750-milliliter bottles but may cost less.

> *To figure out how many cases of bottles you'll need, divide the gallons of finished wine by 2.4. To find the actual number of bottles, multiply your case count by 12.*

Buying corks. New corks can be pricey—up to half a dollar each—but unfortunately there aren't many alternatives. If the cost gives you shivers, at least consider screw caps, also available at brew shops. Lined inside with a long-lived and flavorless plastic, screw caps are starting to show up on top-tier commercial wines, a sign of their reliability. You just twist them on—no tool required—and they make a perfect airtight seal. However, bottles with matching threads may not be as easy to find as standard wine bottles. And together they destroy the romance of the cork-and-corkscrew ritual. Synthetic corks—that is, plastic stoppers molded to look like natural corks—are an option, though not a perfect one. The plastic resists being compressed, making them difficult to drive down the neck of a bottle with a corker. And once in place, they're not as good at conforming to the neck, possibly leaving you with some bottles that "weep," or leak. In fact, when you use imitation cork you come to appreciate the wonders of the real thing.

If standard grade-A corks strike you as too costly, see if you can find composite corks—cork bits bonded together and capped at each end with a slice of real cork.

Should you buy a corker? Check out the handheld corkers sold at brew shops. They're inexpensive but a little awkward to use—fine for small bottlings. The best corkers have a tripod base that hugs the floor without wobbling and a stout lever that in one smooth motion compresses the cork and pokes it into place in the bottle. It's a well-designed gadget and a tempting purchase for anyone who likes using simple tools. But a corker, like lot of winemaking equipment, sits idle for months and then serves briefly, perhaps for a few hours, before being mothballed again. So you might consider borrowing a floor corker or renting one from a brew shop, at least for your first few vintages. Put any money you save toward the best grapes you can find.

You may, however, want to invest in a bottling wand, a cheap tool that's simply a piece of stiff plastic tubing with a valve at one end. Plugged into your siphon, the wand makes it easy to start and stop the flow of wine from the carboy. Simply plunge the wand to the bottom of an empty bottle and lift as the wine rises into the neck. The only drawback is that the wand itself displaces a tablespoon or so of wine, and you can end up under-filling the bottles (see "Bottling Dos and Don'ts," facing page). A final poke against the neck lets out enough wine.

> *When bottling, wait for the corks to dry, and then with a waterproof pen write the year on the cork and the year and grape variety on each case.*

AGING GRACEFULLY

There's a definite thrill in declaring your wine done and ready to drink. But is it actually ready to drink as soon as it's bottled? The answer is yes—and no. On one hand, many red wines grow conspicuously softer and more complex as they age, and you'd be a fool to un-cork the whole vintage before it has a chance to "develop in the bottle," as connoisseurs say. On the other hand, if the wine's good enough to bottle, it's good enough to drink, and in fact it's part of your duty (and pleasure) as a winemaker to study it as it evolves. So keep your corkscrew handy. You'll have the chance to taste what vintners call bottle sickness, a brief phase just after bottling when the wine can taste strangely awkward and unpleasant. You'll then notice it settle down into a stage when it's at its freshest, with the flavors of the fruit at the fore. And you'll witness the steady shift toward maturity—softer tannins, and the more subtle and complex aromas that wine experts have dubbed *bouquet*.

Your wine cellar. The bouquet that old wines develop isn't necessarily better than the bright fruit character of young wines, it's just different. To enjoy the intriguing evolution is one reason for making your own in the first place—so take at least a few steps toward creating a spot for your bottles to age. You don't need an actual cellar, but your wine will age most gracefully if it's kept someplace consistently cool. A wine stored in a site that's alternately cool and warm may suffer just as much as one kept slightly warm for long stretches. Wine expands as it warms and shrinks as it cools, drawing smidgens of air—oxygen—past the cork and into the bottle.

What difference does that make? A lot, potentially. I showed up for a meal at a friend's house with a ten-year-old bottle of our Cabernet, only to find that he'd put out a bottle of the same wine, which I'd given him years earlier. There were several guests, so we opened both bottles. The wines were amazingly different. His had a brownish tint and tasted dull while mine, still purple, had a lively flavor and a nice bouquet. I asked where he'd kept his bottle, and he pointed to a high shelf in a pantry off his kitchen. Near the oven. Across from big south-facing windows. Around the corner from a

Bottling Dos and Don'ts

You'll feel more confident of your wine's chances of a long, healthy life if you follow through on a few little details.

- Rinse but don't otherwise treat your corks. Soaking and boiling are simply unnecessary, and immersing the corks in sulfite solution can actually weaken them and possibly cause them to leak or let air into the bottle. A brief rinse gets rid of any cork crumbs or dust that might end up in the bottled wine. And the water slightly softens and lubricates the corks so they slide in easily.

- Take your time. If you're hurrying, it's easy to overfill bottles, knock over uncorked ones, or lose the suction in the siphon. Bottling goes most quickly if two people work together, with one person filling while the other corks and sets up the empties.

- Don't overfill the bottles. You want just half an inch of space in the neck between the wine and the cork. Air may be the enemy of wine, but the smidgen in the bottle is an essential cushion that lets the wine expand and contract slightly with temperature shifts. Overfull bottles may weep.

(continued)

(continued)

- Rack before bottling. That is, never bottle from a carboy with sediment in it, and never bottle wine that hasn't received a recent sulfite dose (unless you know the free sulfur dioxide level; see page 198).

- Don't let a carboy stand half full. There's no reason you can't spread the job of bottling over days or weeks— but always empty any carboy you start or pour any leftovers into smaller bottles and *fill them full*.

- Let the newly filled bottles stand upright for a day or two. If you immediately lay them on their sides, air under pressure beneath the corks may force wine to seep out.

- Don't place unused rinsed corks in a plastic bag. Damp cork turns moldy in a closed container. Instead, seal the stoppers in a clean paper bag so the moisture can evaporate.

wood-burning stove. My bottle had spent its decade in a dark cellar.

It's a sharp indictment of careless aging. I say "aging" because storing a bottle in your kitchen or pantry for several days or even a couple of weeks won't hurt it. However, leaving any wine in warm conditions for months or years really will shorten its life. Wine scientists say the ideal storage temperature is a constant 55°F. Realistically, though, anything under 70°F—a closet, back room, or basement—is better than storing the wine in the part of the house where you live year-round. Remember to lay the bottles on their sides so the corks remain wet and watertight.

POURING YOUR WINE— WITHOUT POURING IT ON

Our wine cellar, such as it is, is simply a cool basement room with a wall of wine cases stacked on their sides, corks out. All I need is a prompt that dinner guests are coming, and I'm down there on my knees, recalling the personalities in each box: the tough and tannic Cab that has finally turned nice; the berryish Zinfandel that's aging prematurely; the food-friendly Syrah that's vanishing fast. More guests than I care to think of have seen me emerge from the cellar with a bottle in hand and a grin on my face—a sign of impending danger.

There's not much difference—maybe just a glass of wine's worth—between a cheerful wine lover and an insufferable bore. Home winemakers are more than wine lovers—we're proud wine lovers. We love our wines and want our friends to enjoy them too. So we bring bottles to celebrations and potlucks, and give them as presents. We haul out old gems, still delicious after all those years. We wait like obedient retrievers to be praised and rewarded while at the same time, deep inside, we know we're being ill-mannered at the table. A casual remark about a just-opened bottle can unleash a flood of facts on the vineyard site, the grapes' sugar and acid levels, the yeast variety, the fermentation temperature, and on and on.

The classiest labels are simple. Think about naming your winery after a local landmark—Sleepy Creek or Corcoran Lagoon—and give just the year, grape variety, and place of origin.

If there's a rule for talking about your wine in polite company, it's this: don't even start. When pouring your wine for family and friends, name the grape and year, thank them humbly for any compliments, and then do what you can to change the subject. Your guests may pose a question or two as if they're actually interested. But accept that expression as a courtesy that in no way reflects a desire to know the trouble you had in deciding whether to rack right after fermentation or to boost the wine's complexity by letting it rest on the lees. To the uninitiated, winemaking's fine points are inscrutable and, beyond a certain point, obnoxious. Too many times I've caught myself mid-soliloquy—on malolactic bacteria and buttery flavors, on the impact of pH levels on free sulfur dioxide, on rootstock varieties and potassium levels in ripening grapes—and had to stop and remember winemaking's most basic guideline: it's just wine. Let it speak for itself.

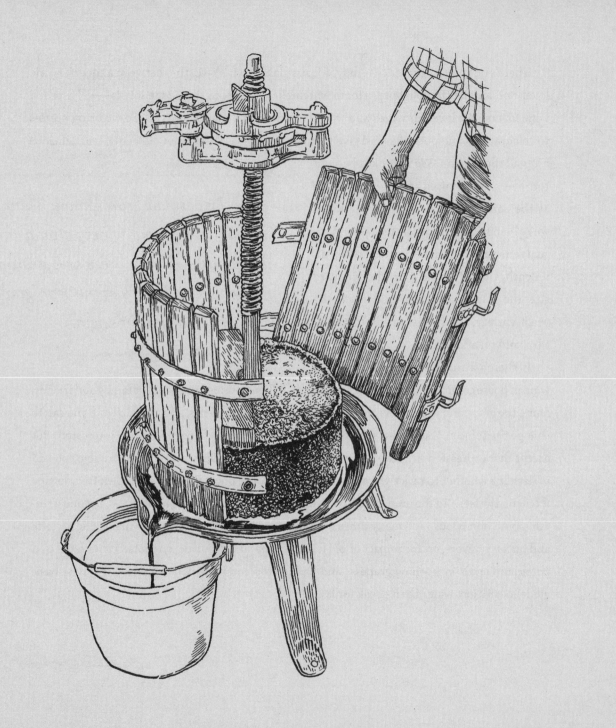

9

VIVE LA DIFFÉRENCE!

AFTER YEARS OF MAKING ONLY RED WINES, my wife and I finally delved into whites and rosés. What changed? Nothing, really. We simply stepped through a gate that had been chained shut by misconceptions—that the making would be troublesome, the details overwhelming, and the wines insipid. We were wrong. It's true, making white wines requires some extra choices and steps, especially before fermentation, and it definitely helps to have gone through the crushing, fermentation, pressing, and racking of a red wine so that you're practiced in the arts of checking temperatures, adding sulfite, topping up carboys, and so on. But after that there's nothing especially tricky about whites. For your efforts, you're rewarded with a range of bright fruit flavors and floral aromas—with wines that outshine reds alongside many foods.

Breaking down the basket on a basket press after the first pressing,
revealing the partly dry skins to be removed, loosened, and pressed again
in the reassembled press.

A BUNCH OF OPTIONS

You start, naturally, with white grapes—or, more precisely, varieties of wine grapes with just a hint of pigment in their skin so that their color at ripeness ranges from pale pink to gold to light green. Chardonnay, Sauvignon Blanc, Pinot Gris, Riesling, and Chenin Blanc are some of the classic grape varieties that produce distinctive white wines. As with reds, however, the only way to make good wine is to bring home good fruit. You can't tell the grower how to prune or when to pick, but you can at least expect to be promised clean grapes with decent levels of sugar and acid.

Some "white" wine grapes contain enough pigment to appear pink or greenish at harvest. Little of the color remains in the juice when the grapes are pressed right after crushing.

Crisp and fruity or rich and buttery? Beyond picking a grape variety, you'll want to decide up front whether you want your wine to go through malolactic fermentation, that stage in which special benign bacteria transform sharp malic acid into gentle lactic acid. Virtually all red wines are allowed—or encouraged—to undergo this fermentation, but for whites it's an option, a key style choice. Malolactic bacteria not only soften the wine's apparent tartness, but they also add a compound that gives the wine a distinctive buttery flavor. Many of the Chardonnays you've tasted have gone through malolactic fermentation.

In other whites, however, the secondary fermentation is frequently discouraged, letting the wine keep the crisp acidity and fruit flavors of the fresh grapes. To complicate matters, some vintners divide the same batch of grapes into two lots, encourage malolactic in only one, and blend the two wines at the end, thereby getting just a hint of butteriness. There are also ways to stop a fermentation so that only some of the tart malic acid is converted to mild lactic. Those steps take some special effort, however, and perhaps another additive (see page 221).

If you're a lover of rich, full-flavored Chardonnays, you may want to inoculate your wine with cultured malolactic bacteria, available at brew shops. (For more on malolactic fermentation, see pages 19 and 183.) If, on the other hand, you'd rather make a crisper wine—and that doesn't rule out Chardonnay—you'll want to skip the inoculation and take steps to stop freelance bacteria in your winery from launching the fermentation. Or, if you're a gambler, you can ignore the whole business. The one risk in taking the laissez-faire approach is that dormant bacteria might someday come to life in the bottled wine, turning it fizzy or possibly cloudy and rank.

A touch of sweetness? The malolactic decision isn't your only style option. Unlike red table wines, some whites are bottled with an evident hint of the grapes' original sweetness. In many cases this residual sugar helps boost the wine's fruit flavors and balance its tartness; and in fact some of the world's great table wines, notably Riesling and Gewürztraminer, are usually bottled with a bit of sugar—in some up to 3 percent or more. Likewise, many American standards, including Chardonnay and Sauvignon Blanc, may be finished with a percent or so of sugar. As with the malolactic fermentation, it's a matter of taste and style. And similarly, making that choice can mean going to some extra trouble. That's because in many cases the sugar-loving yeasts are happy to knock off all but the last bit of sweetness, leaving the wine completely dry—that is, with 0.2 percent sugar or less. A white wine that ferments to a stop won't necessarily taste sour. Some white fermentations leave up to 1 percent sugar. What's more, the alcohol itself lends a degree of sweetness, while acid levels and fruit aromas may heighten or diminish the taste of any sugar residue. If you've ever sipped a brisk Pinot Grigio from Italy or a tart Sancerre from France, chances are you've tasted whites fermented dry.

If you do decide to make a wine with residual sugar, a simple method is to let the wine go dry, chill and clarify it, and then add a bit of sugar (see page 227). Or you may want to do as commercial vintners do and track the falling Brix readings, preserving a touch of sweetness by cutting short the yeasts' activity. The twist in that approach is that it typically involves chilling the entire batch of wine, adding a stiff dose of sulfite, and fining or filtering to remove any residual yeasts (see page 222). Some home winemakers also add a chemical that keeps the yeasts from multiplying (see page 229). Since these are aggressive interventions, a fine option is to leave well enough alone and just bottle the wine as it is. Crisp, fruity white wines are superb with seafood and poultry dishes, or lovable and refreshing on their own.

Settled or unsettled? No matter what, by the time you launch the fermentation, you'll also need to decide whether to let the pulp settle in the carboys, and then siphon off the almost clear juice, or simply start the fermentation right away. Many winemakers skip the settling, insisting that the bits of drifting pulp add desirable complexity. But others argue that clarified juice yields cleaner-tasting wines with fruitier aromas. They warn that the pulp is a potential reservoir of stinky sulfur compounds and spoilage microbes—a definite worry if the grapes were moldy or, worse, a little vinegary. Because I like whites that are light and fresh, I take the second route and let the pressed juice stand before fermentation, having filled the carboys to the top so there's little exposure to air. I then siphon out the clarified juice and leave the pulp behind.

Which yeast? Last and perhaps least is the choice of yeast. Brew shops carry several varieties with evocative names—Côte des Blancs, Premier Cuvée, Pasteur Champagne, and more. Each has a special pedigree, such as exceptional cold tolerance or protection of the grapes' fruit aromas. Feel free to study up on the differences (see page 177) and pick one that sounds ideal. Just keep in mind that almost any yeast that thrives at cool temperatures and ferments slowly will do—and that's what to seek out. Bring home one 5-gram packet for each 5 gallons of juice you plan to ferment.

CRUSHING AND PRESSING WHITE GRAPES

White-wine making starts the way red-wine making does—with mechanically crushing the grapes—but then the differences mount. You immediately bucket the crushed grapes into a basket press and squeeze, so you end up with jugs of mostly pure grape juice (destined to become wine) and big piles of skins and stems (destined for the compost pile). Because there is no skin and pulp in contact with the juice during fermentation, there is no punching down for white wine. And there's no need for a big open-topped fermenter.

The pressing can differ, too. Crushed white grapes are full of sticky pulp and don't readily release their juice. So some winemakers leave the stems in with the crushed grapes when filling the press, on the theory that the springy stems open channels between the skins and help the juice drain. These winemakers arrange to rent a crusher with only a hopper and rollers, no stemmer. Some brew shops carry them. But other winemakers—I'm one of them—use standard crusher-stemmers and simply discard the stems, which are high in astringent tannins that could add rough flavors to delicate white wines. It doesn't matter what kind of container you crush into—the must won't stay there long—but it should be clean. And remember to rent a basket press at the same time.

A dose of prevention. Before you get down to the job of pressing—and with unfermented grapes it's a tougher job—you'll want to add a dose of sulfite. If protection is prudent when making red wines, it's essential with whites. Crushed white grapes are especially susceptible to browning and oxidation, and what's more, common practice calls for letting the newly pressed juice sit overnight while the suspended pulp and detritus settle out. As with red grapes, it's easiest to measure the sulfite into a cup or two of water, and then splash the solution onto the crushed grapes bit by bit as they fall into your bin. (If you're buying pressed white juice, there's a good chance the supplier already added some. But if not, simply

Two Ways to Make Pink Wine

Scorned for decades as dull wines for dim people, rosés have been reborn in recent years. Wine lovers have discovered their pleasing flavors—like those of whites but with a little extra intensity—while winemakers have begun experimenting with rosés and blush wines from a variety of grapes. There are two traditional ways of making pink wine (apart from tinting a white with a slug of red). Both start with red grape varieties. Classic varieties include Grenache and Zinfandel, but Pinot Noir, Cabernet Sauvignon, and other red grapes make fine rosés. Here's how to do it.

- Option 1: Crush red grapes as usual, but don't add yeast. Let the must stand for several hours or perhaps a day, depending on how much color seeps from the skins; and then press the raw must and start the fermentation in settled juice as if you were making white wine. Thereafter, follow the methods for making white wine through bottling.

- Option 2: Start the fermentation in a batch of crushed red grapes, but after several hours—check the color—drain off a quantity of fermenting juice and handle it as if you were making white wine. (The remaining red must will now have a higher ratio of skins to juice, giving that wine a color and flavor boost.)

dissolve a dose in a small amount of water and stir it in.)

How much sulfite is enough? Because of white grapes' special vulnerabilities, it's wise to add a little more than you did to your red must—2 grams of sulfite per 50 pounds of grapes, for a sulfur dioxide level of about 60 parts per million—assuming, that is, that your grapes arrived free of rot, mold, or vinegar taint. If you've noticed that some berries have turned brown or are showing a fuzzy white growth, then you'll want to add 3 grams of sulfite per 50 pounds of grapes, for a sulfur dioxide level of about 90 parts per million. (For more on sulfite and sulfur dioxide, see chapter 14.) When you sprinkle it in, you'll notice the sulfur dioxide's usual burned-matches smell before it fades into the mix. Remember, the cultivated yeasts you're about to add won't suffer from this modest shot, and meanwhile your wine will taste fresher, look brighter, and last longer in the bottle. But make your measurements carefully: too much sulfite can harm the color, flavor, and aroma of the finished wine or even impede the fermentation.

Press twice. Once you've stirred in the sulfite dose, you're ready to press. Scoop the crushed and sulfited grapes into the press basket—put a pail under the spout!—and let the juice drain. About half the grapes' juice will flow out this way. Depending on the kind of grapes and their condition, the color of this free run will range from pale gold or green to khaki. Don't worry if the juice looks tan; some browning of the pulp is inevitable. As the pails fill, pour the juice into clean carboys.

Keep adding crushed grapes to the basket until it's nearly full. Put in the plunger plates and press down gently with your hands, upping the pressure until juice stops running. Pull out the plungers and add another scoop of grapes, if necessary, and then assemble the whole rig and start pressing. Crank the press, wait, and then crank again, keeping at it until the lever begins to fight you. Release the tension and dismantle the basket. Transfer the still-moist skins into a tub or onto a sheet of clean plastic, crumbling them with your hands. Re-build the basket, pile in the loosened skins and stems, and press again. Fill the carboys (or smaller jugs) right to the top, so there's no air space, stopper them tightly, and set them in your home's coolest place.

Is the sugar okay? While the juice in your carboys begins settling, return the (washed) crusher and press to the brew shop and hurry home. Use your hydrometer now to find the sugar content of your juice. If the reading falls between 20.5 and 22 Brix, great. That's right around the level many winemakers consider ideal for dry white wines. If it's a degree or two above 22, that's fine, too—your wine will simply be richer and rounder (and higher in alcohol). If it comes in much under 20.5, however, you may want to add some sugar to bring the Brix up into the mid-dling range (see page 174). And if your grapes are very sweet—say, 26 Brix—adding a precise amount of water (see page 45) could help bring the sugar into balance.

Let the juice settle for several hours—or better, overnight—and use the time to work out the sugar correction, if necessary. Think about the acid level, too. Your supplier should have given you the reading for your grapes at harvest. If you're making a table wine, the broad target for white grapes' total acidity is 0.80 to 1.0 gram per 100 milliliters (8 to 10 grams per liter). As with red table wines, the acid and sugar guidelines are flexible, depending on the nature of the wine you plan to make. Is your juice high in acid? One good option for achieving a balanced wine is to ferment the juice as is, and then finish the wine with a touch of residual sugar. (Find details in chapters 14 and 15, pages 189 and 203.) Is the juice low in acid? You may want to add a bit of tartaric acid at this stage (see page 172) or wait and taste the dry wine, making your choice then.

Let the juice clarify before making any adjustments. Don't forget that once you've siphoned the juice away from the sediment, you'll have less than you started with. Take care not to siphon up the brown layer of pulp and to fill the fresh carboys only two-thirds to three-fourths full. You want room above the liquid because some yeast varieties foam extravagantly, sometimes causing carboys to bubble over. Also, the air in the carboy's upper third provides some essential oxygen to the yeasts during their initial population boom.

A quick tip: Pour the brown sediment remaining in the carboys into a gallon jug (or jugs) and refrigerate it overnight. By morning the pulp will settle even further, leaving a layer of clear juice on top. Suck up the juice with your wine thief or a pipette and add it back to the main batch. *Now* pour out the sediment and wash the jugs.

IN GOES THE YEAST

The juice's sugar and acid are in balance? Your carboys are partly full? Find your thermometer and your packets of wine yeast—as for making red wine, one 5-gram packet per 5 gallons of juice or must. For each 5 grams of yeast, warm a half cup of water to at least 95°F but not more than 104°F. (Don't use deionized or distilled water, which deprive the yeasts of dissolved minerals they need as they rehydrate.)

Now open your yeast packets. Sprinkle the yeasts into the warm water and wait five minutes. Stir gently, and then let the mixture stand for up to half an hour. Meanwhile, take the temperature of the juice. If it's under 60°F, it's a good idea to help the rehydrated yeasts acclimate to their chilly new home. Using your wine thief, draw out enough juice to match the quantity of the yeast-water mixture. Over the course of a minute, slowly mix the juice into the rehydrated yeasts, and then pour equal quantities of this mixture into each partly full carboy. Don't stir it in, instead leaving the yeasts on the surface so they get plenty of oxygen. Put a ferm lock in each carboy, and call it a day.

The early stages in the making of a white wine are crucial. The risk of a warm, overactive fermentation is greatest at Brix readings between 20-something and about 10.

It will be at least a few hours or perhaps a day or more before the yeasts start their growth spurt, producing a good cap of foam.

Above all, stay cool. Unlike red wines, which benefit from the warmth of the fermentation, white wines come out best—with the freshest fruit aromas and tastes—when the yeasts multiply slowly at cool temperatures. Modern commercial winemakers have a big advantage here. Their fermentation tanks come equipped with stainless steel jackets through which liquid coolant circulates. The winemaker sets a thermostat, as if adjusting a refrigerator, and for weeks the yeasts simmer quietly along at approximately 55°F—although some whites are fermented at higher temperatures.

Remember, yeasts begin to swoon when the thermometer drops below 50°F, so just placing your carboys outdoors and hoping for a chilly autumn isn't a great strategy. A cool basement or an air-conditioned room can be ideal—if the temperature remains in the 60s. But it may be simplest to keep your carboys in the garage and cool them individually. Don't expect to hold the juice temperature down to the 50s. Instead, strive to keep it below 65°F. I place each carboy inside a small garbage can or plastic tub, and add water and ice cubes to create a cold moat around the fermenting wine. The water in the moat absorbs heat from the carboy, and the combined volume of liquid responds slowly to warmth in the room—if, say, the temperature in the garage climbs during the day. It's a humble system, but it spares me from having to buy a refrigerator.

When adding yeast food, divide the dose into small portions and add them in stages before the fermentation reaches its midpoint. Adding food later can invite spoilage.

Feed your yeasts. Because clarified white grape juice is low in nutrients and because nutrient-starved yeasts may pump out stinky sulfur compounds or fail to finish fermenting, it's wise to add modest doses of yeast food at stages during the fermentation (see page 54). Remember not to add too much. Large doses can provoke the yeasts into giving off more warmth than you want in a slow, cool fermentation. Here's a feeding schedule for white wines, based on directions for the product Superfood (page 181). Note that it differs from the schedule for feeding red-wine yeasts in chapter 4. It's best to weigh out the powder, but a measuring spoon will do. (For each 1 gram of yeast food called for, instead add a half teaspoon.) Simply dissolve the yeast food in a little water, pour it into the carboys, and replace the fermentation locks.

Day 1 (yeast starter added): 5 grams food per 5 gallons juice

Days 5–7 (lots of bubbles; Brix about 18): 2 grams food per 5 gallons juice

Days 10–14 (still bubbling; Brix not lower than 10): 1 gram food per 5 gallons juice

If you're adding malolactic bugs. Aiming for a buttery Chardonnay-style white? There's no one perfect time for adding cultured malolactic bacteria, available from brew shops. Many vintners choose to add the bugs—along with a small dose of a special malolactic nutrient mix—right when the yeast fermentation reaches its peak, usually several days after the first signs of life in the carboys. Others wait until the yeasts finish up. Because different shops stock different breeds of bacteria, it's best to follow precisely the directions for whichever kind you buy. Remember to keep the packet frozen or refrigerated and to use the whole quantity as soon as it's open. Don't worry about overdosing on the bugs, even if you're making a small amount of wine. The more you add, the more likely they'll finish the job promptly.

Following through. Once a white wine fermentation is rolling—foam on the surface, bubbles rising in the juice, ferm locks burping actively—there's really not much to do. The wine will look truly awful, like dirty dishwater, but it's a passing phase. Ideally, you should note the temperature every day, taking samples with a wine thief. But it's most important just to keep the fermentation rolling at a slow, steady pace. If you've decided to cool the carboys in a water-filled tub, regularly check the water temperature and add ice if it rises toward 70°F. And keep an eye on the sugar. Once the sugar's half gone, you're heading down the home stretch.

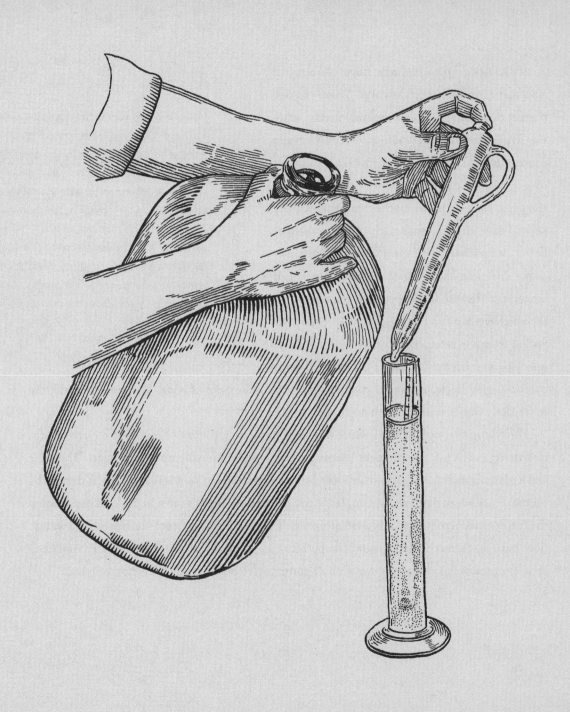

10

CLEAR AND CLEAN

Because white wines ferment in narrow-necked carboys, literally out of reach, there's something remote and a little clinical about the fermentation—no twice-daily punching down, no sticky hands in thick must, no aromatic blasts of carbon dioxide from an open-topped fermenter. The sugar just ticks away, the yeasts' life reaching a modest crescendo of bubbles and foam before easing back to slumber as if it had all been a dream. Take it easy, you've been saying, don't hurry, stay cool. But now, as the action fades, *you* need to hustle a bit. The wine is in danger.

When the foam fades. After a week or two of roiling and bubbling, the yeasts will weaken and stop generating enough carbon dioxide to protect the wine reliably from air and spoilage microbes. It's wise at this stage, as the sugar falls toward zero, to merge the carboys' contents. The goal is to minimize air contact by filling each active carboy into the neck. This is not a racking: you should transfer the entire contents of the carboys—both wine and sediment.

Taking the Brix, or sugar percentage, of a carboy of fermenting white wine that is nearing the end of the active primary stage. From here on, air is the wine's enemy.

Working out the details can be tricky. Say you started with two carboys, each two-thirds full. If you pour from one into the other, you'll end up with one completely full and the other just a third full. The solution? Divide the third-full carboy into gallon jugs, place stoppers and ferm locks on every container, and let the fermentation wind toward completion at its slower pace.

TO RACK OR NOT TO RACK

White wines made in the crisp and fruity style—that is, without malolactic fermentation—usually finish up within a couple of weeks. You'll see fewer and smaller bubbles until eventually the ferm locks go quiet, your sign that the fermentation is ending. Don't rely on the bubbles as your sole gauge, however. Instead, become a demon with your wine thief and hydrometer, checking the sugar every day. Taste the cloudy wine, too, if only to educate your taste buds as the Brix readings sink through the single digits. The readings may eventually fall *below* zero as accumulated alcohol lowers the wine's density to less than that of water.

Once the sugar is at zero or below and the ferm locks are quiet, get set to rack and add sulfite. Procrastination, as in most things, courts trouble. Often, freelance malolactic bacteria are ready to start attacking the malic acid about the same time the yeasts polish off the sugar. So even if you didn't add malolactic bugs, you could find yourself watching while some wild ones kick off a fermentation in spite of you. That's not a disaster—you may simply end up with a softer, more buttery wine than you set out to make. But to discourage malolactic fermentation, it's wise to rack as soon as the wine is dry. Remember that if you're planning to make a wine with residual sugar, as detailed in chapter 15, let it go dry and clarify, and then add some sugar (see page 227).

To start the first racking, lift the full carboys up onto a bench or table and let the lees settle. Next measure out a dose of potassium metabisulfite—1.5 grams per 5 gallons of wine.

A shot of sulfite at this stage cools the ardor of any microbes-in-waiting and helps protect the wine from browning. Simply weigh it out, stir each dose into a small amount of water, and pour it into each empty carboy. As you start the wine flowing, give the carboy a gentle swirl to mix in the sulfite. Put on clean ferm locks and place the carboys someplace cool and calm.

If you've added malolactic bugs. On the other hand, if you want to encourage malolactic fermentation, postpone the racking and sulfiting and let the carboys warm slightly until they are between 65°F and 70°F, the temperature range where the acid-loving bugs thrive. (For more on encouraging malolactic fermentations, see

> *Keep the water in your fermentation locks fresh by adding a tiny pinch of potassium metabisulfite.*

page 183.) You may or may not witness the shift as the yeasts hand over the command to the bacteria. Sometimes the two fermentations overlap, sometimes they don't. Malolactic fermentation is most often accompanied by many tiny bubbles that release just enough gas to joggle the ferm locks a few times an hour.

After several weeks at approximately 70°F, the carboys will turn dead quiet, your signal that the malolactic bugs have done all they're going to do, regardless of whether they've converted all the malic acid to lactic. In other words, if the bugs aren't reproducing—having been treated to conditions they love—they probably can't be coaxed into going further, and you can safely begin the march toward bottling. If you like, you can confirm the malic and lactic acid levels with a chemical test (see page 161), but the results will do more to satisfy your curiosity than to inform a decision. Simply rack and add sulfite, as in the paragraph above. Your wine is made.

Forecast: a light haze. As the days roll by, don't feel shocked or disappointed when your new wine remains stubbornly cloudy. The first racking disposed of a thick layer of settled yeasts. But still adrift in the wine is a cast of much smaller and lighter characters, including yeast fragments, dead or dormant bacteria, and microscopic clumps of protein or pale pigment. Hazes persist for complicated reasons, including the particles' size and electrostatic charge (positive or negative), the wine's viscosity and acidity, the amount of dispersed protein or pigment or tannin, and more. Even when white wines clear up by themselves, as some do, they may turn cloudy later—when they're chilled before serving, for instance. That's why it's wise to stabilize wines before bottling.

CLEARING THINGS UP

The first step is to cool or chill the wine in the carboys. White wines, even more than reds, are prone to spontaneously producing crystals of potassium bitartrate, known as tartrate. Tartrate crystals form readily at temperatures around 40°F, so one option is to place each carboy in the refrigerator for a couple of weeks. Or simply leave the carboys in the coldest place in your home, ideally before spring arrives. Tartrates may or may not form, but if and when they do they'll take at least a bit of the haze with them as they settle. Rack for the second time and add sulfite immediately, while the wine is still chilled. Cold stabilization not only disposes of sediment, it also slightly lowers the acid content of the wine, helping to ready it for fining or filtering.

Chilling your wine to about 40°F—a step called cold stabilization—not only helps it clarify but also slightly softens the flavor.

Most commercial wineries filter their white wines (and often their reds, too). That is, they use powerful pumps to force the wine through progressively finer layers of sterile cellulose or other porous material, capturing nearly every suspended particle, from residual yeast cells and bits of grape pulp down to the tiniest bacteria. Although some vintners swear filtering removes precious color, aroma, and flavor, many others accept the possibility of minor losses in intensity for what they get in return: superclear wine, now virtually sterile so it won't spoil in a warehouse or shipping container.

Home winemakers, especially those who love pricey gadgets, can follow suit if they like. Brew shops usually stock all the home filtering necessities: pumps, hoses, couplings, housings, and replaceable filter pads or cartridges. But before you shell out for the gear—and entangle yourself in gizmos and fine points—stop and think twice. Handmade red wines rarely benefit from filtering. With whites, you'll possibly harm the wine's flavor and color. You'll spend extra hours maintaining the gear. You'll lose some wine. And besides, almost all of what you can do with filters can be achieved simply by racking and fining.

Fining white wines. The term *fining* refers to clarifying hazy wines by adding one or more of several materials that are able to snare the microscopic flotsam. Philip Wagner, in his classic *Grapes into Wine,* notes that fining and filtering are flip sides of the same coin. "When a wine is fined a sort of veil of the fining material is drawn down through the wine, dragging all the suspended matter with it," he writes. "When a wine is filtered the veil, a porous wall or membrane, is fixed and the wine is forced through it." In both instances the "veil," as he calls it, stays involved only briefly, leaving nothing behind that would flavor, color, or otherwise taint the wine. At home the winemaker gives the wine weeks or months to clear itself as much as it can, and then adds one of several possible agents—a common one is a special kind of clay—and waits for the agent and the particles it captured to settle, and disposes of

Is Your Wine Truly Clear?

Have you ever watched sunlight break through a rain cloud and seen golden rays slanting toward the ground? You can see the sun's rays right then, but not in clear weather, because tiny raindrops or moisture particles in the air below the clouds intercept some sunlight and bounce it toward you. Likewise, new wine that looks quite clear at a glance often contains microscopic particles that show up as a faint haze when a flashlight or other light is pointed through it. Before declaring your wine ready to bottle—either before or after fining—pour a generous sample into your tasting glass, set it in a shady place, and shine a strong light through it from the side, perpendicular to your line of sight. If you can see the light beam in the wine, you may want to help the wine clarify further.

the sediment in the third racking. Without fining, white wines may fail to turn brilliantly clear.

How does adding a murky material like clay help a wine turn clear? Magnetism, in a word. Many of the haze molecules have either a positive charge or a negative one. When both are present, they glom onto each other and fall to the bottom. But when the hazy bits are all positive or all negative, any that bump into one another ricochet off in opposite directions, staying too active to sink. The best way to settle them down is to add something that carries the opposite charge.

Because positively charged molecules—especially grape proteins—are a common cause of cloudiness in white wines, a standard approach is to add a negative agent after the second racking, and then sit tight for up to a week while it sponges up the haze and drags particles to the bottom. My first choice is bentonite—the special clay mentioned above—because it's cheap, natural, easy to use, widely available, and often stunningly effective. A follow-up option is Sparkalloid (Scott Laboratories), a seaweed extract mixed with diatomaceous earth, a claylike powder composed of the skeletons of minute marine organisms called diatoms. But there are at least a dozen fining agents—some attracted to proteins, others to tannins—including gelatin, egg white, milk protein, and, believe it or not, purified sturgeon's bladder. Some winemakers add two or more in succession. Others fine first, and then filter. My advice is to start with bentonite alone, and in later vintages move on to different materials and methods. (For details on preparing and adding bentonite, see page 122; for details on Sparkalloid and other agents, see page 222.)

Looking ahead to bottling. Ideally, once your wine is truly clear, it's done and ready to bottle. You'll want to taste it, of course, giving it a full sensory once-over, paying special attention to its aromas and tartness. The wine should have a clean, fruity scent, with no trace of rotten-egg smell or other off odor. And as for the tartness, it's a judgment call, a matter of opinion. No one likes wines that are frankly sour, a possibility if the grapes were low in sugar and high in acid and fermented totally dry. But that shouldn't be an issue if the sugar and acid were in balance before you added the yeasts. If you simply prefer wines with a touch of sweetness, now's the time to add some sugar (a step detailed in chapter 15, page 227).

> *The fining agent bentonite—named for Fort Benton, Montana, near where it was first identified—is a clay derived from weathered volcanic ash. It's now mined in Wyoming.*

At last, into the bottles. Any wine, red or white, can be bottled—and served and enjoyed—once it's clear, clean-tasting, balanced, and stable. There's really no set timetable, and in fact some home vintners hold off, "bulk aging" their wines in stoppered carboys for months or even years. That said, white wines are usually best when bottled and corked promptly, preferably before the weather warms up in June. The goal is to prevent oxidation and to save the fresh fruit flavors and aromas for that happy moment when you pull the cork. That means minimizing rackings. So far in this chapter, I've suggested racking and adding sulfite to white wines three times: at the end of fermentation, again after cold stabilization, and a third time after fining. Whether it's helpful to rack again before bottling depends on the wine itself—whether it has thrown sediment since the third racking, whether there are some off odors or trapped gases that might blow off with agitation. If after its final spell in the calm, cool room the wine seems clean and good enough to drink, give thanks to Bacchus and start lining up bottles, corks, and a corker.

It's wise at this prebottling stage to give the wine a final small dose of sulfite. You'll be tempted to skip it, but keep in mind that much of what you've added is no longer helping. Some of it went away with the pressed skins, brown pulp, and yeast lees, while the measures added in later rackings have by now lost much of their potency. To prevent oxidation and spoilage in the bottle, weigh out 1 gram of sulfite per 5-gallon carboy. Before adding it, check to make sure there's no sediment in the carboys, and then simply stir in the sulfite with your racking wand. If there is obvious sediment, do a fourth racking into fresh carboys, adding the sulfite as usual, and start bottling.

Bottling is bottling whether the wine is white

or red (see "Bottling Dos and Don'ts," page 99), with the one proviso that with whites it's especially prudent to limit oxygen exposure. Commercial wineries "sparge" their wine bottles, forcing the air out of them with a shot of nitrogen gas, which itself is forced out when the wine pours in, leaving just a squeak of inert gas under the cork. You don't need to go that far—you'll drink your whites soon. Just avoid splashing the wine, drive the corks in promptly, and never a let a carboy of wine stand around half full.

the lid, and switch the blender on at a low speed (caution: hot steam can escape). Remove the lid and, with the motor still running, sprinkle in the bentonite. Blend for at least 2 minutes.

- Transfer the slurry to a clean, odor-free jar or other container with a tight lid, and refrigerate overnight or up to 24 hours. Do not skip this step; it's necessary to "open" the clay so it can snare haze particles.

- Thoroughly stir, shake, or otherwise mix the slurry before measuring it. It should be thick and smooth, like whole milk or half-and-half, possibly with a few sandy grains.

- Pour 2 tablespoons of this mixture into each 5 gallons of wine, and stir vigorously with your racking wand. Seal the remaining bentonite slurry in the jar and return it to the refrigerator.

- Let the wine settle for three days, and then check its clarity (see page 120). If the wine is still cloudy, add 2 more tablespoons of the slurry and allow the wine to settle for a week. If the wine remains cloudy, you may need to use more bentonite or possibly add a different agent (see page 222).

- When the wine is clear, rack and add sulfite— 1 gram per 5 gallons. Try not to aerate the wine during racking—that is, keep the outflow end of the siphon in the wine as each carboy fills.

Part One Recap

WINEMAKING STEP BY STEP

HERE'S A RUNDOWN on the winemaking stages detailed in chapters 3 through 10. Although the main actions are highlighted, you'll want to turn back to the chapters to find specific guidelines and especially explanations. These steps assume you've already chosen, ordered, and received between 50 and 500 pounds of wine grapes or 5 to 40 gallons of white wine grape juice.

CRUSHING GRAPES FOR RED WINE *(CHAPTER 3, "WHEN RED MEANS GO")*

1. Rent a crusher-stemmer from the nearest brew shop.

2. Have on hand four additives: genuine wine yeasts; yeast food to keep the yeasts nourished during their population boom; freeze-dried malolactic bacteria, benign microbes that'll follow up after the yeasts and break down harsh acids so your wine tastes softer; and potassium metabisulfite, to limit oxidation and discourage rogue microbes.

3. Crush your grapes into a clean 30- or 55-gallon food-grade plastic drum or garbage can, filling it no more than three-fourths full so there's room for the rising cap of grape skins. Clean the crusher-stemmer with copious water and a scrub brush before returning it.

4. During crushing, add enough potassium metabisulfite to give about 30 parts per million sulfur dioxide, or up to 90 parts per million if more than a few of the grape bunches were moldy or spoiled. (For sulfite guidelines, see page 19.)

5. Measure the sugar and, if possible, the total acidity levels of the juice. The sugar level, measured with a hydrometer before fermentation, should be between 22 and 25 Brix. Ideally, the total acidity reading will have been furnished by your grape supplier. It should be between 0.60 and 0.80 gram per 100 milliliters. (For sugar and acid correction guidelines, see page 42.)

STARTING AND RUNNING THE FERMENTATION
(CHAPTER 4, "THEN A MIRACLE HAPPENS")

1. Gently stir your packaged wine yeast into water warmed to 94°F to 105°F—not hotter! For each 5-gram packet of yeast, use a half cup of water. Let the mixture stand for 30 minutes.

2. Pour the rehydrated yeast into the fermenter full of crushed grapes. Cover loosely and let stand undisturbed for about a day in a room that is neither hot nor cold. Insulate the fermenter if the batch of crushed grapes is small and the room is cooler than 60°F.

3. Check the fermenter for signs of yeast activity (foam, gurgling noises), and then stir the must thoroughly with your arm. Thereafter, punch down the buoyant cap of skins at least twice a day until the fermentation slows.

4. Add yeast food at the first signs of fermentation, about 5 grams per 5 gallons of must. In addition, make one or two smaller additions, 1 to 2 grams per 5 gallons, at or near

sugar levels of 18 Brix and 12 Brix. Near the end of fermentation, also mix in the dry contents of one small (1.5-gram) packet of freeze-dried malolactic bacteria.

5. Regularly check the must's temperature and sugar levels during the one to two weeks of active fermentation. The temperature should rise to between 80°F and 90°F, while the sugar level should steadily fall to close to zero Brix. If necessary, insulate the fermenter to help the must retain its heat.

PRESSING *(CHAPTER 5, "A PRESSING ENGAGEMENT")*

1. As the fermentation slows and the cap grows less dense, continue to check the must's sugar level. Prepare to press when the Brix reading is near or below zero. Make sure you have on hand clean pails, clean carboys, and a carboy-size funnel.

2. Rent a basket press from the nearest brew shop, checking to be sure you receive all the parts. Assemble the basket and place a clean pail under the press's spout.

3. Scoop the mixture of skins, seeds, and wine from the fermenter into the basket, letting the wine drain between additions. Stir the skins to free more juice, adding more skins until the basket is almost full. Put in the plungers and blocks.

4. Decide whether to keep the press wine and free-run wine separate, and then carefully wind down the cast-iron ratchet and begin pressing, taking breaks after several pulls on the lever. Loosen and press the skins a second time.

5. Fill the carboys to just above the shoulders. In the mouth of each carboy place a drilled stopper and fermentation lock filled with water. Set the carboys in a room or enclosure with a constant temperature of 65°F to 70°F.

6. Check the scent of the pressed wine, and if you detect a strong rotten-egg odor, consider siphoning the wine off the sediment.

THE SECONDARY FERMENTATION AND FIRST RACKING
(CHAPTER 6, "THE QUIET STAGE")

1. Keep the filled carboys at a constant 65°F to 70°F for two to three weeks.

2. Watch for small carbon dioxide bubbles rising through the wine, evidence that the yeasts are fermenting the last bits of sugar and possibly that bacteria are carrying out the secondary, or malolactic, fermentation.

3. When the bubbles slow markedly or stop completely, determine whether the malolactic fermentation is complete using either a sensory (taste and smell) test or a chemical test (see page 161).

4. Lift the carboys onto a table and, using a clean three-eighths-inch hose, siphon the wine into empty carboys, taking care not to suck up the sediment on the bottom. Splash the wine down the inside of the carboys to aerate the wine and drive off funky odors.

5. During racking, add 1.5 grams of potassium metabisulfite to each fresh carboy. First dissolve the grains in a small amount of water, and then swirl the solution into the first few inches of wine. Fill each carboy into the neck, and stopper each with a fermentation lock or solid stopper. Move the full carboys to a cool, quiet place.

THE SECOND AND THIRD RACKINGS
(CHAPTER 7, "WATCHFUL WAITING")

1. Do a thorough sensory check of your wine. Using a wine thief or pipette, dip into a carboy and withdraw some wine—about 2 ounces, or enough to fill a wineglass to a depth of an inch or so. In bright light, tilt the glass so the liquid spreads up the side, and then inspect the sample against a white background. Check for cloudiness and dissolved gases (minute bubbles), and note color hue and intensity. Swirl and sniff the wine to detect any off aromas, and taste to evaluate its astringency, viscosity, and acidity.

2. Carry out the second racking about a month after the first. Add 1 gram of dissolved sulfite to each empty 5-gallon carboy, fill each carboy into the neck with wine, put on a ferm lock, and set each in a cool place.

3. If you wish, chill each carboy to encourage tartrate crystals to precipitate.

4. Consider giving the wine a touch of oak flavor by adding oak chips or another commercial oak product. Taste the wine frequently and rack before the oak taste becomes too bold.

5. Within a few months—ideally after the wine has become clear—rack for the third time. Transfer the wine while it's still cold, to leave any tartrate crystals and other sediment behind. As before, add 1 gram of sulfite per 5 gallons and mix it in thoroughly.

THE FINAL STEPS *(CHAPTER 8, "BOTTLING AND BEYOND")*

1. Prepare to bottle when the wine is clear, clean-tasting, balanced, and stable. Rack for the fourth and final time about seven or eight months after the fermentation is complete, possibly in May or June. To prevent oxidation and spoilage in the bottled wine, add 1 gram of sulfite to each 5-gallon carboy during racking; or check and adjust the free sulfur dioxide level (see page 193).

2. Using a siphon and corker, bottle the wine in new or newly washed 750-milliliter wine bottles. Rinse but don't otherwise treat the new corks. Take your time during bottling, and be careful to fill each bottle into the neck so that no more than a half inch of air remains between the wine and the cork. A bottling wand can speed the process.

3. Using a waterproof pen, write the vintage year on each cork and the year and variety on each case of wine. Leave the cases standing upright for a day to allow the air compressed under the cork to come to the same pressure as the outside air.

4. Lay the cases on their sides in a cool, dark cellar or closet.

FERMENTING A WHITE WINE
(CHAPTER 9, "VIVE LA DIFFÉRENCE!")

1. Decide what style of white you want to make: crisp and fruity or rich and buttery. Have on hand packets of cold-tolerant yeast, potassium metabisulfite, yeast food, and, if desired, cultured malolactic bacteria.

2. Rent a crusher-stemmer and a basket press from the nearest brew shop, checking to be sure you receive all the parts.

3. Crush your grapes into a clean food-grade plastic drum or garbage can. During crushing, add 2 grams of potassium metabisulfite per 50 pounds of grapes for a sulfur dioxide level of about 60 parts per million, or up to 90 parts per million if more than a few of the grape bunches were moldy or spoiled. (For sulfite guidelines, see page 19.)

4. Immediately press the crushed grapes. Assemble the basket press and place a clean pail under the press's spout. Scoop the crushed grapes from the drum into the basket, letting the juice drain between additions. Stir the skins to free more juice, adding more until the basket is almost full. Press, taking breaks to let the juice drain. Break apart the cake of pressed grapes, refill the basket, and press again. Before returning the basket press and crusher-stemmer to the shop, clean them with a scrub brush and water.

5. Pour the newly pressed juice into clean carboys, filling them into the necks. Stopper the carboys and allow them to stand in a cool place so the grape pulp can settle.

6. Measure the sugar (and, if possible, the total acidity) of the juice. The sugar level, measured with a hydrometer before fermentation, should be between 20.5 and 22 Brix. Ideally, the total acidity reading will have been furnished by your grape supplier. It should be between 0.80 and 1.0 gram per 100 milliliters. (For sugar and acid correction guidelines, see page 42.)

7. Using a siphon hose, transfer the clarified juice to clean carboys, filling each new carboy only two-thirds to three-quarters full. Discard the muddy sediment left behind.

8. Gently stir your packaged wine yeast into water warmed to 94°F to 105°F—not hotter! For each 5-gram packet of yeast, use a half cup of water. Let the mixture stand

for 30 minutes. Pour the rehydrated yeast into the partially full carboys. Cover loosely and let stand undisturbed in a room that ideally is no warmer than 60°F.

9. Check for signs of yeast activity (foam, bubbles). At the first signs of fermentation, add yeast food, about 5 grams per 5 gallons of juice. In addition, make one or two smaller additions, 1 to 2 grams per 5 gallons, at or near sugar levels of 18 Brix and 12 Brix. If desired, also mix in the contents of one small (1.5-gram) packet of freeze-dried malolactic bacteria near the peak of fermentation.

10. Regularly check the must's temperature and sugar levels. During the active fermentation the temperature should remain at 65°F or below, while the sugar level should fall steadily. Place the carboys in tubs of cold water to help the fermenting juice stay cool.

FINISHING A WHITE WINE *(CHAPTER 10, "CLEAR AND CLEAN")*

1. Continue to check the sugar as the fermentation slows. When the wine is no longer giving off abundant carbon dioxide—usually after one to two weeks—merge the contents of the carboys so they are full into their necks.

2. Allow the wine to ferment completely dry. When the Brix is near or below zero, prepare to rack. Lift the full carboys up onto a bench or table and let the lees settle. Measure out a dose of potassium metabisulfite—1 gram per 5 gallons of wine. Stir each dose into a small amount of water, and pour it into each empty carboy. As you start the wine flowing, swirl each carboy to mix in the sulfite. Put on clean ferm locks and place the carboys someplace cool and calm.

3. If you want to encourage malolactic fermentation, postpone the racking and sulfiting and let the carboys warm slightly to between 65°F and 70°F. Watch for tiny bubbles that release just enough gas to joggle the ferm locks a few times an hour. After several weeks, the carboys will turn quiet. Rack then and add sulfite as in the paragraph above. (For more on malolactic fermentation, see pages 113, 183, and 220.)

4. To encourage tartrate crystals to precipitate, refrigerate each carboy for a week or two or leave the carboys in the coldest place in your home, ideally before spring arrives. Rack for the second time and add 1 gram of sulfite to each carboy while the wine is still chilled.

5. Let the wine stand undisturbed for several weeks or a few months to clear itself. If any trace of cloudiness remains—do a careful sensory inspection—add a fining agent such as bentonite. (See page 122 for hints on preparing and adding bentonite, and page 222 for advice on using other white-wine fining agents.)

6. Decide whether to adjust the sugar level of the finished wine (see page 227) before preparing to bottle as you would for a red wine. Allow the wine to fall perfectly clear, and then rack for a third time, adding 1 gram of sulfite to each carboy. During racking, avoid aerating the wine by keeping the outflow end of the siphon in the wine as each carboy fills. Likewise, keep the wine from splashing during bottling and never let a carboy stand partly full. Mark the bottles and cases and store them in a cool place.

Part Two

MAKING EVEN BETTER WINE

As much as I've loved the many wines we've made—and in 25 years we've never made a nasty one—some have been more likely to end up on the table at special dinners. What does it take to make excellent wine every time? If that question had a short answer, you'd have heard it by now. But in fact there are refinements—call them insiders' tricks—for every step, starting with the grapes themselves and carrying on, more or less, in stepwise order through the various ways a wine can be fermented and aged.

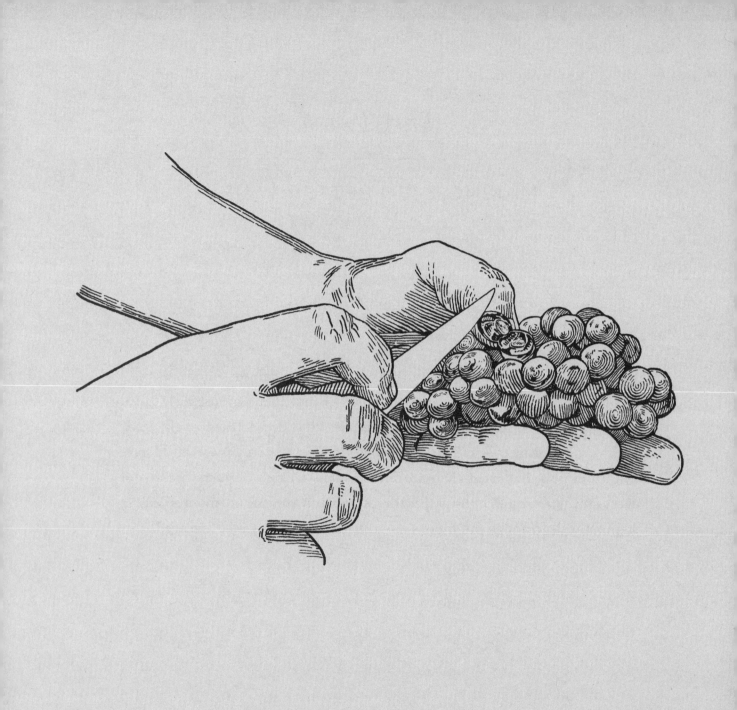

11

GETTING A GRIP ON YOUR GRAPES

Winemakers love to spout self-deprecating homilies: "The grapes make the wine." "Great wines are made in the vineyard." "Winemaking is a custodial endeavor." They're all true, mostly—the grape's the thing, as the playwright might have said. But great fruit doesn't just pop from the ground. Winegrowing is both an art and a science, and it demands a fanatic's attention to detail: the age and health of the vines, microclimate, soil type, vine density, irrigation schedule, trellis system, pruning regimen, and the yearly ups and downs of the weather. Expert grape growers have become latter-day sorcerers, managing the impact of the year's rainfall and sunlight on the vines and fruit, sometimes withholding water or applying nutrients, sometimes choosing to trim off leaves and expose the grapes, sometimes deciding to "drop fruit" (lop off and discard a percentage of the ripening clusters)— all to concentrate and balance the key flavor elements of the remaining grapes.

But chances are you won't get to take evening walks among the vine rows with several dif-

Checking maturity in a cluster of Cabernet Sauvignon grapes recently harvested in Sonoma County. Key signs are liquefied pulp and browned, or lignified, seeds.

ferent growers, prodding them for their thoughts on the forthcoming harvest. The grower's decision on when to pick is as often as not a torturous, last-minute compromise in which ineffables such as the threats of frost or rain and the availability of a harvest crew are weighed against the grapes' steadily evolving levels of sweetness, acidity, astringency, and flavor.

GAUGES OF RIPENESS

In all top-notch vineyards, quality, not quantity, is the watchword. That is, the number of tons of grapes grown on each acre of land is deliberately kept low so the vines can put more energy, and ideally better flavor, into fewer bunches. There's no single benchmark, but premier American vineyards usually yield from two tons of grapes an acre to six. Wouldn't two always be better? Not necessarily. What's true for hundred-year-old Zinfandel in Northern California isn't necessarily true for Riesling or Seyval Blanc in upstate New York or for Norton in Missouri.

Four main gauges of grape ripeness are judged before harvest: sugar content, total acidity, pH, and flavor maturity. Only the fourth gauge— flavor—can't be easily quantified.

The real sign of quality is what's inside the grapes themselves. The grower's decisions in the vineyard in the months before harvest come down to four crucial traits in the ripe fruit—three that can be measured plus one that can only be sensed: sugar content (or Brix), total acidity (also known as titratable acidity), pH (a separate acidity measure), and flavor maturity. Brix and total acidity levels are discussed in chapters 3 and 12 (pages 37 and 151). And on page 141 you'll find details on winegrowers' evolving focus on pH. But in the meantime, what's the big deal with the mysterious "maturity"? Are winemakers turning back the clock?

Measuring maturity. Naturally, what matters most is the overall character of the finished wine, and that's why there's a new focus on a time-honored gauge of ripeness. Wherever possible—wherever grapes mature readily—vintners are pushing growers and vineyard managers to zero in on sensory cues. One obvious sign is color. Ideally, red-wine grapes at harvest are uniformly dark, with few or no pale berries. Fully ripe white-wine grapes show a yellow tint and may be somewhat translucent. But color is just the start. In pursuit of mature grape flavors, vintners now ramble through the vineyard in harvest season, plucking and chewing individual berries to gauge the tastes of the skin and pulp. They also judge the texture of the flesh, the color and firmness of the developing seeds, and the color and dryness of the stems that bind the berries into bunches. In the centuries before numerical sugar and acid tests became common, winegrowers decided when to pick using mainly these signs.

Vintners now ramble through the vineyard in harvest season, plucking and chewing grapes to gauge the tastes of the skin and pulp.

Grape seeds start out green and soft, for instance, but by the time they're ripe turn brown and hard or brittle. Meanwhile, the pulp's texture goes in the opposite direction, changing from thick to almost runny. The many compounds that give fine wines their flavors and aromas also shift, some fading away, others stepping forward. Cabernet Sauvignon typically shows the flavors of citrus rind and green apple when unripe. As the berries ripen, the mix evolves to cherry and strawberry, in ripe grapes to plum and blackberry, and eventually in overripe

Cultivating Grape Growers

Above all, you want to find a supplier who offers quality fruit and treats you with courtesy and respect. Just remember that grape growers are hardworking farmers, dedicated to the land and proud of their work. If you fail to show up on harvest day, they may well cut you off. Here's how to get off on the right foot.

- Near harvest season, check bulletin boards or listings in brew shops in your area for notices from other home winemakers or winemaking clubs who are seeking or offering fresh grapes. Ask how you can get in on their order.

- Call local wineries and ask for the general manager, vineyard manager, assistant winemaker, or winemaker. Ask whether they sell grapes (either whole or crushed) in harvest season to home winemakers. Or drop in at tasting rooms in your area, ask the winemaker's name (or check the winery's Web site), and call later about the possibility of buying grapes at harvest.

- Ask each local winery if it holds an annual open house. Wineries sometimes use these semipublic events to introduce steady customers to their favorite contract growers—your chance to go straight to the source. Make it clear that you're a serious, experienced winemaker.

(continued)

ones to prune and raisin. Mingled with these flavors are tannins from the skins and seeds, the source of red wines' astringency—not a flavor technically but a puckery or rough sensation in the mouth. The tannins change, too, becoming gentler or softer as the grapes mature.

The hang-time dilemma. Unfortunately, these changes rarely happen in lockstep, nor do they precisely keep pace with the evolving levels of sugar and acid. Vineyardists often sample grapes that by the numbers look ready but still taste green ("leafy") or harshly astringent ("leathery"). And often these days, the decision in such cases is to give the grapes more "hang time," or days on the vine—never mind that the sugar is creeping up and the acid down. This kind of vineyard brinksmanship can make for intense, full-flavored (if high-alcohol) wines; but it's also creating headaches for home winemakers, who sometimes find themselves dealing with table-wine grapes that are very high in sugar (up to 27 Brix) or low in acid (less than 0.6 gram per 100 milliliters) or both. What's more, some grape varieties produce unlikely strong flavors when left too long on the vine. If the grower is distracted, inexperienced, or careless, a delayed harvest may mean the winemaker gets raisined grapes if the days are hot and dry or moldy ones if the weather turns wet or muggy. And if your supplier is overly devoted to sensory cues, you could get grapes that are out of balance and troublesome.

Beyond sugar and acid: the power of pH. Acidity, of course, is the backbone of a wine's character. For our purposes, total acidity is simply the degree to which grapes, musts, or finished wines taste sour: the higher the acidity, the more tart the flavor. But if acid's only impact on wines were to their taste, vintners might not show as much interest in the second acidity scale, pH—a measure of the concentration of free hydrogen (H) ions in a liquid. It's those ions that actually make things acidic; and so pH is also known as effective acidity. Total acidity and pH typically go hand in hand. That is, if you stir a big dose of tartaric acid into your wine, both measures will leap toward the acid end of their scales. But sometimes—and this is why winemakers watch pH carefully—the total acidity reading suggests one acid strength, while the pH suggests another. And it's usually the pH that matters most in the wine, especially in

- Use your computer's search engine to scour the Internet for professional grape growers in your area. Many wineries employ freelance management companies to run their vineyards. Search "grape growers," "winegrowers," "vineyard management," "viticulture," and "vintners' association" along with a location, such as a state, a region, or a county. Or look in the yellow pages under "fruits and vegetables, wholesale," and see if any of the companies will order fresh wine grapes for delivery in harvest season.

- Inquire about grapes from the state of Washington and from California's Lodi region, which are often shipped to faraway parts of the country. You may have to pay in advance.

Once you've found a grape grower, you may want to talk through your deal and then note the important matters in a written agreement. Here are some items to consider.

- Is a deposit required? When is the balance of payment due—before, on, or after delivery of your grapes?

- What are the agreed-upon targets for sugar, total acidity, pH, and flavor development?

(continued)

(continued)

- What are the contingency plans if rain or frost is forecast for the harvest?

- Will the grower harvest and deliver, or are you expected to supply a harvest crew and pick the fruit yourself? Will the grape-laden bin(s) be on a truck bed or placed for you on the ground?

- Will delivery be at the edge of the vineyard, at a winery's crush pad, or elsewhere?

- How soon after the start of picking does the grower promise to fulfill the entire order?

- What percentage of the delivery can be "material other than grapes"—that is, grape leaves, stems, insects, dirt clods, and other detritus?

- What guarantees does the grower make about the grapes' condition at delivery? Can you inspect the fruit before accepting it? Can you refuse a portion of the delivery if it's moldy, raisined, overheated, soured, or otherwise spoiled?

maintaining sulfite's protective power. (For tips on measuring pH and on determining its effect on free sulfur dioxide levels, see pages 159 and 193.)

It's important to stop and explain a strange disparity. Total acidity is simple: 10 is high acid, 5 is low. But the pH scale, which runs from zero to 14, works in exactly the opposite way: the higher the pH reading, the *lower* the acidity, and vice versa. (The pH of pure water, at 7, is in the middle.) What's more, the range on the scale that matters to winemakers is quite slim. Grape juice so high in acid that it's puckeringly tart might have a pH of 3.0 or 3.1. Juice from supersweet, low-acid grapes might have a pH of 3.9 or 4.0. In other words, those little tenths make a huge difference.

Yet in ripening grapes, as in just about everything, balance is key. In California and most other western regions, the rough harvest targets for red grapes have traditionally been in the range of 22.5 to 24.5 Brix, a total acidity of approximately 0.6 to 0.8 gram per 100 milliliters, and a pH of 3.3 to 3.5. Grapes for white wines might be picked at a Brix of 20.5 to 22, a total acidity of 0.8 to 1.0 gram per 100 milliliters, and a pH of 3.1 to 3.4.

Such targets may define harvest-ready grapes for many winemakers in the West, but in cooler regions—and in cool-climate grape varieties—they aren't always realistic. Consider these sugar readings taken near harvest in a New York vineyard near Lake Erie in 2003: Chardonnay, 19.8 Brix; Riesling, 18.8; Viognier, 20; Merlot, 20; Pinot Noir, 19.8; and Syrah, 18. The readings aren't bad—those are predictable sugar levels for that area—and besides, home winemakers could easily add some sugar to nudge the Brix up before fermentation. But in cool climates, high acidity is as common as low sugar. In those same grapes, total acidity ranged from 1.29 grams per 100 milliliters in the Merlot to 1.8 in the Syrah. Meanwhile, the pHs were bracingly low: 3.17 to 2.89.

Red grapes should show fully mature tannins along with adequate acidity. White grapes should have fairly high acidity but also good aromatic qualities.

So how can you be sure you get good grapes? What you're seeking—as is every other savvy vintner—is perfectly ripe fruit grown to modern standards in a scientifically managed vineyard. Red grapes should be picked when they show fully mature tannins along with adequate acidity. White grapes should have relatively high acidity but also good aromatic development. As a small-scale winemaker you're likely to bump into at least some farmers who are out on the fringe: hobbyists with a yard full of unruly vines, mavericks devoted to odd varieties and unorthodox practices, or fast-talking businessmen who are only too happy to charge you top dollar for grapes brushed off by other winemakers. So before settling on a particular source, see if you can find a grower who knows how to get the most from the fruit in the vineyard.

Vineyard acreage is mushrooming in the United States, and European-style wine grapes now grow coast to coast. As a result, for the first time in U.S. history home vintners in nearly every state can go straight to the source of their fruit, placing themselves squarely in the tradition of making wine that reflects the character of a place. No one has to look to California—or even to Oregon, Washington, or upstate New York—to find grapes good enough to make table wine. We're a vineyard nation now, and most home vintners can reasonably hope to find a source of respectable grapes within a day's drive.

Nationwide, there are now more than a million acres of vineyards putting out some 3 million tons of wine grapes each year.

"Respectable grapes," however, means different things in different parts of the country. The classic European wine grape, *Vitis vinifera,* can be tricky or nearly impossible to grow in regions where winters are icy or where summers are warm and damp. Hard freezes can kill dormant vines, while frosts in late spring may ruin the developing grapes. Sultry or rainy summer weather gives molds and mildews precisely the humid conditions they need to thrive in the grapes' tight clusters. And in many places, endemic pests are just waiting to bore through the vines' roots or infect their sap. Thomas Jefferson tried again and again to grow European wine grapes at Monticello in Virginia but admitted defeat in the face of such challenges. Yet by the late nineteenth century viticulturists had begun hybridizing grape varieties, striving to meld the refined flavors of Pinot Noir, Chardonnay, and other European classics with the disease resistance and cold hardiness of wild North American grapevines (see "What About Native American Grapes?" opposite).

The offspring of these durable European-American hybrids and many further crosses and backcrosses are now planted widely in the United States. In fact, in many places where experts swore premium wine grapes would never thrive, maverick growers have been pulling out native grapes and replacing them with hardy hybrids such as Chambourcin and Seyval Blanc, which yield table wines with more pleasing flavors. Meanwhile, in other promising locales, both natives and hybrids are giving way to new plantings of the more adaptable European varieties—Chardonnay, Cabernet, and Riesling, among others—in hopes that they can be coaxed into turning out first-rate fruit. And to a degree no one believed possible a couple of decades ago, they are.

Finding a supplier. Yet getting your hands on just the right amount of excellent grapes can be a challenge. For one thing, commercial wineries are understandably stingy with grapes they grow for themselves, as are the "contract" growers who sell their produce to the same wineries year after year. What's more, back-yard growers often lack the viticultural know-how to produce well-balanced fruit, and even some commercial

What About Native American Grapes?

More than 15 grape species, all in the genus *Vitis,* are native to North America. Some of them have been cultivated since colonial times and are still made into wine in many parts of the country. Here's a rundown on the virtues and vices of the principal natives.

Norton and Cynthiana *(Vitis aestivalis)* are two names for—and possibly distinct clones of—a dark-skinned wild variety first cultivated in Virginia in the early 1800s. Now widely recognized as a superb American red wine grape, Norton is essentially free of the foxy and musky flavors that turn most winemakers away from other native grapes (below). It is vigorous, highly disease-resistant, and fairly cold-hardy (to −20°F). One downside: The fruit may ripen with high total acidity *and* high pH, a potentially troublesome mix for winemakers. Although some wineries in Missouri and Virginia are renowned for their outstanding Norton wines, the variety is also grown commercially in Arkansas, Florida, Georgia, Illinois, Indiana, Kansas, Kentucky, Louisiana, Maryland, New Jersey, North Carolina, Oklahoma, Pennsylvania, Tennessee, Texas, and West Virginia.

Concord, Catawba, Delaware, and Niagara are well-known varieties and hybrids of the native species *Vitis*

(continued)

(continued)

labrusca, grown widely in New York State and other parts of the East. Prolific, disease-resistant, and cold-hardy, these vines produce grapes with a distinctive—some say peculiar—aroma and flavor that in red wines are often described as like those of wild strawberries or animal fur. The chemical constituents of this "foxy" scent have been isolated and named: methyl anthranilate and o-amino acetophenone. For whatever reason, wines bearing these compounds are most pleasing when finished with a significant percentage of residual sugar.

Muscadine grapes, principally *Vitis rotundifolia,* are grown throughout the southern United States, from Delaware down along the coastal plains to Florida and as far west as Texas. The grapes are large—an inch or more in diameter—with thick, loose skins and, often, a musky taste. There are hundreds of varieties, among which Scuppernong, a bronze cultivar, has traditionally been a favorite of southern winemakers, although Carlos (bronze), Noble (red), Magnolia (bronze), and several others also make likable sweet wines. Muscadine vines are resistant to most of the pests and diseases that plague European and hybrid vines planted in warm, humid regions, but they thrive only where temperatures hardly ever sink below 10°F. Their bitter

(continued)

farmers who supply both pros and amateurs unscrupulously boost their profits by "overcropping," or managing their vines to turn out big loads of grapes that may look fine but make feeble wine.

If you're lucky, a brew shop near you orders grapes from local growers and supplies them in harvest season to home winemakers. Typically, you're notified several days before the harvest date to show up at the shop or a drop-off point at a set time. You'll pay for this service, of course, but it can be worth it if the shop proprietors take the trouble to line up good fruit. That's a big *if.* Before you place your grape order, ask some questions: Where, exactly, are the grapes grown? (Preferably in a professionally managed vineyard in an area known for its premium wines.) Do any respected wineries buy grapes from the same grower? (See if you can find some of the wines and taste them.) What are the sugar and acid targets for the grape harvest? (Most large-scale grape buyers tell the growers what they hope to get.) What ripeness data does the grower or brew shop furnish with the grapes? (Ideally, the Brix, total acidity, and pH.) Have any winemakers had problems with the grapes in past vintages? (That is, have the grapes ever been delivered underripe, overripe, or moldy?)

Perhaps most important—especially if the shop brokers several grape varieties or offers grapes of the same variety from several vineyards—ask the staff which grapes they would choose and why. Ask, too, if they can put you in touch with any winemakers who have bought the same fruit before. With luck, you'll get the chance to taste and pass judgment on a Cabernet or Chardonnay made from previous harvests of the grapes you have your eye on.

Finding your own grapes. Of course, if you're sure about the type of grapes you're looking for, you can sail right past the brew shop and cut your own deal. Look first for a winegrower who's used to supplying home winemakers (see "Cultivating Grape Growers," above). Growers who make their living selling grapes by the ton may not be in a hurry to start doling them out by the pound. Keep in mind that beyond cash on the barrelhead growers get a number of perks when they deal with wineries. They often leave to the winemaker some responsibility for the risky decision on when to harvest. They may enjoy the glory of seeing their grapes used in special

skins, thick pulp, and somewhat low sugar levels can make them hard to vinify. The grapes can also be low in available nitrogen, requiring an extra addition of yeast nutrients during fermentation.

Wild riverbank and sand grapes (*Vitis riparia* and *V. rupestris*) are of huge importance to winemakers—not so much for the wine they make but for their immunity to phylloxera, the soil aphid that kills European vines not grafted onto pest-resistant roots. These native species have been key sources of the rootstocks on which most of the world's premium grapevines now grow. Although grapes from these varieties are sometimes made into wine—a winery in South Dakota makes a "full-bodied, semi-dry" wine from wild *riparia* grapes—the fruit lacks the European grape's notable flavors and its natural balance of sugar, acid, and tannin. The common red hybrid Baco Noir is a cross between *V. riparia* and Folle Blanche, a white European variety.

"vineyard-designated" wines. They may get to hobnob with famous patrons at seasonal winery functions.

All that said, grape growers do have a strong incentive to supply home winemakers: the ton of grapes they might offer to wineries (or brew shops) for $2,000 ($1 a pound) could bring them $4,000 ($2 a pound) when sold in 100-pound lots to home winemakers. One way to keep your own costs low—and also make it easy for growers to do business with you—is to join with other winemakers and place a grape order in the one- to several-ton range.

> *A ton of grapes usually produces 150 to 170 gallons of finished wine. A 100-pound lot of grapes—about a gallon crushed— yields 7.5 to 8.5 gallons of wine.*

Picking 'em. The other twist in dealing directly with growers is that when it comes time to bring your grapes home, you may need to think big. Fresh grapes are often hauled from the vineyard in large food-grade plastic containers called harvest or field bins, each holding about half a ton of bunches. Picture your bin arriving—five feet up from the pavement on the bed of a big truck. Is the truck equipped with tailgate lift and pallet jack to get the bin to the ground? Or is there a forklift (and driver) on hand? Will you rent or borrow a truck to get the heavy load home? Or will you divvy up the order into boxes, buckets, or 40-pound totes you can stack in a pickup or minivan?

Meanwhile, as you shop around for grapes, it's possible you'll someday be offered the option of picking the fruit left hanging in the vineyard by the professional harvesters. This practice, known as gleaning, goes back at least as far as the Middle Ages, when peasants were allowed to scavenge just-harvested fields for the scattered remainders of grains or other produce. Nowadays pickers are trained not to take the grapes called the second crop, or secondary clusters that are slower to mature than the large bunches. They're pedigreed, all right, but troublesome—small, widely spread among the vines, and potentially low in sugar and high in acid if not given extra time to ripen. If you're not an exceptionally crafty winemaker, you'll end up validating another of those old sayings: "You can't make good wine from bad grapes."

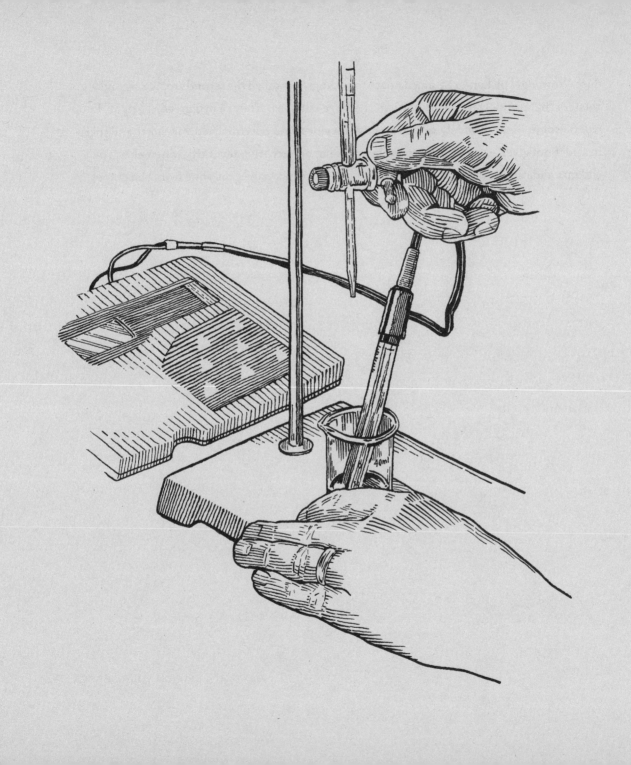

12

TESTING, TESTING

NO MATTER HOW MUCH PROFESSIONAL VINTNERS glorify the grapes they ferment, and their own intuition as well, they still depend heavily on laboratory tests as they turn the raw fruit into wine. Every winery worth its corks has at least a small chemistry lab, and many make liberal use of independent analysis laboratories. These outfits, which take in juice or wine by courier or express mail and e-mail or fax back the results, do superb work as a rule, and they have helped legions of winemakers turn out better wine. But off-site testing takes time—a day or two at least—and it can stall the smooth progress from crushed grapes to fermentation. It isn't cheap, either, running as much as $10 to $25 a test. Besides, many of the evaluations are now easy to do at home, and the equipment keeps getting handier and cheaper.

The following five tests—for sugar content (Brix), total acidity (TA), pH, malolactic completion, and residual sugar—are the cornerstones of a basic but reliable home wine lab. For the price of a year or two's worth of professional lab tests (and shipping fees), you can buy

---

Testing for total acidity using a titration burette and a benchtop pH meter. The burette holds a dilute sodium hydroxide solution, the beaker a small amount of wine.

the goods to run these checks. They demand a bit of attention to detail but provide all the data you need to make the several key additions and subtractions spelled out in chapter 13. Meanwhile, one other crucial aspect of good winemaking—testing for and controlling sulfur dioxide levels—is treated in chapter 14.

Still, there may be times when you want deeper information. Professional labs (see page 233) offer a boggling roster of tests for winemaking problems, including volatile acidity (vinegar taint), hydrogen sulfide, acetaldehyde levels, infections by *Brettanomyces* and *Lactobacillus*, metal contamination, and many, many other technical concerns. Most of these are beyond the scope of this book—and beyond the ability of most home winemakers to correct. The important thing is to use the knowledge and tools you have to make the best wine you can.

SUGAR REFINED

When you order fresh wine grapes or juice, you should ask to be given the harvest data—Brix, total acidity, and pH. However, as Ronald Reagan once said in another context, trust, but verify. Harvest conditions aren't always benign, vineyardists aren't always mindful, and vines aren't always healthy or well suited to their site's *terroir* (its soil, slope, and climate). What's more, even when the grower's own data look glorious, there's many a twist between the vine and the fermenter. You may inadvertently be delivered grapes from the only row of vines that was under- or overripe. Or the picker who filled your bin may have taken many unripe bunches. Or grapes that showed a nice middling Brix in the vineyard may after they're crushed "soak out" to a higher one as extra sugar seeps out into the must from pockets of raisined berries.

How sweet are they? Virtually all of these shortcomings can be fixed, but only if you know what you have—in your own fermenter at home. Measuring your must's sugar content is easy to do with a hydrometer. But the basic version, which typically shows the sugar level, or Brix, from zero to 35, is a fairly crude tool. A more precise kind can come in handy, especially in that first reading on which you'll base immediate decisions about adding water or sugar to adjust the must's sweetness. Most wineries keep their test lab stocked with fine-gauge hydrometers. For these, the makers choose a short segment of the full scale and then stretch it out in 0.1 gradations so it's easy to tell, for example, whether a must at 24 Brix is actually 23.6 or 24.8. You can buy these hydrometers in a variety of ranges: –5 to +5, zero to 8, 8 to 16, and 16 to 24 (or similar ranges, plus a late-harvest scale from 30 to 65). Fine-gauge hydrometers aren't quite as easy to find as the old workhorses—and they're sometimes quite a bit larger—but they can help you

> *For each degree Fahrenheit above your hydrometer's calibration temperature, add 0.03 to the Brix measurement. For each degree below, subtract 0.03 Brix.*

refine your winemaking. Probably the wisest way to sharpen your Brix measurements without buying the whole battery is to get a 16 to 24 hydrometer for fine detail before fermentation and a –5 to +5 to help at the end, when sugar readings can fall below zero.

Another way to ensure exact sugar readings is to keep a sharp eye on the must's temperature. Most winemaking hydrometers are calibrated for Brix measurements at 60°F. At cooler temperatures, hydrometers read artificially high; at warmer temperatures, they read low. So at, say, 55°F a sugar reading should be tweaked down a bit, and at 65°F it should be tweaked up. The formula: for each degree Fahrenheit above the hydrometer's calibration temperature, add 0.03 to the Brix. For each degree Fahrenheit below, subtract 0.03 Brix. This formula also works to correct readings from hydrometers calibrated to other temperatures, usually 68°F.

Though seemingly tiny, these fixes can matter. Suppose you have a small batch of unfermented Cabernet must that sat for a day in a hot garage and has now warmed up to 75°F.

TABLE 4 *Corrections for Hydrometers Calibrated to 60°F*

Before taking a Brix measurement, strain or settle the juice to remove any bits of skin or pulp, which can skew the reading. Use the clarified juice for measuring both the temperature and the Brix. In the left-hand column below, find the juice's temperature, and then look across to the right to find the value to subtract or add to correct the Brix. No correction is needed at 60°F because at that temperature the hydrometer reads true.

JUICE TEMPERATURE (°F)	SUBTRACT FROM THE SUGAR READING (BRIX)
40	0.60
45	0.45
50	0.30
55	0.15
60	—

	ADD TO THE SUGAR READING (BRIX)
65	0.15
70	0.30
75	0.45
80	0.60
85	0.75

When checked with a fine-gauge hydrometer, it shows a Brix of 24.6. However, after the correction for temperature is added, the actual sugar turns out to be over 25—high enough, possibly, to warrant bringing down the sugar a degree or so with a small amount of water. Chardonnay juice that when chilled to 40°F measures 22.5 Brix is really at 21.9—and is in line, perhaps, for a small sugar dose, depending on the style of wine to be made.

THE ACID TEST

The second key to ensuring your grapes' future as wine is to measure the total, or titratable, acidity (TA) so that you can adjust it if necessary into the right range (see page 172). With the simple test kits sold in most brew shops, it's possible, if a bit tricky. You use a graduated syringe or pipette to add neutralizer (dilute sodium hydroxide) to a bit of wine into which you've placed a few drops of an indicator solution called phenolphthalein. The indicator turns the juice or wine pink when just enough neutralizer is added to cancel out its acid. The exact measure of added neutralizer points to the total acidity—say, 0.7 gram per 100 milliliters.

The kits work well for white wines and some juices, although precisely measuring out the neutralizer takes practice. But for red wines, or for juices that have picked up color from the skins, they're less reliable. That's because the dark pigment obscures the crucial color change at what's called the end point of titration. Some winemakers invent workarounds—lightening the wine's color with water, and then rejiggering the calculations, or training themselves to see nearly invisible color shifts in intense light. And in some kits, acid-sensitive litmus paper is used instead of phenolphthalein to find the neutral endpoint, but the results can be iffy.

There's a great way out of this bind. If you really plan to be an expert winemaker, shell out for a good pH meter, which gives you the neutral end point of titration on a digital readout. Luckily, pH meters aren't as pricey or as tricky to use as they once were. Basic handheld meters run from $50 to $200, while more elaborate and precise benchtop meters cost $250

Sodium hydroxide, used in total acidity tests, absorbs carbon dioxide from the air, impairing its power to neutralize acids. Store yours tightly sealed in the refrigerator.

to $500. To check out the choices, type "pH meters wine" into your computer's search engine and see what pops up, or ask what's on hand at the nearest brew shop. Hanna and Oakton are reputable companies that make a variety of economical meters. Just keep in mind that all pH meters are electronic gizmos that demand scrupulous care. The electrode—the part you dip into the wine to detect the hydrogen ions—can be easily fouled or damaged. The electronic unit it connects to (a miniature computer, really) can be ruined by too much dirt or moisture. And the meters have to be calibrated before each use—a minor distraction— but you'll need to lay in a supply of at least two calibration solutions, known as pH buffers, one with a pH of 4.01, the other with a pH of 7.0.

At the same time you pick up your pH meter, buy a titration burette, which is a sophisticated (but easy-to-use) version of the clunky measuring syringe in most brew-shop test kits. For the price of a case of good wine, you kill two birds with one stone. Total acidity tests become a piece of cake—directions follow—and you can now measure pH, which would otherwise be impossible.

How to run a total acidity test using a pH meter. The titration burette is a gizmo you might have used in chemistry class. It's a graduated glass tube with a stopcock, or valve, at the business end. The burette is clamped to a tall stand so it can easily be set in place over a beaker or jar. Volume marks on the burette run upside down: high at the bottom, low at the top.

For this version of a TA test, the neutralizer (sodium hydroxide, or NaOH) is added until it fills the burette to the zero-milliliter line. A wine sample is set below, and the pH probe placed in it. Neutralizer is added slowly until the pH meter reads 8.2. The milliliters of sodium hydroxide dripped from the burette are used to find the total acidity (details below). A version of the test that skips the math is also given; it uses sodium hydroxide of a different concentration. (Concentrations commonly available at winery supply shops and laboratories include 0.01, 0.067, and 0.1 N.) Always buy sodium hydroxide in small amounts, tightly reseal the containers and store them in the refrigerator to protect the compound from oxygen and preserve its potency, and replace your supply every year.

The first method uses 0.1 N sodium hydroxide. (N is the measure of concentration.) Although the method looks intricate, it's actually easy to do. The illustration at the beginning of this chapter (page 150) shows a TA titration in process. Necessary equipment (available at shops or labs that sell supplies; see page 233) includes the following:

- pH meter and calibration solutions (buffers)
- 0.1 N NaOH, minimum of 50 milliliters
- a 5- or 10-milliliter pipette
- a 10-milliliter titration burette, with stand and clamp
- a few small (50- or 100-milliliter) beakers or clean jars
- deionized or distilled water
- squeeze bottles with spouts
- a pocket calculator

1. Calibrate your pH meter according to the manufacturer's directions.

2. Fill a squeeze bottle with fresh 0.1 N sodium hydroxide. Make sure your solution is 0.1 N, *not* 0.01 N (one tenth as strong). Label the bottle "NaOH" so you can't mistake it.

3. Fill the burette to the zero line with 0.1 N sodium hydroxide.

4. Fill another squeeze bottle with deionized water.

5. Using a pipette, add 10 milliliters of deionized water to a 50-milliliter beaker.

6. Using the same pipette, add 5 milliliters of the juice or wine to be tested to the same beaker. (Always strain any solids from the raw grape juice before testing.)

7. Place the beaker beneath the titration burette and immerse the pH meter probe in the liquid.

8. Add sodium hydroxide bit by bit to the diluted juice or wine, stirring gently with the pH probe.

9. Watch the pH reading. As you add sodium hydroxide the number will rise slowly, and then rapidly as you approach the end point, 8.2. Toward the end, add the solution one drop at a time, stirring and checking the pH after each addition.

10. Stop adding sodium hydroxide when the pH reading just reaches 8.2. If the final drop sends the pH over 8.2, don't worry; it's close enough.

11. Write down the number of milliliters of sodium hydroxide you added—it should be in the range of 4 to 6 milliliters—and then enter that value into your pocket calculator and multiply by 0.15. That gives you the total, or titratable acidity, expressed as grams per 100 milliliters. Example: 4.8 ml NaOH × 0.15 = 0.72 g/100 ml.

12. Repeat the whole test to confirm your results. (Remember to refill the burette.)

13. As soon as you've finished, drain and dispose of the sodium hydroxide from the burette. Pour the sodium hydroxide in the squeeze bottle back into the original bottle. Using the squeeze bottle filled with deionized water, rinse the burette, leaving the stopcock open so the burette can drain and dry. Tightly seal the partially full bottle of sodium hydroxide and store it in the refrigerator.

14. Using the squeeze bottle filled with deionized water, carefully rinse the pH probe and store it as specified in the owner's manual.

The second method uses 0.067 N sodium hydroxide and avoids the math.

1. Follow the steps above using 0.067 N sodium hydroxide instead of 0.1 N. It will take more milliliters of sodium hydroxide to reach the neutral end point of 8.2 on the pH meter.

2. Write down the number of milliliters of sodium hydroxide needed to neutralize the acid in the juice or wine. That number is the total, or titratable, acidity of the juice or wine. Example: 6.8 ml of NaOH is added to reach pH 8.2. So the TA = 6.8 g/l or 0.68 g/100 ml.

WHY pH MATTERS

Checking your wine's total acidity is a bit like confirming your hat size: it's useful information—but only on rare occasions. Knowing your wine's pH is another matter. There are several good reasons why you can't help but make better wine when you keep track of the pH along the way. First, as noted before, pH shows you the wine's effective acidity, which itself acts as a natural preservative. Wines with low pH (2.9 to 3.1) can also be sour and harsh on the tongue, and they may be too acidic to let the acid-softening malolactic bacteria get started. On the other hand, wines with high pH (3.7 to 4.2) may taste flat and look drab. Only wines with their pH in the happy midrange (3.2 to 3.6) have balanced flavors and show bright, stable color.

And if that's not enough, consider this: high-pH wines are exceptionally vulnerable to spoilage, and even big doses of sulfite can't protect them. That's because there's a direct link between the wine's pH and the sulfur dioxide actually set loose to squelch microbes and oxidation. The higher the pH (the lower the effective acidity), the less protection you get from any sulfite you add. And without protection from the sulfite—and from the acid itself—your wine is a sitting duck for every bad bug that ever hitchhiked on a stopper or wine thief. In other words, without some sense of your wine's pH you're gambling with your entire investment of time, energy, and money. (For full details on pH and protective sulfite levels, see chapter 14, page 189.)

It's of course helpful to learn the pH of the raw grapes at crush. But thereafter, in the winemaking, the pH commonly goes *up*. The shift occurs mainly during malolactic fermentation, with the change of tart malic acid to mild lactic, and to a lesser degree during the chilling stage, when some tartaric acid gets bound into potassium bitartrate and settles out as tartrate crystals. The pH rise is often slight, but it can be drastic. If, for instance, your grapes come in from the vineyard with an especially high level of malic acid and minimal tartaric acid, a full-bore secondary fermentation could cause the pH to soar. All of which means that a one-time reading is a good start, but it's only a piece of the picture.

Extra potassium in grape juice or wine can raise its pH, lowering its effective acidity. That's one reason some problematic musts have both high total acidity and high pH.

So why not just buy the meter and skip the total acidity tests? For a variety of reasons, grapes sometimes ripen with high total acidity *and* high pH. You're right: It doesn't make sense—the pH should be low in high-acid grapes. But it's not an uncommon event, and in fact the native grape variety Norton is notorious for ripening in this condition, as are other varieties grown where the soil is rich in the mineral potassium. (Excess potassium in must and wine raises the pH without changing the total acidity.) If you, the vintner, know only the must's pH, you could be moved to bring it down with a big dose of tartaric acid, unwittingly turning the wine unlikably sour.

MINDING THE MALOLACTIC

It's of course key to get a good profile of the grapes *before* the primary fermentation, since that's when corrections may be needed. (For details on adding acid, sugar, and water, see chapter 13.) But after the grapes are wine, when the urgency of the crush has given way to watchful waiting, testing can be just as important. Beyond the pH, which governs the sulfite's protective power, you'd like to know whether the malolactic fermentation is complete or still under way. And you're interested in the wine's sweetness, especially any residual sugar your hydrometer is too crude to show (more on this in a bit). It's also crucial to confirm the true, active level of sulfur dioxide in the wine (see page 189).

Malolactic bacteria, either naturally occurring or added as an inoculant, typically launch the secondary fermentation as the yeasts running the primary fermentation are polishing off the last of the sugar. In a burst of reproduction that can take days, weeks, or months, the benign bacteria turn the wine's harsh malic acid into gentle lactic acid, giving off carbon dioxide gas in the process. Several seat-of-the-pants signals can hint that the fermentation is winding down. The fizz of fine carbon dioxide bubbles slows, and then stops. The total acidity falls to below its level at crush, or the pH rises, or both. A tart flavor of green apples in the new wine gives way to a grapey or even buttery one. And the wine turns clear.

These are significant clues, but they're often misleading, and expert winemakers rarely count on them. A wine that, in vintner's lingo, has gone only partly through malolactic is a potentially unstable one in danger of coming back to life in the bottle, turning the wine spritzy or possibly cloudy. Ideally, the bacteria convert virtually all the malic acid to lactic. Ripe grapes, remember, ideally have a total acidity of 6 to 10 grams per liter (0.6 to 1.0 gram per 100 milliliters). Depending on the grape and the growing conditions, malic acid can make up as much as 90 percent of the total or as little as 10 percent. Sophisticated "enzymatic" tests commonly run at wine labs (but not practical at home) show how much of the actual malic acid, or "malate," is left after fermentation. When the bacteria have done their job, the malate level falls to between 0.2 and 0.1 gram per liter or even lower, into the hundredths of a gram. (Tartaric acid doesn't change much.) Although it's great to receive such clear and precise results, malate tests can run as much as $15 to $20 a sample.

Blessedly, you can get roughly the same information at home from a different kind of malolactic test that's offered as a kit in brew shops for $30 to $50 and serves for dozens of samples. Called chromatography, or paper chromatography, the test exploits the fact that malic, lactic, and tartaric acids have different molecular weights. That is, if you could weigh the acid molecules as you do apples, ten lactics would weigh less than ten malics.

In the test, wine samples are dabbed onto a sheet of special paper. The paper is placed on edge in a strong solvent, which slowly wicks up through the fibers, dissolving and carrying along the acids from the wines. When the solvent reaches the top, the paper is dried, eventually showing as many as three fuzzy ovals above each wine spot—one for each acid, with heavy tartaric at the bottom, middling malic in the middle, and light lactic at the top. The winemaker hopes to see strong lactic and tartaric spots and no malic spot at all, proof that the bacteria have finished up and left little or no malate.

To make the most of your malolactic chromatography tests, run more than one wine at a time and include a commercially made wine or two for comparison.

Although a chromatography test takes several hours, the steps are easy, and for all but a few minutes you're free to do something else. Gauging the results is simple, too, because the kits typically come with small vials of pure malic, lactic, and tartaric acid solutions to be used as standards.

Necessary equipment (available at shops or labs that sell supplies; see page 233) includes the following.

- chromatography paper, no. 1
- test jar with tight lid, about 1-gallon capacity
- malolactic test solvent, at least 50 milliliters
- small-bore capillary tubes or micropipettes (20 microliters), at least 24
- standardized malic, lactic, and tartaric acid samples, liquid, 0.3 percent
- stapler
- pencil, straight edge, and stiff scrap paper

Wipe off and thoroughly dry the table or counter where you do the prep work. Never crumple or crease the special paper, and hold it only along the edge. Make sure the paper fits in the jar without bending or overlapping; if not, trim it to size. Keep the wine spots smaller than the diameter of a pencil eraser by quickly and lightly touching the sample tube to the paper. And for the sake of your loved ones, dry the solvent-soaked test paper outdoors.

1. Lay out a piece of chromatography paper on a clean surface, with a long side of the rectangle toward you.

2. Using a sharp pencil, draw a straight line across the width of the paper about an inch up from the bottom, and mark small, light Xs at three-quarter-inch intervals along the horizontal line.

3. Below the leftmost X write *tartaric*, under the next write *malic*, and under the third *lactic*. These will be where you put your reference acid samples. Below the remaining Xs write names or numbers for the wines you'll be testing. Set the paper aside.

4. Make a holder for the capillary tubes you plan to use by folding a small piece of stiff scrap paper in zigzags so that you end up with as many pleats as tubes.

5. Dip a separate capillary tube into each reference acid—the liquid should rise more than halfway up each tube. Do the same for each wine to test. As you go, place each tube in the paper tube-holder, wet end out, in the order in which they'll be dabbed on the chromatography paper.

6. Lay the chromatography paper in front of you. Gently touch the tartaric tube to the tartaric X. Set the tube back in the paper holder, and proceed down the line, placing a small spot of each sample on each X. Wait a few minutes for the spots to dry.

7. Repeat the spotting for each sample six or more times—try to use all the wine in each tube—waiting for the spots to dry before adding more or proceeding with the test. (While you wait for the final dab to dry, throw the capillary tubes away.)

8. Gently roll up the chromatography paper so that the sides are just touching, and with the stapler fasten the paper into a tube. The ends should not overlap.

9. Set the large test jar on a flat surface where it can stay undisturbed for several hours. Remove the cap from the solvent (it will have a strong odor) and, by holding the small jar *inside* the big jar, slowly pour out the solvent without splashing to a depth of half an inch. Put the cap back on the solvent jar. Wash and dry your hands.

10. Carefully lower the paper tube into the test jar, trying to keep the paper from touching the sides. Place the lid tightly on the jar and let it stand. Check it every few hours.

11. When the solvent has climbed to within a quarter inch of the paper's top edge—up to eight hours—remove the paper from the jar and hang it in a dry, well-ventilated place, preferably outdoors. Pour the remaining solvent back into the small jar; wash and dry the large jar. Let the paper develop overnight, or until it strongly shows an overall greenish color and evident rows of yellow spots.

12. Each reference acid will have left a single egg-shaped spot. The tartaric spot will be at the lowest level, malic midway up, and lactic nearest the top. (Ignore any stretched-out traces or trails.) Each wine sample will show a spot that lines up with the tartaric reference (virtually all grape wines contain tartaric acid). The wines will also show spots that line up with the malic and/or lactic standards. If a wine's lactic spot is weak and its malic spot strong, the malolactic fermentation is not yet done. If, however, there's a bold lactic spot and no, or hardly any, malic—congratulations! You can scratch "check for ML completion" off your list of duties.

TESTING FOR RESIDUAL SUGAR

Even when yeasts roar with gusto through a batch of sweet must and the hydrometer drops below zero, new wine often retains some sugar. You can't count on your taste buds to tell you how much, since fruit flavors and high alcohol can trick them with phantom sweetness, while strong acidity can make faintly sweet wines taste drier than they are. Nor can you rely on your hydrometer, which shows a wine's sugar (dissolved solids) by gauging its density. The less sugar, the lower the density—but alcohol lowers the density, too. (Its density, or specific gravity, is 0.8 to water's 1.0.) So by the time a wine reads dry, with a Brix below zero, the alcohol is heavily skewing the reading. The sugar percentage could really be above zero—too sweet to bottle without taking precautions against a new fermentation kicking off. Professional winemakers dodge the problem by sending samples to the lab for a chemical ("enzymatic") test that measures the glucose and fructose, the two types of sugar that combine to make ordinary sugar.

Meanwhile, home winemakers opt for a simpler method invented to help people with diabetes check for sugar in their urine; many brew shops now sell an easy-to-use kit under the name Clinitest. (Dextrocheck, a related version, is no longer available.) To run the test, you drop a pill, called a reagent tablet, into a small sample of wine, watch as the wine changes color, and then check the sample against a chart with sugar percentages for a range of colors from deep blue (0.0) to bright orange (1.0). Dry wines typically have about 0.2 to 0.3 percent sugar (that is, 0.2 to 0.3 gram of sugar per 100 milliliters of wine), although many winemakers rate anything under 0.7 or 0.8 as dry enough to bottle without worry. Slightly sweet, or "off dry," wines may run from 1 percent sugar to as high as 5 percent, with dessert wines even higher. Clinitest kits aren't as precise as the enzymatic lab tests, but they're simple and cheap—about $30 for a hundred tablets, a color chart, a few vials or test tubes, and a couple of small pipettes.

How to run a residual sugar test. Although a reagent-tablet test takes just seconds and is easy to do, there are a couple of twists. The tablet reacts violently with the wine in the test tube, generating enough heat to actually boil—so keep your fingers away from the hot zone. And watch closely during the boiling stage to see whether the color passes through orange to deep brown, an event that means the wine has more than 1 percent sugar and is too sweet to check unless it's first diluted.

Necessary equipment (available at shops or labs that sell supplies; see page 233) includes the following.

- Clinitest reagent tablets, at least 2
- 0.5-milliliter pipette or eyedropper

- small test tube or vial

- color chart calibrated with sugar percentages, 0.0 to 1.0 percent

You may also need some deionized or distilled water.

1. Using a pipette, place 0.5 milliliter of wine in the test tube or vial.

2. Add a Clinitest reagent tablet, holding the tube above the liquid level.

3. Watch the reaction—don't shake the tube—checking to see if the color passes through orange (1 percent sugar) and turns brown. If you do see the color shift past orange to brown, the wine has more than 1 percent sugar and will need to be diluted and tested again (details in step 6).

4. If in the boiling stage you don't see the orange-brown "pass-through," give the tube a gentle shake and wait 15 seconds.

5. In bright light, estimate the sugar percentage by holding the tube near the chart and looking for the color that most closely matches the sample. Write down the sugar percentage, and then pour the liquid into a sink drain and flush with water (caution: the liquid is corrosive and may still be hot).

6. Start over with a clean tube if you saw an orange-brown pass-through. Place 0.1 milliliter (2 drops) of wine in the tube along with 0.4 milliliter (8 drops) of deionized or distilled water. Add a Clinitest reagent tablet. Read the percentage from the color chart, and then—to adjust for the added water—multiply that number by 5 to find the actual sugar percentage. Repeat to verify.

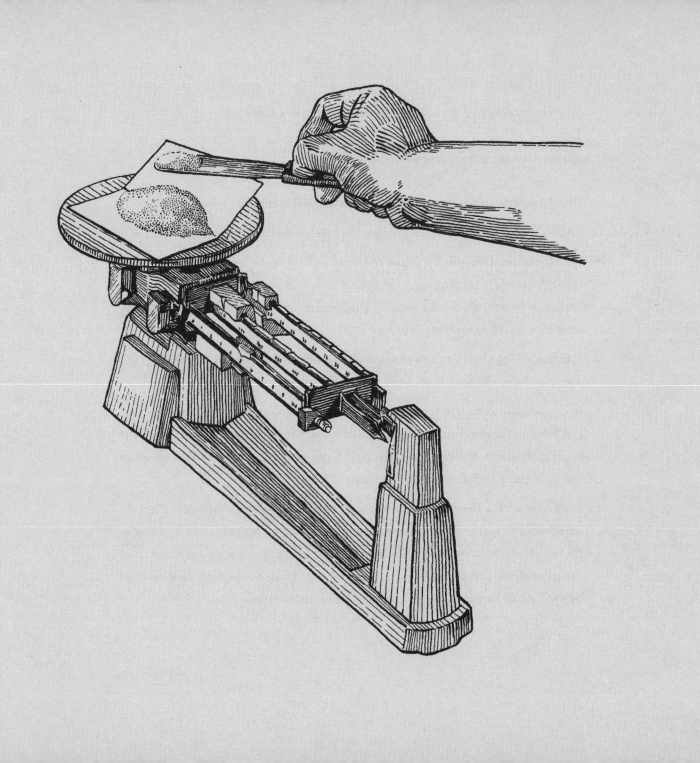

13

TAKING CONTROL

WINEMAKERS LIKE TO TOUT THEIR PRODUCTS' PURITY—"wine is just grapes, nothing but grapes"—but of course that's not true, and it never has been. Yeast, yeast nutrients, malolactic inoculants, water, tartaric acid, and sugar are all ingredients that winemakers may add at or near the start of fermentation. It's of course always best to intervene as little as possible, refraining from adjusting grapes that are already great. But as noted in chapter 11, different enologists define ideal ripeness in different ways, and some otherwise good grapes fall outside even the most liberal limits. So you may find yourself having to decide whether to ameliorate—that is, to add water, tartaric acid, or sugar before fermentation. (To decide whether to explore some of these options, turn back to "Gauges of Ripeness," page 138.) And you'll want to make sure you're in control of the fermentation by managing the yeasts and malolactic bacteria.

Weighing out tartaric acid on a triple-beam balance scale. The scale has been calibrated to read zero when a square of creased stiff paper is placed on the platform.

ADJUSTING MUSTS

Although there are no absolute standards, here are some traditional targets for well-balanced red and white grapes destined to become dry table wines.

Red grapes: 22.5 to 24.5 Brix, 0.6 to 0.8 gram per 100 milliliters total acidity, pH 3.3 to 3.5

White grapes: 20.5 to 22 Brix, 0.8 to 1.0 gram per 100 milliliters total acidity, pH 3.1 to 3.4

So should all grapes outside these ranges be adjusted? Absolutely not. Many vintners regularly make superb dry red wines from grapes harvested at higher sugar levels. Likewise, lots of excellent white wines are made from fruit that has ripened well into the red grape range. There are benefits and risks. Extra-ripe grapes can make rich, full-bodied wines. They may also be more vulnerable to problems during fermentation and if they're low in acid can yield wines with a dull color and flabby flavor. In other words, when you step out of the middle of the road, you may find either a glorious patch of ripe berries or a tangle of thorns. It all depends on your judgment and experience.

Numerical targets for grape ripeness are not ironclad rules. Many makers of red wines are happy to ferment grapes with sugar levels of 25 or 26 Brix.

Cutting the sugar in overripe grapes. Chapter 3, on making red wines, includes a table showing how much water to add to lower high-sugar musts to 24.5 Brix, a generally safe maximum at the start of fermentation. What if your grapes are unusually sweet—say, 27 Brix—but you're aiming for a different target? Using a simple formula, it's not hard to figure how many gallons or liters of water to add—with one crucial twist: you can't do your calculation using the original volume of must. Remember, the must is a mixture that includes the grapes' juice, skins, and seeds. But only the juice itself becomes wine; the solids will be removed and discarded. If you don't also remove the skins and seeds from your calculation, you'll end up adding too much water. Standard practice is to reckon water additions using the predicted volume of finished wine.

California winemakers who work with large quantities of grapes have found that they get 150 to 170 gallons of finished wine from each ton, or 2,000 pounds, of grapes. Scaled down and rounded off for home winemaking, that's about 8 gallons (7.5 to 8.5 gallons) of finished wine from each 100 pounds of grapes. Those 100 pounds, when crushed, yield about 10 gallons of must. In other words, each 10 gallons of must should give you about 8 gallons of wine—roughly 80 percent of the original volume.

Never adjust the sweetness of a must by calculation alone. Always add any water or sugar in stages, checking the Brix at intervals after thorough mixing.

So here's one method for figuring how much water to add. First, multiply your undiluted must volume by 0.8 to find the predicted volume of finished wine. Next, divide the Brix reading of your undiluted must by the Brix you want for fermentation. Then multiply that number by the finished wine volume in gallons or liters. Finally, subtract from that number the finished wine volume in gallons or liters. Stated as formulas, this method goes as follows.

volume of must × 0.8 = volume of finished wine

([original Brix / desired Brix] × volume of finished wine) – volume of finished wine =

volume of water to add

Suppose you have 40 gallons of must at 27 Brix. You want to dilute it to 25. The calculations would go like this:

$$40 \times 0.8 = 32 \text{ gallons of finished wine}$$
$$([27 / 25] \times 32) - 32 = 2.6 \text{ gallons of water to add}$$

It's always wise to pour in just part of the water, stir the must *thoroughly,* and then check the sugar with your hydrometer before adding the whole amount. And because musts from over-ripe grapes may possibly include shriveled berries full of especially thick and sticky juice, it's best to check the Brix again after the must has stood for several hours or overnight. Often in such cases, more sugar "soaks out," raising the Brix and necessitating another, though smaller, water addition.

Acidulating diluted musts. Remember that anytime you dilute a must you should also bring its acid level back up. In chapter 3, to keep things simple, I suggested adding 7 grams of tartaric acid for every liter of water you add, or 26.5 grams for every added gallon. That approach assumes that 0.7 gram per 100 milliliters is ideal total acidity. An alternative approach is to acidulate to the must's exact original TA. The universal formula reads like this:

$$\text{gallons of water added} \times 3.785 \text{ [liters per gallon]} \times \text{original TA of must [in g/100 ml]}$$
$$\times 10 = \text{grams of tartaric acid to add}$$

Say you added 2 gallons of water to a must with a TA of 0.75 gram per 100 milliliters. The calculation would go:

$$2 \times 3.785 \times 0.75 \times 10 = 56.8 \text{ grams of tartaric acid to add}$$

It's possible, however, that you actually want to lower both the sugar and the acidity. In that case, the best practice is to make your water addition, and then to run both total acidity and pH tests on the diluted must. If the acid level is now in the right range, great. If not, then you can simply act as if the grapes' acidity needed a boost after harvest and bring the TA to whatever level you want.

Raising the total acidity in over-ripe grapes. The rule of thumb for total acidity additions is that adding 1 gram of tartaric acid to 1 liter of wine raises the TA by 0.1 gram per 100 milliliters. Remember, however, that you need to think in terms of the amount of finished wine, *not* the original volume of must. Recast the rule above as a formula that assumes you're working in gallons, and you get this:

Some winemakers make their must dilutions with bottled springwater or purified water from the market. Others boil tap water to drive off any chlorine. These steps may or may not help the fermentation but can buy peace of mind.

$$\text{volume of must} \times 0.8 = \text{volume of finished wine}$$
$$(\text{desired TA} - \text{original TA [in g/100 ml]}) \times \text{gallons of finished wine} \times 3.785 \text{ [liters per gallon]} \times 10 = \text{grams of tartaric acid to add}$$

Suppose you have 30 gallons of must with a TA of 0.52 gram per 100 milliliters, and you want to raise it to 0.65.

$$30 \times 0.8 = 24 \text{ gallons of finished wine}$$
$$(0.65 - 0.52) \times 24 \times 3.785 \times 10 = 118 \text{ grams of tartaric acid to add}$$

Dissolve the tartaric acid in a cup or two of water or some juice drawn from your fermenter, and stir it into the must. Note that raising the total acidity will usually—but not always—lower the pH by a proportional amount. The rule of thumb is that adding 1 gram of tartaric acid per liter of wine lowers the pH by 0.1. In other words, that gram of acid you add per liter to raise the total acidity by 0.1 gram per 100 milliliters also lowers the pH by 0.1—but check it with your pH meter.

Raising the sugar in undersweet must or juice. A confession here: in 25 years of winemaking I've never needed to add sugar to a must. In California, where I live, grapes ripen readily—sometimes too readily—and in fact I've come to appreciate the amazing job the grapevines do. Ripe wine grapes are some of the sweetest fruit anywhere. By weight the juice is 20 percent to 25 percent sugar (each percent equals roughly one unit on the Brix scale). But I've learned a great deal about the steps involved in sweetening musts, and I'm certain those insights can help you. Here are some key points.

> *Adding tartaric acid to raise a must's total acidity will also lower its pH, although the pH shift won't always be proportional to the change in acidity. For certainty, use a pH meter.*

- Sugar-addition formulas vary wildly. Even the most direct and elemental approach has uncertainties. In theory, adding 1 gram of sugar to 100 milliliters of juice (or 10 grams per liter) will raise its Brix one degree. By that reckoning, adding 37.85 grams of sugar per gallon of juice (10 grams per liter × 3.785 liters per gallon) will do the same. Unfortunately, it's not that simple. For complex reasons having to do with the way solids (sugar, acids) dissolve in water, more sweetener may actually be needed. A standard formula (below) assumes that 0.125 pounds (56.7 grams) of sugar are required to raise the Brix of a gallon of juice by one degree. In other formulas the Brix is raised one degree by adding 1.5 ounces (42.45 grams) of sugar to each gallon of must.

- Calculate sugar additions based on the volume of actual juice, without the grape skins and seeds, or of finished wine, which is roughly 80 percent of the must volume.

- Use ordinary white table sugar from the supermarket. Ignore any advice you may read about adding corn sugar or special "invert" sugar. It's not necessary to prepare white sugar for fermentation by, say, heating a mixture of sugar and water with a bit of acid to separate the sucrose into glucose and fructose. Yeasts have enzymes to do that job.

- Always dissolve the sugar in water to make a syrup. The unfermented must will be too cold to readily accept much granulated sugar into solution. Measure the sugar into a clean saucepan and add just enough water to submerge the granules. Place the pan on the stove over low heat and stir with a clean stainless steel spoon, adding a little water if necessary, until the sugar dissolves. Allow the syrup to cool to room temperature.

- Do your sweetening by touch. That is, use the formulas (below) to calculate how much syrup to make, but then make the actual addition in stages, checking the Brix of the must after thorough mixing. Stop adding syrup when your hydrometer shows you've reached the desired Brix.

Here are two sugar-addition formulas, both adapted from the venerable handbook *Making Table Wine at Home* by George Cooke and James Lapsley of the University of California, Davis.

$$(\text{desired Brix} - \text{original Brix}) \times 0.125 \text{ [pounds per gallon]} \times \text{gallons of juice or finished wine} = \text{pounds of sugar}$$

Suppose you have 40 gallons of must at 19 Brix and you want to raise it to 22.

$$40 \times 0.8 = 32 \text{ gallons of juice}$$
$$(22 - 19) \times 0.125 \times 32 = 12 \text{ pounds of sugar}$$

A slightly more precise formula—based on weight, not volume—goes like this:

$$(\text{desired Brix} - \text{original Brix}) \times \text{weight of must} / (100 - \text{desired Brix}) = \text{pounds of sugar}$$

Suppose you have 400 pounds of must at 19 Brix and you want to raise it to 22.

$$400 \times 0.8 = 320 \text{ pounds of juice}$$
$$(22 - 19) \times 320 / (100 - 22) = 12.3 \text{ pounds of sugar}$$

Reducing the total acidity in high-acid must or juice. If your crushed must or pressed juice has a total acidity of 1.0 or higher, you may want to take steps to bring the acid down before fermentation. Keep in mind that reducing the total acidity will likely raise the pH, so you may have to compromise. Here are four options.

- Blend some low-acid wine-grape must or juice into the original batch—the ideal approach, but a tricky one because it may be impossible to line up a new batch of grapes on short notice.

- Use a specialized yeast, such as Lalvin 71B-1122, that metabolizes malic acid. This technique won't help much if the must's acid is mostly tartaric, with little malic, but it's worth trying.

- Treat the juice with a product called Acidex, sold in brew shops, which lowers both tartaric and malic acids. A small amount of the unfermented juice to be treated is stirred slowly into the measured dose of Acidex, and then the mixture is mixed vigorously into the entire batch of must. (For detailed dose-per-volume instructions, see the data sheet that comes with the product.)

- Add water, and then bring the sugar back up to its original level—an option for extreme cases only, because you're inevitably diluting the wine's flavor. This method works best in must or juice with high acidity and low pH. Keep any water addition under 15 percent. This is the formula:

$$\text{volume of must} \times 0.8 = \text{volume of finished wine}$$

$$([\text{original TA} / \text{desired TA}] \times \text{volume of finished wine}) - \text{volume of finished wine} =$$
$$\text{volume of water to add}$$

After adding the water, measure the total acidity and add a little more, if necessary. Next, check the Brix, and then adjust it using the sugar-addition formula above.

ALL YEASTS ARE NOT CREATED EQUAL

Some yeast strains supposedly "enhance color and spiciness" or "add citrus and floral notes." But they can have these effects only when you tightly control winemaking's other variables.

Rummage in old winemaking books, and you'll eventually run across a recipe for fruit or grape wine that calls for baking yeast. Ridiculous? Not really. Bread, beer, and wine yeasts are all in the species *Saccharomyces cerevisiae* (formerly *ellipsoideus*) or *S. bayanus*. Dumped out of a foil packet they all look, feel, and smell the same, whether bought in the supermarket or in the brew shop. They all thrive in sweet juice. And they all happily turn grapes into wine.

But they aren't interchangeable. As with wine grapes themselves, hundreds of separate varieties or strains have been identified and selected, each with its own special traits. In the United States, Lallemand (Lalvin), a multinational company, offers some 35 different yeast strains bred for winemaking, though just a handful of them are widely available in brew shops. Meanwhile, the Red Star, Wyeast, and White Labs companies each put out about half a dozen varieties useful to makers of table wines; some are identical except for the brand or variety name. Most come dry in 5-gram packets—the right amount for 5 gallons of must—but Wyeast's yeasts come as liquid cultures in soft pouches, usually 8 to 32 ounces. While the companies all describe their products differently (see page 233 for Web site addresses), there are six especially important criteria to keep your eye on when yeast shopping.

Overall vigor. If you don't need a yeast with specialized traits—that is, your grapes are healthy and at standard ripeness—look simply for a strong, even fermenter with good alcohol tolerance and a tendency to ferment all the available sugar. For red wines, Pasteur Red (from Red Star and Wyeast) is a stalwart that does a great job of bringing out the intense flavors of Cabernet, Merlot, Syrah, and other rich reds. Bourgovin RC212 (Lalvin), isolated in France's Burgundy region, is popular for Pinot Noir. Premier Cuvée (Red Star) and EC1118 (Lalvin) are vigorous fermenters that produce low amounts of foam, making them good choices for whites or rosés; however, they can suppress malolactic fermentation.

Cold tolerance. Slow, cool fermentations at temperatures of 60°F or below—commonly used for bright, aromatic white wines—require cold-tolerant yeast strains. Fine choices are Pasteur Champagne (Red Star and Wyeast), Steinberg (Wyeast), and ICV-D47 (Lalvin).

Residual sugar. If you're making a white that you hope will end up with a touch of residual sugar, consider Côte des Blancs (Red Star, a.k.a. Epernay 2) and ICV-D47 (Lalvin). Côte des Blancs is somewhat sensitive to cold, meaning that chilling late in the fermentation can help preserve some sweetness.

Flavor enhancement. For fruity, high-acid wines, 71B-1122 (Lalvin) is a good choice. It can actually soften high-acid musts by metabolizing up to 40 percent of the original malic acid. To accentuate flavors in Chardonnay, try ICV-D47 (Lalvin). To highlight the fresh-fruit flavors of white varieties such as Sauvignon Blanc, Chenin Blanc, Pinot Gris, and Seyval, try K1V-1116 (Lalvin).

Alcohol tolerance. Musts with a Brix of 25 or higher—big Zinfandels, late-harvest wines, and the like—should be inoculated with a yeast that readily tolerates high levels of alcohol. Pasteur Champagne (Red Star and Wyeast), as well as Premier Cuvée and EC1118, fits the bill, as do L2226 and K1V-1116 (Lalvin), both of which can also be used when you're trying to restart a stuck fermentation.

Hydrogen sulfide. Montrachet (Red Star) is a fine general-purpose yeast for both full-bodied reds and whites such as Chardonnay, but it may give off hydrogen sulfide gas during fermentation. If you already know your grapes are prone to making sulfide—if, for instance, the vines were dusted with sulfur late in the season or you have reason to believe they're low in nutrients—you may want to choose another variety.

Of course, there are many more cultured yeast strains that possess what the *Oxford Companion to Wine* calls "real or fancied minor differences." The twist is that most of them—including red-friendly strains such as Lalvin's ICV-D254 and L2056—come in hefty 500-gram packages (about a pound), enough to inoculate 2.5 tons of must. And shops that stock the big packages won't usually break them up. So if you're dead set on using a special strain, you may want to find other winemakers to share in the bounty. Beware: only when stored dry at room temperature in an *unopened* (not resealed) package do yeasts remain fully viable from one year to the next. One other tip: because the yeast strains ferment on their own schedules and absorb nutrients at different rates, it's unwise to mix them, experts say. If you're striving for complex flavors, divide your batch of must, ferment each lot with a different yeast, and then blend the finished wines.

THE TAO OF YEAST FOOD

Matching the attributes of the grapes and yeasts doesn't guarantee a trouble-free fermentation. In fact, even the most glorious grapes won't always meet the yeasts' nutritional needs. In particular, fresh grape must is often low in nitrogen and may also lack vitamins and minerals. Yeasts need nitrogen to grow hundreds of millions of new cells during their initial population boom and to keep their metabolic engines running during fermentation. When shortchanged, they may fail to convert all the sugar to alcohol. Or they may merely struggle, in the process generating obnoxious hydrogen sulfide gas. The solution is to help the yeasts along.

There are three approaches. The first, outlined for red and white wines in chapters 4 and 9, is simply to assume your grapes are somewhat low in nutrients and automatically add modest doses of yeast food during the first half of the fermentation (see pages 54 and 112).

The second and slightly more refined method is to make an educated guess about whether your must's nitrogen is actually low. You should definitely feed your yeasts if

- you're fermenting clarified juice for white wine.
- the grapes' sugar level was 25 Brix or higher (even if the must was subsequently diluted).
- grapes from the same vineyard have in past vintages given off hydrogen sulfide or failed to complete their fermentation.

- you plan to let wild or native yeasts launch the fermentation.

- the vines were threatened in the months before harvest by drought or disease.

- the grapes are from a vineyard in the East or Midwest (that is, a cold-winter area).

- the grapes are Muscadines or another native variety.

The third and most exact approach is to delay the start of fermentation while you rush a sample of the juice to a professional lab to be tested for yeast-available nitrogen (YAN). Technicians there will run tests for ammonia nitrogen and for alpha-amino nitrogen (NOPA). The sum of the two measurements equals the total nitrogen available to the yeasts. According to researchers at the yeast company Lallemand, readings from just-crushed grapes most often fall between 80 and 400 parts per million (i.e., milligrams per liter). Experts differ on how much nitrogen the yeasts need to sustain their fast lives in the fermenter. But in "normal" grapes at 21 to 24 Brix, YAN scores around 250 parts per million are widely considered good, with a minimum of 300 parts per million for grapes crushed at 25 Brix or higher.

In other words, if the lab reports that your grapes at an original Brix of 23.5 had a YAN of 100 (low), or grapes at 25 Brix had a YAN of 260 (also low), it's time to set up your gram scale and measure out some yeast food. The goal is to bring the nitrogen up into the beneficial range while maintaining or even building up levels of other essential nutrients.

Feeding by design. You're likely to find yeast foods made by Red Star and Lallemand. Brew shops and labs that sell supplies often carry at least one brand or the other. Diammonium phosphate, or DAP, is a generic source of nitrogen for yeasts. Both Red Star and Lallemand offer DAP and also include it in their multinutrient blends. Superfood is the proprietary name for the main blend distributed by Red Star and trademarked by the Wine Lab (listed under Gusmer Enterprises on page 235) in California's Napa Valley. It contains DAP, yeast extract (a.k.a. T154), yeast hulls (a.k.a. Nutrex 370), minerals, and vitamins. The other common product, Fermaid K (sometimes labeled simply Fermaid), is Lallemand's blend. It contains inorganic nitrogen (DAP), organic nitrogen (autolyzed yeast, a.k.a. yeast extract), inactive yeast (yeast hulls), minerals, and vitamins.

Because nutrient-deficient musts generally need vitamins and minerals as well as extra nitrogen, some winemakers add an exact amount of DAP plus one (but never more than one) of the brand-name nutrient blends. Keep in mind that Superfood and Fermaid K are similar but not identical. Most important: Fermaid K contains roughly twice as much DAP. Here are some guidelines for their use.

- Follow the maker's directions exactly, even if they seem brutally complex. Suppose a lab test found that your undiluted must is low in yeast-available nitrogen. Standard advice is to raise the YAN to approximately 250 parts per million—simple enough. But if your grapes were harvested at 25 Brix or higher, or if they have some of the high-risk attributes listed above, you should probably aim somewhat higher.

- Always figure out the total amount of DAP and nutrient blend you plan to add before adding any. Adding 0.25 gram of DAP per liter of must provides roughly 50 parts per million of yeast-available nitrogen. So to raise the YAN of a gallon of must by approximately 50 parts per million, add about 1 gram of DAP (0.25 gram per liter × 3.785 liters per gallon). Remember, though, that the brand-name nutrient blends are mixtures of DAP and other nutrients. Fermaid K is relatively high in DAP, Superfood relatively low. Adding 0.75 gram of Superfood per liter of must (2.8 grams per gallon) will raise the YAN by 50 parts per million. But just 0.38 gram of Fermaid K per liter of must (1.4 grams per gallon) will provide those same 50 parts per million of YAN. For more information on these (and other) fermentation products, see the Red Star and Lalvin Web sites (addresses on page 234).

- Base your additions on Brix readings taken before any dilution to reduce high sugar levels. Remember that high-Brix grapes need more nitrogen while low-Brix grapes need less.

- Add the nutrients in a series of separate small doses, never all at once. Large nutrient doses can cause rampant yeast growth and high temperatures, possibly leading to a stuck fermentation.

- When a substantial dose is needed, make your additions once a day instead of every few days. Warning: Nutrient overdoses can kill yeasts, generate off flavors, or promote the growth of spoilage microbes. Do not add more than the maker recommends.

- Mix the nutrients into a small amount of water before stirring them into the must.

- Add the final nutrient dose before the sugar falls below 10 Brix.

- Never add DAP, Superfood, or Fermaid K to the water when you rehydrate the yeasts.

- Buy fresh nutrients every year. Most of these products are extremely hygroscopic— they grab moisture out of the air—and readily turn into dense cakes that will not dissolve or disperse.

SEVEN WAYS TO SEDUCE A MICROBE

Of all the winemaking innovations of the past few decades, perhaps the most dramatic and helpful has been the creation of pure cultures of malolactic bacteria. Dry wine in a cold cellar is not a happy home for microbes—the reason Louis Pasteur praised wine as the "most hygienic of beverages." And in the old days, as many wines failed to go through malolactic fermentation, enologists blamed the "fastidious" bacteria, unable to endure the high levels of acid and alcohol. That whole picture has changed. Newly selected strains of the wine-tolerant bacteria *Oenococcus oeni* (known until the late 1990s as *Leuconostoc oenos*) are able to thrive in dry wine, not only softening the wine's acidity but at the same time diminishing its bitterness, heightening its fruitiness, and improving its body.

The chemical effects are especially significant. One gram of malic acid, when transformed by the bacteria, becomes 0.33 gram of carbon dioxide gas and 0.67 gram of lactic acid. In other words, there's now just two thirds as much lactic acid as there was malic, and on top of that the lactic acid is weaker. It's what's known to chemists as a monoprotic acid—that is, each lactic molecule frees just one hydrogen ion to the diprotic malic's two, giving the wine after secondary fermentation a lower effective acidity. In a must that starts out with a high level of malic acid, total acidity can fall by as much as 0.4 gram per 100 milliliters—from, say, 0.9 to 0.5. Meanwhile, pH may rise by as many points, bringing a wine's pH of, say, 3.2 to 3.5 or possibly 3.6.

Winemakers who once welcomed such marked changes as a stroke of good luck or a benevolent act of God now have the choice of launching the malolactic fermentation with either a liquid or a freeze-dried culture. Lallemand alone offers about a dozen different strains, including one that prospers in wine with alcohol at 15 percent and acidity at pH 3.0—conditions that were at one time deemed far too harsh for the fussy microbes. Another maker, Chr. Hansen, offers three freeze-dried varieties in its Viniflora brand: Oenos, a multipurpose strain; CH-16, for high-alcohol reds; and CH-35, for white and rosé wines, especially those fermented with *bayanus* yeasts or having low pH. On top of this, enologists have figured out the bugs' nutritional needs, and the companies now offer special malolactic nutrients—a wise investment if you plan to inoculate.

Which wines benefit. Virtually all dry red wines are candidates for malolactic fermentation, not only to round out their flavors but also to guarantee that they will be stable after bottling. Wine in the bottle is constantly evolving, chemically speaking, and conditions that are initially unfavorable to *Oenococcus* bacteria can shift to favorable ones. (The free sulfur dioxide level slowly falls, for instance.) Once the dormant bacteria spring to life, they can launch an assault on the wine's malic acid, generating off odors and producing enough gas to carbonate the bottles or possibly drive out the corks. But red wines that have gone through malolactic fermentation are stable and can be bottled with lower sulfur dioxide levels.

In white wines, as noted in chapter 9, malolactic fermentation is optional—a style choice that hinges not only on the bacteria's acid-busting talents but also on their tendency to produce diacetyl, a highly aromatic chemical that's identical to one used in the vegetable oil on "butter-flavored" popcorn. That smell you associate with busy movie theaters? That's diacetyl. All *Oenococcus* strains make diacetyl—even in red musts—but for complex reasons it's not always evident in the finished wine. For one thing, amid red wines' rich and forward flavors, the compound is rarely conspicuous. What's more, once the bacteria finish converting the malic acid, they turn around and start chewing up the diacetyl they just made, changing it into other chemicals. Yeasts, too, can degrade diacetyl. Vintners hoping for extra-buttery white wines inoculate with malolactic bacteria *after* the primary fermentation (possibly even racking first), monitor the secondary fermentation closely, and then rack and sulfite as soon as the malic acid is gone. Others wanting just a slight dose of diacetyl inoculate with malolactic bacteria near the end of the primary fermentation, and then—to let bugs and yeasts remove some of the compound—leave the wine unsulfited on its lees for several days at the end. (It's also possible to stop a malolactic fermentation midway; see page 221.)

Timing the inoculation. These manipulations are somewhat controversial—in fact, everything about the timing of malolactic inoculations is arguable. Some winemakers favor adding the bacteria at the height of the yeast fermentation, when the must is comfortably warm and low in alcohol, and there are plenty of nutrients. Others wait until near the fermentation's end, when the raging yeasts are tapering off and leaving elbow room for other forms of life. Still others insist that with the new, more adaptable strains of bacteria, there's no need to rush. In fact, they say, there are strong reasons to postpone the inoculation until the wine goes dry.

Malolactic bacteria that start early and convert all the malic acid before the end of the yeast fermentation can on occasion turn into troublemakers. Having run out of their favorite food, they attack the sugar in the must, in the process giving off acetic acid and other noxious compounds known collectively as volatile acidity—a bad thing in any wine. Meanwhile, the *Oenococcus*-friendly environment of warmth, diminishing yeast activity, rising pH, low sulfur dioxide, and significant sugar is also an open door to spoilage microbes, in particular *Lactobacillus, Pediococcus,* and *Brettanomyces*. That's why many winemakers prefer to wait until the yeasts have run through all but the tiniest bit of residual sugar—perhaps as low as 0.2 percent—before inoculating with a modern strain of malolactic bacteria that's willing and able to do its acid-munching in dry wine. Then, when the bacteria are done, the vintners promptly rack and sulfite to keep the spoilage bugs at bay.

So there are three inoculation options: middle, late, and after, with no final word from the experts. The bug-breeders really are trying to help—it's not a conspiracy to complicate your life—and in fact winemakers everywhere have benefited from the reliability of the malolactic cultures. But the timing questions hand you the decision-making power—an opportunity to refine your craft.

To run successful malolactic fermentations (usually in red wines or full-bodied whites):

- Hold sulfite additions at crush to no more than 60 parts per million total sulfur dioxide (see page 191).

- Adjust the Brix of the must or juice to 24.5 or below so the alcohol doesn't rise above 14 percent.

- Inoculate the must with cultured malolactic bacteria and follow the supplier's directions, adding special malolactic nutrient if it's recommended. (Note: The bacteria can't use DAP.)

- Try to start the primary fermentation in must that has a pH between 3.2 and 3.5.

- Don't add sulfite to the dry wine after pressing (red wines).

- After fermentation, keep the wine at a constant temperature between 65°F and 70°F.

- Rack and add sulfite only after the malolactic fermentation is complete.

To discourage malolactic fermentations (usually in white or rosé wines):

- Add up to 90 parts per million of sulfur dioxide at crush.

- Try to start with the pH of the must or juice below 3.2.

- Use a *bayanus* yeast strain (which deprives bacteria of nutrients).

- Ferment at cool temperatures (below 60°F) and keep the wine cool after fermentation.

- Rack to clarify the wine immediately after primary fermentation.

- Don't age the wine in a barrel where a malolactic fermentation has occurred before.

- Add enough sulfite to keep the free sulfur dioxide (see page 198) above 20 parts per million, or 30 if the pH is 3.6 or higher.

- Treat the wine with lysozyme after the primary fermentation (see page 221).

14

MASTERING SULFUR DIOXIDE

"CONTAINS SULFITES." Those blunt words, required by law, grace the label of virtually every bottle of wine sold in this country. The declaration puts sulfur dioxide on the table, so to speak, and makes wine lovers meet it face-to-face, like it or not. It's a chemical preservative, and that's bad—we'd all prefer our food and drink to be as pure as possible. But it also makes any wine live longer and taste better.

So honorable winemakers add only the smallest amounts needed to protect their wines. Adding none isn't a realistic option. In fermentations run without added sulfites, the yeasts themselves generate about as much sulfur dioxide as a tightfisted winemaker might use. But if wines make their own, why add any? Now we're at the heart of the matter. In one study of 15 unsulfited wines, enologists found that the small amount of natural sulfur dioxide was all in the inactive or "bound" form that gives wines little or no protection from spoilage.

Swirling and sniffing the wine to check for the scents of hydrogen sulfide, volatile acidity, excessive sulfur dioxide, or other flaws.

WHAT'S SO GOOD ABOUT SULFUR DIOXIDE?

If you harbor any lingering doubts about the benefit that restrained and respectful use of sulfur dioxide brings to wines, consider what the compound does in mere parts per million. Sulfur dioxide

- helps release variety-specific flavor compounds, flavonoid polyphenols, from the grapes when added at crush;

- inhibits the grape enzymes that contribute to browning and oxidation of musts;

- binds with and deactivates acetaldehyde, a common fermentation by-product that can give wines an unpleasant oxidized or sherrylike aroma;

- inhibits spoilage microbes and wild yeasts, ensuring clean, complete fermentations;

- enables cultured yeasts to use the must's sugar better and to multiply rapidly with ample oxygen;

- helps red wines retain their deep purple color and whites keep their pale gold or green;

- reacts with and neutralizes the oxygen introduced during rackings;

- and scavenges oxygen from the air bubble left in the wine at bottling, preventing premature aging.

In other words, keeping sulfur dioxide under tight control is among the best ways to make sure you come out with excellent wine—right up there with procuring the best possible grapes, keeping your equipment spotless, and reminding yourself to top up.

The ins and outs of sulfur dioxide. Life would be far easier for winemakers if the crystalline powder commonly known as sulfite were nothing but pure sulfur dioxide. But no such luck. Potassium metabisulfite ($K_2S_2O_5$) is really only 57.6 percent sulfur dioxide (SO_2). (The leftover potassium ions disperse into the wine.) In other words, 1 gram of sulfite produces just 0.576 gram, or 576 milligrams, of the real thing. Stir that gram into a liter of water and you get a sulfur dioxide solution of 576 milligrams per liter, or 576 parts per million. Now put those same 576 parts into 19 liters of water—the amount in a standard 5-gallon carboy—and you end up with 30 parts per million (576 divided by 19). That's why 1 gram of potassium metabisulfite powder added to a carboy of wine gives a total sulfur dioxide level of 30 parts per million. Note that the *sulfite* powder is weighed out in grams, but the dissolved *total sulfur dioxide* level is noted in parts per million. Also remember that sulfite is not the same as *sulfide,* the common name for hydrogen sulfide, a gas with a rotten-egg smell sometimes given off by yeasts during fermentation.

Sulfite and sulfur dioxide are two different things. The most common form of sulfite—potassium metabisulfite—contributes about 58 percent of its weight as sulfur dioxide.

If 30 parts per million of total sulfur dioxide is a good rule of thumb for additions to dry wines at various stages, 150 to 175 parts per million total sulfur dioxide is about as much as it's wise to let your several additions add up to during a wine's trip from crusher-stemmer to bottle. At levels above that you may begin to smell and taste it—a great reason to keep a running tally of how much you've added.

Actually, however, these rules of thumb don't guarantee optimal protection for your wine. That's because, as noted above, the sulfur dioxide itself isn't 100 percent effective. About 50 percent of what you first add becomes chemically bound up by one or more of 50 different compounds in the must or wine, including acetaldehyde (oxidized alcohol), sugar, yeast, bacteria, phenols, and proteins. That leaves about half of the sulfite dose free to do the job of defeating microbes and limiting browning and oxidation. And to complicate matters, only a fraction of this "free" sulfur dioxide actually does the real antioxidant and antimicrobial work. This tiny but mighty portion is known as molecular sulfur dioxide. Whenever you can detect the burned-matches smell of sulfur dioxide in a solution or a wine, you're sensing these highly reactive free-floating molecules of pure sulfur dioxide gas.

Potassium metabisulfite isn't the only kind of sulfite. Sodium metabisulfite ($Na_2S_2O_5$) is slightly more potent, yielding 67.4 percent sulfur dioxide, and should be added in smaller doses.

The crucial role of pH. Vintners' lives would also be much easier if every wine's free sulfur dioxide level pointed straight across to its level of molecular sulfur dioxide. Again, no such luck. A wine's molecular sulfur dioxide level is under the influence of two things: its free sulfur dioxide level and its pH. As the pH goes up, less and less free sulfur dioxide is turned loose as protective molecular sulfur dioxide. At pH 3.0, about 6 percent of the free sulfur dioxide is molecular, but at pH 3.6, just 1.5 percent is.

What does that really mean in the wine? At pH 3.6, any amount of sulfur dioxide is less than half as effective as it would be at pH 3.2. To unleash more molecular sulfur dioxide, you can either boost the free sulfur dioxide by adding sulfite, or lower the pH by adding tartaric acid or blending the wine with one that has a lower pH. Because adjusting the pH can be tricky, most winemakers prefer to adjust the free sulfur dioxide by adding sulfite.

But the goal is to add as little as you can. The minimum level of molecular sulfur dioxide that enologists agree will keep dry wines safe from spoilage is between 0.5 and 0.8 parts per million—with the smaller amount most often for red wines and the larger one for whites. Wines with their alcohol at 12 percent or less—and that means many whites—need some extra molecular sulfur dioxide. It's true that higher amounts would offer better protection, but there's a catch. Molecular sulfur dioxide becomes a problem—you can smell and taste it—around 2.0 parts per million or even a little less. The standard approach is to confirm the wine's pH, choose the right molecular sulfur dioxide level for long-term protection, and then determine how much free sulfur dioxide is needed.

Here's how to use table 5 (page 194). Say you have a batch of Cabernet Sauvignon that finished malolactic fermentation and needs to be racked and sulfited for the first time. (That is, you've added no sulfite since you crushed the grapes, and the small dose you did add then has since become 100 percent bound.) There's enough wine for several 5-gallon carboys. The pH is 3.3, and you're going for a molecular sulfur dioxide level of 0.5 parts per million. Using table 5, scan down the left-hand column for the pH, and then look across to find the suitable level of free sulfur dioxide: 16 parts per million. That's what you want distributed in each carboy.

Adjusting the free sulfur dioxide level. Remember, you can't directly add free sulfur dioxide—only potassium metabisulfite. And there are two stages between the powder and the free sulfur dioxide in the wine.

The protective power of the sulfite you add is directly governed by the wine's pH. At any sulfur dioxide level, the wine receives less and less protection as the pH rises.

If you start with 1 gram of sulfite, you get just 0.576 gram of actual sulfur dioxide. And some of that total sulfur dioxide gets bound up by compounds in the wine—usually about 50 percent—leaving just half of the 0.576 gram, or 0.288 gram, of free sulfur dioxide. So to make up for the fact that every gram of sulfite contributes less than a third its weight as free sulfur

The higher your wine's pH, the higher the level of free sulfur dioxide needed to achieve a protective dose of molecular sulfur dioxide. First, find the pH of the wine using a pH meter or by sending a sample to a test lab. Next, decide on the right level of molecular sulfur dioxide—either 0.5 parts per million (red wines) or 0.8 parts per million (white wines). Finally, look up the necessary parts per million (ppm) of free sulfur dioxide (SO_2) in this table. Caution: that's not the sulfite dose. To determine the grams of sulfite to add, use the formulas in the chapter text.

pH	FOR 0.5 PPM MOLECULAR SO_2, FREE SO_2 SHOULD BE:	FOR 0.8 PPM MOLECULAR SO_2, FREE SO_2 SHOULD BE:
2.9	7 ppm	11 ppm
3.0	8 ppm	13 ppm
3.1	10 ppm	16 ppm
3.2	13 ppm	21 ppm
3.3	16 ppm	26 ppm
3.4	20 ppm	32 ppm
3.5	25 ppm	40 ppm
3.6	31 ppm	50 ppm
3.7	39 ppm	63 ppm
3.8	49 ppm*	79 ppm
3.9	62 ppm	99 ppm

* Shaded boxes show additions that could possibly raise the total or molecular sulfur dioxide to the level at which it can be tasted or smelled. In this range, it's better to lower the pH than to raise the free sulfur dioxide.

dioxide, a constant, or multiplier, is needed. The multiplier is 3.5 (that is, 0.288 times 3.5 equals 1). Got that? Here's the formula for using parts per million of free sulfur dioxide to find out how much sulfite to add.

(free SO_2 ppm [from table] × 3.5 [multiplier] × gallons of wine × 3.785 [liters per gallon]) / 1,000 = grams of $K_2S_2O_5$ to add per 5-gallon carboy

You want 16 parts per million of free sulfur dioxide in 5 gallons of unsulfited wine. How much sulfite should you add?

$$(16 \times 3.5 \times 5 \times 3.785) / 1{,}000 = 1.06 \text{ grams per 5-gallon carboy}$$

That makes sense. The rule of thumb is to add 1 gram of sulfite to 5 gallons of wine to achieve 30 parts per million of total sulfur dioxide. And about half of that total ends up free. So by the formula, a smidgen over 1 gram of sulfite gets you a free sulfur dioxide level of 16 parts per million. Bingo! Everything fits. But there's a twist. Suppose the wine's pH is not 3.3 but 3.6. If you check table 5, you'll see that the wine now needs not 16 but 31 parts per million of free sulfur dioxide to bring the molecular sulfur dioxide to a safe level.

$$(31 \times 3.5 \times 5 \times 3.785) / 1{,}000 = 2.05 \text{ grams per carboy, or about twice as much sulfite}$$

If you ignored the molecular sulfur dioxide and the pH and added your sulfite solely to hit a target of 30 parts per million of total sulfur dioxide, you'd add just 1 gram of sulfite—that is, your wine would get *half* the protection it needs. And you'd have no idea how much sulfur dioxide was active in your wine.

Unfortunately, this formula for adding sulfite, as handy as it is, is reliable only for that first post-malolactic dose. Why's that? Because the formula assumes (via the multiplier) that exactly 50 percent of the sulfur dioxide is bound and 50 percent of it is free. In fact, as you keep adding sulfite to the wine during the subsequent rackings, more and more of the sulfur dioxide stays in the free form. Enologists' estimates differ, but once you've added more than about 60 parts per million *total* sulfur dioxide, as much as 100 percent of the sulfur dioxide from each new sulfite

Parts per million means the same thing as milligrams per liter. A tenth of a gram (0.1 gram, or 100 milligrams) of a substance dissolved in a liter of liquid equals 100 parts per million.

dose remains free. If, for example, you later add 1 gram of sulfite per carboy (30 parts per million total sulfur dioxide), it may in fact contribute up to 30 parts per million free sulfur dioxide.

At the same time—as the months roll by while the wine clears and stabilizes—the free sulfur dioxide is doing what it's supposed to do: reacting with oxygen, capturing acetaldehyde, immobilizing bacteria and rogue yeasts. In other words, while you're steadily nudging the free sulfur dioxide *up*, other forces are dragging it back *down*. If your wine has been racked and sulfited a few times—and especially if you're about to bottle—it's wise to run a test to find the actual level of free sulfur dioxide (testing methods appear later in this chapter). Once you know how much is free in your wine, you can subtract that number from the target level of free sulfur dioxide in table 5. Then you know how much to replace (or not—your wine may have plenty). So for any late-stage sulfite additions, you need both a new multiplier and a new formula.

([free SO_2 ppm (from table) - free SO_2 in wine] × 1.75 [100 percent multiplier] × gallons of wine × 3.785 [liters per gallon]) / 1,000 = grams $K_2S_2O_5$ to add per 5-gallon carboy

Suppose the test shows that your Cabernet's free sulfur dioxide level is 6 parts per million. That's 10 parts per million short of the 16 you want before bottling a red wine at pH 3.3. How much sulfite should you add?

([16 - 6] × 1.75 × 5 × 3.785) / 1,000 = 0.33 gram per 5-gallon carboy

If you used the original multiplier (3.5), you'd add 0.66 gram—twice the amount that's needed to protect the wine. There's no denying that these calculations are cumbersome and have built-in uncertainties. But the minor guesswork involved in using the formulas is far more reassuring than the guesswork involved in just guessing.

HOW TO MEASURE SULFITE AS A LIQUID

In the winery where I've worked, we used sulfite exactly as I do at home: for each planned dose, we used a pocket calculator to figure out how much was needed, and then weighed out the powder on a scale, dissolved it in a small amount of water, and immediately added it to the wine. We poured the fresh solution into each stainless steel tank through a hatch at the top and stirred it in using a motorized mixing tool poked into the wine through a valve on the tank's side.

As easy as that same process is on the scale of carboys and kegs, some home winemakers find it more convenient to add the compound as a ready-made liquid. That is, they weigh out a set amount of sulfite and dissolve it in a set amount of water to make a stock solution of known strength. They then use a pipette or graduated cylinder to add however much is needed.

The most common stock solution is 10 percent sulfite. That is, 1 liter (1,000 milliliters) of the solution contains 100 grams of sulfite. (Remember, as above, we're talking about sulfite the powder—potassium metabisulfite—not sulfur dioxide the chemical.) Or to put it another way, each 100 milliliters of the solution contains 10 grams of sulfite, and each 10 milliliters contains 1 gram. So to add 1 gram of sulfite to a carboy at racking, you simply pipette up 10 milliliters of the solution and dribble it into the empty carboy just before you start the wine flowing.

Making a sulfite solution. To make a stock 10 percent sulfite solution, first weigh out 100 grams of potassium metabisulfite, and then mix into it enough tap water to make exactly 1 liter. (Don't first measure out 1 liter of water and mix the sulfite into it, or you'll end up with more than 1 liter and your solution will be too weak.) Stir the mixture until the sulfite dissolves completely. Pour the solution into a screw-top glass bottle (plastic is too porous), seal it tightly, and store it someplace cool and dark out of the reach of children.

Stock solutions have their good and bad points. They're arguably a little easier to use than dry sulfite, since you weigh and dissolve the powder just once and thereafter make each sulfite

Tips for Minimizing Sulfite

The first rule is always to know how many grams of sulfite you've added to the wine. The second is to know what your combined sulfite additions equal in total, free, and molecular sulfur dioxide. Here are some other guidelines.

- Record additions of dry sulfite in grams and 10 percent stock solution in milliliters.

- Track total, free, and molecular sulfur dioxide levels in parts per million.

- At crushing, add only enough sulfite for 30 to 45 parts per million of total sulfur dioxide, or 1 to 1.5 grams of sulfite per 100 pounds of grapes or 5 gallons of juice, and mix it in thoroughly.

- Never add any amount of sulfite during the primary fermentation.

- Always repeat sulfite calculations—or, to paraphrase the carpenter's adage, calculate twice, add once.

- Make relatively few sulfite additions so that each relatively large dose produces an effective level of molecular sulfur dioxide.

- As a rule of thumb, add 30 parts per million total sulfur dioxide (1 gram of sulfite per 5 gallons) at each

(continued)

addition in a quick single step. But the solutions lose potency over time, and they slightly complicate your sulfite calculations. To add 1.7 grams of sulfite, you have to use 17 milliliters of 10 percent solution.

TESTING FOR FREE SULFUR DIOXIDE

The great thing about testing for free sulfur dioxide is that you're rarely in a hurry for the results. Your wine is cooling its heels in your carboys, kegs, or barrels. You've added sulfite at intervals since the first racking, and the wine smells clean and looks bright. You can afford the time—just a few days, really—to pull out a sample, ship it off to a lab, and wait for the results to come back. And in fact, of the several ways of finding out your wine's free sulfur dioxide level, sending for a lab test is by far the easiest and most reliable. (For a list of labs, see page 235.)

Two types of lab tests. Depending on the sophistication of the lab you choose, you'll probably be offered one of two types of free sulfur dioxide tests. The more precise and reliable version is called an aspiration/oxidation (a/o) test. A small sample of wine is placed in a stoppered flask linked by hoses to a light-duty air pump akin to the kind you might use on a home aquarium. The sample is acidified to make it give off sulfur dioxide gas, which is then swept up, or aspirated, into nitrogen gas or air. This gas mixture is bubbled through a flask of hydrogen peroxide, creating an acid whose strength is in direct proportion to the initial free sulfur dioxide level. The newly created acid is titrated with sodium hydroxide—the same way a wine sample is titrated to find its total acidity—and the volume of sodium hydroxide drained from the burette is plugged into a formula that indicates the free sulfur dioxide, ideally in a range between 5 and 50 parts per million.

racking, and then before bottling test the free SO_2 level and add enough sulfite to bring the molecular sulfur dioxide to at least 0.5 parts per million.

- Keep a running tally of your sulfur dioxide additions, and try not to add more than 150 parts per million total.

- Remember that in wines above pH 3.6 it may not be possible to add enough sulfite to reach an effective molecular sulfur dioxide level without exceeding 150 parts per million total sulfur dioxide in a dose or two.

- Buy a fresh batch of sulfite every year.

The second way of measuring free sulfur dioxide is known as the Ripper method, which for many years was the most common test. A starch indicator is added to a small sample of wine, and then the pH is adjusted with a strong acid. Using an ordinary titration burette, an iodine reagent is dripped into the wine until a blue end point is reached. The volume of reagent added is used to calculate the free sulfur dioxide level.

The Ripper method has a long rap sheet of shortcomings. Some of the sulfur dioxide gas blows off and is lost as the reagent is dribbled in, while at the same time the reagent reacts in the wine with red pigments, tannins, ascorbic acid, and other compounds other than sulfur dioxide, producing readings with a margin of error as high as 10 parts per million. That is, your results from the lab could be either 10 parts per million too high (more likely) or 10 too low (less likely), and you would have no way of knowing. What's more, in all but the lightest red wines, the blue end point can be hard to see. In reds, as a general rule, Ripper tests tend to overestimate the free sulfur dioxide, so it's possible to invent a fudge factor and simply assume that the real level is a few to several points lower. Still, if you have a choice when sending wine samples to be tested, ask for the aspiration/oxidation test (sometimes also called aeration/oxidation). Sticklers may object that the a/o test can also overestimate free sulfur dioxide in red wines—especially young reds—because some of the compound that's initially bound by grape pigments is liberated during the procedure, raising the reading. True, but the error usually isn't large.

> *The only completely foolproof way to tell how much of the sulfur dioxide in your wine is unbound or "free"—the only effective form—is to have the wine tested. Luckily, time is on your side.*

The home sulfur dioxide test. Many winemakers have set themselves up to run Ripper tests at home, though the procedure requires getting comfortable with chemistry. (The test calls for strongly corrosive sulfuric acid, among other things.) Others have shelled out for enough gear—a few hundred dollars for flasks, stands, tubing, reagents, and a pump—to carry out their own aspiration/oxidation tests. (For listings of equipment suppliers, see page 233.)

But there's a simpler option. Most brew shops carry handy gadgets for testing free sulfur dioxide. The devices, called Titrets, from the Chemetrics company, come in economical packets of ten with concise, detailed instructions. Each test costs a dollar or two, or a tenth of what you'd pay for the same information from a lab. That's the good news. The bad news is that Titrets are tiny, self-contained Ripper titration units with all the foibles of the full-scale method.

Each unit contains the starch indicator, acid, and iodine reagent sealed under a partial vacuum in a small glass tube, or ampoule, the size and shape of a fountain pen. With each of these tubes comes an accessory bead valve that fits onto the ampoule's sharp tip. With the valve snugly in place, the glass point is snapped off, and the tip of the assembly is dunked in the wine sample. A quick squeeze on the bead valve lets the vacuum in the ampoule suck up a tiny bit of wine, which causes the indicator inside to turn deep blue. Several more bits of wine are imbibed until the blue color vanishes, signifying that the end point has been reached. The ampoule is then turned tip up and the liquid level noted on the side, where a scale shows the free sulfur dioxide in parts per million from 10 to 100.

It's a clever system, although it takes nimble fingers to add just the right smidgen of wine by quickly squeezing and releasing the valve. In an effort to cure that problem, the company offers a molded plastic gizmo, called a Titrettor, that holds the ampoule-and-valve assembly and in theory makes it somewhat easier to start and stop the flow of wine. With or without it, you'll find that using Titrets takes practice, especially on red wines. That's because to find the end point of the test in a Pinot Noir or Syrah, you have to notice when the indicator changes color from blue to clear in liquid that's already deep red or purple. It is doable. Old hands like to note the colors—pure wine first, then the changing shades in the ampoule— against a bright light. Others dilute the wine sample to half strength, and then double the free sulfur dioxide reading.

How accurate are the results? Ripper tests have an error margin of plus or minus 10 parts per million. That means a wine that tests out at 27 parts per million free sulfur dioxide could actually have as little as 17 parts per million or as much as 37. The results are more likely to be high than low, but your own slips in working the valve on the ampoule or in catching the end point in dark wines can skew the numbers in other ways. That's why you may want to send wine samples out to a professional lab for aspiration/oxidation tests, if only to get a reliable point of reference for your home tests.

15

MAKING THE WINE YOU WISH YOU'D MADE

IT'S ONE THING TO MAKE WINE as if you're lighting a roman candle: set it off and let it go. It's something else to do it exactly the way you want. The grapes may be all-important, but the character of the wine they produce can be adjusted or even transformed by a winemaker's decisions: The length of time the crushed grapes stand before fermenting. The yeast strain. The temperature and length of the primary fermentation. The use of yeast nutrients and malolactic inoculants. The amount of force applied in pressing. The size and timing of sulfite doses. The frequency and number of rackings, and the oxygen they add. The decisions whether to add a fining agent or to age the wine in barrels. Obviously, you can carry the manipulations to extremes, and some winemakers do. But what are the crucial choices, the key things that will help you make the wine you'll love?

Start with your own senses. Pour yourself sips of a wine you've made and a comparable commercial wine. That is, if you've made a Cabernet Sauvignon, uncork some respected win-

---

Setting up a blending trial by using a 100-milliliter graduated cylinder
to add precisely measured samples of two wines to a series of identical
clean wineglasses.

ery's Cabernet, ideally one from grapes grown in the same area. Give each glass the whole swirl-and-sniff test, jotting notes as you go. You're not seeking flaws so much as attributes: color, body, aroma, fruitiness, astringency, intensity, complexity, softness, silkiness, oakiness, tartness, and richness. Maybe your wine has a strong, fruit-forward aroma but isn't deeply colored. Perhaps it's beautifully clear but smells a bit yeasty. Maybe you wish it had more richness or body or fresh-fruit character. Or perhaps your wine has what vintners call a short finish, a lack of aromas and mouth-coating sensations that linger after the sip is swallowed. What are the traits you'd like to pursue? Here are some paths to follow once you know.

RED WINES: TAKING COMMAND OF COLOR AND FLAVOR

Makers of red wines are often dismayed to see the intense purple-red of the must at mid-fermentation fade to cherry-red by the time the wine is pressed. The shift is not an illusion. The color of red wines comes from water-soluble pigments called anthocyanins, found almost exclusively in the grapes' skins. (Cabernet Sauvignon grape skins contain some 16 different kinds.) As the fermentation gets rolling, anthocyanins are extracted from the skins; and by the fourth day or so, the must's color can be a stunning deep purple. But wine scientists have found that as even more anthocyanins dissolve into the must, the color doesn't always darken, and it may in fact fade. How can that be? Anthocyanins are inherently unstable, or labile, as enologists say. Some are reabsorbed by the grape skins or taken up by the yeasts, while others are transformed by oxygen or sulfur dioxide. Meanwhile, the free-floating anthocyanins in the must interact with tannin from the grape skins and seeds, combining into stable complexes, called polymers, that are less purple-red and more cherry- or brick-red. This polymerization proceeds fastest in the stages before pressing, but it goes on throughout the wine's life under the influence of the wine's pH, its tannin content, the degree of exposure to oxygen, the sulfur dioxide level, and the cellar temperature. By the end of the first year, 50 percent to 70 percent of the pigments are polymers, and as the years pass all the anthocyanins polymerize, some forming large compounds that may eventually settle as dark deposits in the bottle.

There are numerous twists and turns in the story of wine-color chemistry, not the least of which is that the puckery stuff we refer to as tannin isn't one compound but many—the reason vintners typically use the plural term *tannins*. Also known as polyphenols, tannins are found in the grapes' stems, skins, and seeds. But after crushing, which removes the stems, and the early stage of fermentation, which extracts most of what the skins have to give, it's the seeds that furnish most of a wine's tannins. That's why it pays to press carefully so you don't wring too much from the seeds.

Tannins are the Dr. Jekyll and Mr. Hyde of red wines: They help stabilize the flighty anthocyanins and contribute to the overall feel and flavor of the wine. But they can sometimes be too bold—aggressive, even—turning what would be pleasant wines into brutal monsters. So the goal for deeply colored reds is to get maximum extraction of the anthocyanins while ensuring that the tannin levels rise high enough for prompt and ongoing polymerization but not so high that the wines end up unbearably astringent. The steps below—from cold soaking and long maceration to barrel-aging and blending—are common options. Some are routes to drastically different styles of wine. Others are alternate paths to the same end. Keep in mind that even professional winemakers and enologists disagree on the details. You can expect to see these same techniques explained differently in every winemaking reference you check. To me, that's inspiring. You know you're a vintner when you have to run your own experiments. The only prerequisites? Basic knowledge and a shot of courage.

Cold soaking—for extra color and flavor. Many winemakers believe that adding a step before fermentation, called cold soaking, can boost the intensity and stability of the color of red wines, and may also heighten the aromas and flavors, especially in Pinot Noir and other light, fruity reds. The grapes are crushed into a fermenter as usual, but then the must is promptly cooled and left to stand—no yeasts need apply—for up to four days. Without alcohol around, anthocyanins from the grape skins bond chemically with tannins and other phenols, helping to preserve the color. At the same time, oxygen absorbed at crushing reacts with some tannins, changing them into polymerized forms that may have a softer, more supple feel in the mouth. And other chemical changes help free compounds that contribute to the wine's aroma. Here are the steps to take.

> *Study up on winemaking's fine points so you get what you want, but keep it all in perspective. It's best to manipulate the wine as little as possible.*

- Chill the must to 50°F or lower to keep the fermentation from starting. (At warmer temperatures native yeasts may spontaneously come to life, cutting short the soak.) Try freezing plastic gallon jugs of water and placing them in the must, rotating in new ones as those thaw. Insulate the fermenter with blankets or a sleeping bag.

- Add a smaller-than-usual amount of sulfite—around 0.5 gram per 5 gallons of must for a sulfur dioxide level of about 15 parts per million. Although sulfur dioxide helps protect the must, it also interferes with the reactions that stabilize the anthocyanins.

- Experiment with adding pectic enzymes (pectinase) at crushing. Many winemakers say the enzymes speed the extraction of pigments and flavor compounds from the skins during the soak. For details on the kinds and their uses, check under "Enzymes" on the Web sites of some major fermentation suppliers and labs (see page 233).

- Keep air away from the must, either by laying plastic sheeting on its surface or by blanketing it with an inert gas (see the sidebar "Using Compressed Gas to Protect Your Wine," page 208), and then sealing the fermenter.

- After the second or third day, let the must warm slowly to approximately 60°F, and then add rehydrated yeasts to start the fermentation.

Extended maceration—for more complex flavors. Extended maceration is vintners' high-flown term for the act of letting the skins and seeds steep, or macerate, in the newly fermented wine for days or even weeks before pressing, a procedure most often followed for rich, age-worthy varieties such as Cabernet Sauvignon. The prolonged skin contact adds no extra color to the wine, and in fact the extraction of anthocyanin pigments actually peaks several days earlier, midway through the fermentation. Instead of extra color, the goal is to gain flavor complexity and to soften the wine's mouthfeel by pulling more tannins and other compounds from the spent grapes.

It's a risky approach, however, with uncertain rewards. The skins give up their relatively small amount of tannins very quickly, so after the fermentation ends it's only the grapes' harsh seeds that kick in any extra. Winemakers who aren't exceptionally diligent—who don't taste every day—can end up with "chewy," overextracted wines that are astringent and bitter and more likely to brown as they age. Research enologists, who like to ask whether time-honored traditions live up to their billing, have carefully compared wines pressed promptly with the same wines given extra time on the skins and found little or no benefit. Nor did the treatments help the anthocyanins and tannins polymerize to stabilize the color. Despite these findings, many winemakers swear by the practice. If you would like to see for yourself whether extended maceration can make more complex wines, here's what you need to do.

- When the Brix falls to zero in the new wine, keep air away by either covering the surface with plastic sheeting or blanketing it with inert gas (see the sidebar).

- Allow the wine to stand at room temperature, punching down gently once a day to keep any grapes at the surface wet.

- Taste the wine every day. You should notice the tannins growing gradually harsher, and then suddenly softer—your cue to press. The change could take from one to three weeks.

- Stay hyperalert for signs of spoilage. If you can detect the smell of vinegar (acetic acid) or nail polish remover (ethyl acetate), press promptly. Test to see whether the malolactic fermentation is done, and when it is add 1 to 2 grams of sulfite per 5 gallons (30 to 60 parts per million sulfur dioxide).

Powdered tannins—for more stable color. In hopes of helping to stabilize their wines' color, some vintners add small amounts of powdered

tannins to their musts. The idea is to help polymerize the labile anthocyanins, an approach that at
least some enologists support. Unfortunately, it's
virtually impossible for home vintners to tell in advance how much tannin is enough and how much
is too much—or whether any at all will be helpful.

- Nitrogen is basically air without oxygen. It's lighter than the other gases and so can't settle to form a protective blanket. It works best when used to replace the air completely in a partially full closed tank.

If you want to experiment with adding tannins, available at most brew shops and from many
testing labs, here are a few broad principles.

- Grapes that sometimes make pale or moderately pigmented red wines may benefit most. These include Grenache, Nebbiolo, Pinot Noir, Sangiovese, and Zinfandel.

- Powdered tannins, sometimes sold as condensed tannins, are extracts of grape seeds, oak, or other hardwoods. The many kinds differ in their compositions and react differently in musts. Before you add any tannins, look into the sophisticated products offered by the major yeast suppliers and labs (see page 233).

- Additions generally fall between 0.2 and 1.5 grams of powdered tannin per gallon of must, but add the amount the maker suggests. As a rule, it's better to use too little than too much.

- Tannins are usually dissolved in warm water, and then poured into the must near the start of fermentation. For your own education, taste the mixture before adding it.

Cofermentation—for bolder color. There's yet another way to boost and stabilize the
color of red wines, though it too can be hit-or-miss. The method, known as cofermentation,
calls for crushing and fermenting together two or more grape varieties. The grapes don't have

to be in equal proportion, and in fact it's possible to prompt the color-deepening effect by adding a small percentage of white grapes.

If you've studied the wines of France and Italy, you've probably seen that white grapes have traditionally been part of the blends for dark-red Italian Chiantis as well as for French Rhônes, such as Châteauneuf-du-Pape and Côte-Rôtie. And even in California, where wine-making has deep Italian roots, early vineyards were often planted with a mix of varieties and the resulting "field blend" harvested and fermented together. Did those old winegrowers know a precious secret?

Apparently so. It turns out that in fermenting musts, some anthocyanins combine naturally with colorless grape compounds other than tannins, released from the skins and seeds. Called cofactors or copigments, they form dense stacks of molecules that heighten the bold purple color. Research has shown that the skins of certain white grapes may be rich in these otherwise invisible cofactors while some red grapes may lack them, even when they're well endowed with colorful anthocyanins. In other words, if enough of the right cofactors aren't around in the must early in the fermentation, the wine may remain forever an underachiever, high in anthocyanins that never reach their potential. One study in Italy found that a Sangiovese achieved its deepest color when fermented along with minor amounts of Canaiolo, Malvasia, and Trebbiano (or Ugni Blanc, a widely planted white variety).

So should you crush white grapes with your reds? Usually, no. There's a good chance you'll merely dilute the color. But if you like to experiment and you've had trouble getting rich color from a particular grape variety from a particular source, you could give the method a try. The twist, of course, is that you'll rarely have the chance to bring home two different varieties of grapes on the same day. Here are some approaches.

- Consider ordering two or more kinds of frozen crushed grapes. Or make a white wine, and then freeze the pressed skins to thaw and add later to your next batch of red wine.

- Keep the percentage of white grapes low—20 percent or even much less—so the pale skins don't absorb and carry away pigment from the red grapes.

- Try fermenting two lots—one with and one without the second grape variety—and compare the wines' colors.

Carbonic maceration—for brighter, fruitier flavors. Perhaps the trickiest and most offbeat fermentation method, carbonic maceration starts with filling a fermenter with whole, uncrushed clusters of red grapes, traditionally Gamay or Pinot Noir. The grapes are then flooded with a deep layer of carbon dioxide gas, and the fermenter is sealed and kept warm for up to three weeks. While the trapped gas protects the fruit from spoiling, natural enzymes in the grape pulp start a spontaneous yeast-free fermentation that perks along slowly and may eventually stop. The fermenter is opened and the softened but still intact grapes pressed. The bright red, slightly alcoholic juice is then inoculated with rehydrated yeasts and fermented to completion at a lower temperature.

Why do things in such a strange way? Wines made by carbonic maceration have extraordinary fresh-fruit aromas and flavors, rich color, and very little astringency—all of which you've experienced if you've ever had a superb Beaujolais. In practice, however, and especially at home, most such fermentations are actually hybrids: partly standard, partly carbonic. There are many possible variations—some winemakers simply toss a few whole grape clusters into their must—but here's one method.

- Crush and destem between 25 percent and 50 percent of your grapes and place them in your fermenter. Add rehydrated yeast and the remaining, uncrushed grapes, and then flush the fermenter with carbon dioxide, or another inert gas if you have it. (If you don't, that's okay; the fermentation will make carbon dioxide.)

- Cover the fermenter snugly with heavy plastic sheeting or a close-fitting lid fitted with a ferm lock. Use a heating pad or electric blanket to keep the fermenter at roughly 85°F.

- As the fermentation gets under way, check the sugar in the must several times a week. If you choose to punch down—a judgment call—do so gently, so as not to break the berries.

- At zero Brix or thereabouts, bucket the skins and fermenting grape clusters into a basket press, as if for a white wine, and press and funnel the wine into carboys. Meanwhile, transfer the free-run wine to separate carboys, and let both lots ferment to dryness at approximately 65°F. Blend the finished wines to your own taste.

Don't let the many kinds of fining agents confound you. Some are mainly for red wines, some for whites. In practice, you'll probably ever need only one or two.

Protein fining—to cut astringency. To soften a red wine's mouthfeel, even after other treatments, some winemakers add egg white or gelatin. These proteins combine with a portion of the offending tannins and fall to the bottom as sediment. They may also help "polish" the wine by removing any lingering haze, although red wines, unlike whites, usually clear up by themselves as the grapes' own proteins and tannins interact.

There is a risk: protein fining can lighten a wine's color if it removes tannins that have already linked up, or formed polymers, with the wine's pigments. For that reason, it's generally best to add the fining agent early in the wine's aging, before much of the tannin has had a chance to polymerize. Depending on the initial tannin and color levels, the agent used, and the amount of protein added, the overall effect can be slight or dramatic. Here's how to use egg white or gelatin to fine red wines. (For white wine fining tips, see page 222.) Caution: until you're an old hand at fining, keep your additions at the low end of the ranges. Overfining can turn a wine hazy.

- Egg white. Though messy, egg whites do a superb job of softening astringent wines and tend not to remove much color. Usually added: one-eighth to one-half an egg white per 5-gallon carboy. For each egg white needed, separate the white from the yolk of a fresh egg, or measure 2 tablespoons of pasteurized liquid egg white (from the supermarket). Add 0.5 gram of table salt and about 70 milliliters of water to a beaker or measuring cup, and then stir in the egg white to make 100 milliliters of solution. Add the solution in proportion to the amount of egg white desired: 12.5 milliliters equals one-eighth white, 25 milliliters equals one-quarter white, 50 milliliters equals one-half white, and so on. Throw out any leftover solution. Rack in a week or two.

- Gelatin. More convenient to use than egg whites, gelatin more aggressively removes tannins, color, and aroma. Usually added: 0.1 to 1.0 gram (about 30 to 250 parts per million) of unflavored dry gelatin per gallon. Weigh the required dose, dissolve it completely in a small amount of warm (not hot) water, and then slowly stir it into the wine. Rack in a week or two.

Barrel-aging—for added flavor and suppleness. Wines aged for months in oak barrels not only show gentle vanilla aromas and flavors, but they may also be noticeably softer, darker, and more concentrated than the same wines held in glass or stainless steel—they're better, in other words. That's why virtually all top wineries age their red wines in oak. Even if you turn out a modest amount of wine, you can follow their lead. Barrels permit your wine to oxidize slowly, a process that helps set the color and soften the flavor. The wine will also absorb tannins and other phenols from the wood, boosting these welcome sensory effects. But keep in mind that both water and alcohol escape through the barrel staves—up to 5 percent a year in a standard barrel and 10 percent or more in a smaller one—leaving a vapor-filled space, or ullage, below the stopper, called a bung. To slow oxidation it's wise to keep a regular schedule for replacing the wine lost to evaporation (the "angels' share," some call it). Don't wait more than a couple of weeks, and always use an airtight silicone bung. What else? Here are answers to some common questions.

> *Four simple rules for success in barrel-aging your wine: use a high-quality oak barrel; taste regularly; top up often; and when in doubt, rack early.*

- What's the right kind of barrel? The barrels sold most widely in brew shops are made in the United States from oak grown in Oregon, Missouri, Pennsylvania, Virginia, or elsewhere. But barrels made of French, Canadian, and Eastern European oak are also available. Each of the several oak varieties grown in the different nations and regions can contribute a different flavor to wines. What's more, different makers use different cooperage methods. French oak is typically hand split before being shaped into barrel staves, while American oak may be sawn. On top of this, most barrels' inner surface is lightly charred, or toasted, by exposure to an open flame, and the tastes they contribute to wines can differ dramatically between barrels with light, medium, or heavy (dark) toastings. Medium is a common toasting grade for barrel-worthy wines, with heavy reserved for rich, tannic reds.

One California winemaker says he can discern distinct flavor characteristics in more than 60 different products from more than 20 different barrel makers. Here's how he describes a Seguin-Moreau barrel made with American oak staves and French oak heads: "All the richness of American oak with subtle nuances of finesse from the French heads. The use of heavy toast allows this barrel to produce great smoky dark chocolate aromas and flavors with subtle cinnamon and brown sugar in the background." Many winemakers pursue similar complexity by aging a single batch of wine in both American and French oak. In other words, don't automatically settle for whatever barrel is on hand in your local brew shop. Check the choices at several barrel makers and try to find one that suits the style of wine you're making (see "Suppliers and Laboratories," page 233). A new barrel, depending on its size and provenance, typically costs between $200 and $500.

Wine experts have written volumes on the ins and outs of oak barrels. For a sampling, see the Sonoma County Library's Web site, www.sonoma.lib.ca.us/wine/oak.html.

- Which size is best? If you don't make enough wine each year to fill a standard wine barrel—about 60 gallons (225 liters)—it's fine to buy any size down to about 15 gallons. The basic rule: as the barrel's size goes down, the amount of oak each gallon is exposed to goes up. It's a physical law: for any three-dimensional object, surface area increases with the square of the diameter while volume increases with the *cube* of the diameter. So the smaller and newer the barrel, the more often you should sample the wine to see how oaky it tastes. Once a week is not too often. You want the aroma and flavor to come through as faint hints, not as conspicuous oakiness. A simple insurance policy against overoaked wine: hold out a portion of the vintage so you can blend the lots later. That is, it's smart to buy a barrel somewhat smaller than the batch of wine you plan to make.

Let newly blended wine stand for at least a week before racking and bottling to enable the wines to marry, as vintners say, and to reveal unexpected cloudiness or new sediment.

- How long does a barrel last? Wine aged in a barrel used for four or more vintages won't pick up as much oak flavor, but it will still slowly oxidize. What's more, a well-used or "neutral" barrel can be reconditioned at least once by "shaving," that is, scraping or sanding the inner surface, and then retoasting the oak. Some suppliers sell low-cost reconditioned barrels—a legitimate way to save money—and when the flavor eventually fades, you can make up the difference by adding oak beans, chips, cubes, or staves (see page 88). The only downside: shaved barrels lose more wine to evaporation through their now-thinner staves.

- Don't new or newly shaved barrels need special treatment? Most wineries simply soak their new barrels overnight to make sure they're tight before filling them with wine. Caustic treatment, which is suggested in some outdated barrel-care texts, will simply deplete the oak's flavor. However, it is an option as a way to remove tartrate deposits and to try to save used barrels with faint off flavors or aromas. A standard treatment is about 5 grams of sodium percarbonate (see page 33) per gallon of barrel volume (1.25 grams per liter). Dissolve the powder in warm water, add it to the barrel, and then fill it with water and allow it to stand overnight. Empty the barrel and rinse it several times with hot water before refilling the barrel with a fresh citric-sulfur solution (see page 33) and letting it stand. Empty and rinse again with water.

· What's the right way to store an emptied barrel? Keeping a barrel filled year-round is the best way to protect it from spoilage microbes. However, few home winemakers turn out enough wine to keep a barrel always full. The safest way to protect your investment while waiting for the next vintage is to fill a just-emptied barrel with a water solution of 1.5 grams of potassium metabisulfite and 0.5 gram of citric acid for each gallon the barrel holds. Remember to top up, and replace the solution every few months. And if you find that you're aging more sulfite solution than wine each year, don't abandon the barrel—make more wine.

Blending—for balance and complexity. Many of the world's best wines are blends, even some that pretend they aren't. In most of the United States, premium wines that claim to be made from only one kind of grape legally can and often do contain up to 25 percent of one or more other varieties. The winery can state on the label that it's whatever variety makes up 75 percent—Zinfandel, say, or Pinot Gris—and can declare it to be a 2006 vintage when up to 5 percent of the wine is from another year. This isn't chicanery. Blended wines are often better. Here are some good reasons to try merging the wines from two or more lots of grapes.

How to Set Up a Tasting Trial before Blending

Blends are usually made when wines are otherwise ready to bottle. Before committing yourself, set up a tasting series. You'll need about half a bottle of each of the two wines to be blended, a pen, some masking tape, six identical wineglasses, a 100-milliliter graduated cylinder (or a 10- or 20-milliliter pipette), and a pitcher to spit into. Set it all out in a room that's free of strong odors, and consider inviting a couple of wine-savvy friends. Here's a convenient way to run the tasting.

- With the pen and tape, label one bottle Wine 1 and the other Wine 2—or name them by their grape variety or source.

- Label the empty wineglasses 100/0, 80/20, 60/40, 40/60, 20/80, and 0/100 and set them side by side.

- Add 100 milliliters of Wine 1 to glass 100/0, 80 milliliters to glass 80/20, 60 milliliters to glass 60/40, and so on, leaving the last glass empty.

- Shift to Wine 2 and, skipping over glass 100/0, add 20 milliliters to glass 80/20, 40 milliliters to glass 60/40, 60 milliliters to glass 40/60, 80 milliliters to glass 20/80, and 100 milliliters to glass 0/100. Swirl

(continued)

- To build more complex flavors. Some traditional blends endure because the grapes' flavors are naturally complementary: Cabernet and Merlot, Sauvignon Blanc and Sémillon, Zinfandel and Petite Sirah, Syrah and Grenache. But go ahead and experiment—your nose and taste buds will tell you if you go wrong. Both Cabernet Sauvignon and Merlot meld well with other bold reds, especially Syrah and Sangiovese, as winemakers in Australia and Italy have proved in recent decades. Pinot Noir, by contrast, can lose its delicate qualities when blended. Many northern winemakers find that wines from hybrid grapes often taste better when blended with a modest amount of a vinifera wine.

- To balance acidity and astringency. The best way to soften an overly tart (or low pH) wine is to blend it with a low-acid one. Likewise, the right partner can soften a harsh, overextracted wine or one that picked up too much oak flavor. It's better to break the rules than to make unlikable wine—which is to say there may be times when you're moved to blend the wines from two recent vintages. Don't let anyone tell you you can't.

- To disguise minor flaws. Always blend to improve. There's no virtue in blending a clean wine into one that's spoiled with a large amount of acetic acid or a strong hydrogen sulfide smell. But wines with mild maladies can be saved, especially ones that are low in color or have only faint off odors or flavors. There's a key principle of enology to note here: aroma or flavor dilution always lags behind volume dilution. That is, adding 5 gallons of clean wine to 5 gallons of funky wine will cut the offensive aroma by less than half. That's why it's crucial to run tasting trials (see the sidebar "How to Set Up a Tasting Trial before Blending").

the glasses to blend the wines. Each glass will contain 100 milliliters of wine—enough for several people to taste.

- Carefully swirl, sniff, and taste each wine in the sequence, and then—if you want to have faith in the results—spit out each sip. Make note of which you like best.

- When you've chosen a favorite, take a break and sip some water to refresh your palate. Meanwhile, refine the test by setting up three samples at 10-milliliter increments centered on your choice—say, 50/50, 40/60, and 30/70—and choose again. Repeat at 5-milliliter increments, if you like. Make careful note of the chosen proportions of each wine.

- If one wine began with a high pH, always test the final blend and consider readjusting the mixture until its pH is low enough to bottle safely.

WHITE WINES: ACHIEVING CLARITY AND BALANCE

The harsh tannins that can bedevil the makers of red wines are virtually never a problem in whites. Instead, in the absence of tannins, many newly made white wines have a surplus of protein, which can show up as a stubborn haze. White table wines also often come out with higher acid levels than red wines—especially if the winemaker prevented the malo-lactic fermentation—and when they're fermented completely dry can sometimes taste wickedly sour. So taking better control of white wines' quality mainly means two things: help-ing the wines to become perfectly clear and clean, and achieving a good balance between acid-ity and sweetness.

Adding pectic enzyme—for clarity and for easier pressing. When making white wines, you can try at crushing time to boost the juice's liberation from the grapes by adding a natural compound called pectic enzyme, pectinolytic enzyme, or pectinase, available at brew shops or from one of the big suppliers of fermentation products (or labs; see page 233). It softens the pulp and in theory frees more juice by breaking down the grapes' pectin, the same stuff that makes grape jelly jell. It can also encourage the grapes to release extra flavor and aroma com-pounds, and can help finished wines clear, since pectins are among the constituents of the hazes common in newly made wines. Many winemakers in the eastern United States have found that adding pectinase is helpful in pressing high-pectin, slippery-skinned grapes such as Muscadines. The enzyme is added at crushing, and is then allowed to do its work in the must for up to four hours before pressing. (Pectinase is also sometimes used after fermentation; see below.)

Pectic enzymes come in many varieties, some specially formulated for use in red musts, where the main goal is greater extraction of color and flavor. Because the enzyme products differ—Lallemand makes several, for instance—it's important to follow the instructions for whichever kind you buy. Many winemakers don't like to use pectic enzyme at crushing be-cause it also liberates more grape pulp, which then has to be gotten rid of by racking. In other words, using it may get you more juice but not necessarily more finished wine.

Controlling malolactic fermentation—to preserve acidity and limit butteriness. If you're making a full-flavored Chardonnay-style wine, you may want to let the secondary, or malolactic, fermentation run its course so that virtually all the tart malic acid is converted to mild lactic acid, with the accompanying addition of buttery diacetyl. But what if you want just a touch of that butteriness? One basic approach is to ferment the wine in two lots—one that you inoculate with bacteria (see page 183), the other that you don't. You then stop the second lot from starting a spontaneous malolactic fermentation by sulfiting and chilling. Blend the batches when both are clear and stable. The risk you run is that bacteria from the first batch will go after the malic acid from the second, defeating your efforts and—if the fermentation kicks off in the bottle—possibly spoiling the wine.

A better idea is to fend off or halt the unwanted fermentation with a natural bacteria-killer called lysozyme. It's an enzyme isolated from ordinary egg whites that shatters ("lyses") the bacteria's cell walls, stopping the microbes cold. It has no effect on yeasts, so it can be added at crushing, at the end of the yeast fermentation, or anytime during or after the malolactic fermentation. In other words, you can take the two-batch approach, if you like, using lysozyme to prevent malolactic fermentation in the final blend. Or you can encourage a bacterial fermentation in the entire lot of wine, taste or test as it progresses, and add lysozyme when some or most of the malic acid is gone.

Available as a dry powder, lysozyme is sold by many brew shops and labs. Keep in mind that lysozyme kills only "gram-positive" bacteria, a group that includes the wine spoilage bugs *Lactobacillus* and *Pediococcus* but not *Acetobacter*. In other words, it can't help protect your wine against the most common problem microbes. Additions are usually between 1 and 2 grams per gallon (about 260 to 530 parts per million). Here's how to use lysozyme to control malolactic fermentations.

- Make a 10 percent solution by dissolving 10 grams of lysozyme in enough lukewarm distilled or deionized water to make 100 milliliters. (Adding 10 milliliters of this solution to the wine will add 1 gram of lysozyme.)

- Stir the mixture gently until any lumps dissolve (it can take several minutes). It will look and feel like egg white.

- To prevent malolactic fermentation after a yeast fermentation or to halt an active malolactic fermentation in dry wine, add 300 to 500 parts per million. Remember: 100 parts per million equals 0.1 gram per liter or 0.38 gram per gallon. For 300 parts per million, add 11 milliliters of solution per gallon. For 400 parts per million, add 15 milliliters per gallon. For 500 parts per million, add 19 milliliters per gallon.

- Stir the lysozyme solution into the wine. Allow it to react and settle for up to five days, and then rack.

Fining—for clarity, color, and aroma. Persistent hazes in white wines are most often the fault of unstable grape proteins. But other compounds, including grape pectins and protein-based fining agents, can cause clarity problems. Bentonite, the adsorptive clay, is many winemakers' first choice for clearing up these conditions in white wines, and for that reason it's given full treatment in chapter 10 (see page 122). But it's not your only option—and that's good, because the universal rule about fining agents is that you may need to try more than one to get a good result. Here are three other widely used clarifying agents, plus two others more commonly employed to improve white wines' color and aroma.

- Sparkalloid. A brand-name product from Scott Laboratories (see page 236), Sparkalloid is a polysaccharide extract of seaweed mixed with pulverized diatomaceous earth. It carries a strong positive charge that neutralizes the charge on haze particles so that they no longer repel one another and settle out as a deposit. Sparkalloid won't harm your wine's color or aroma but will form thick lees, meaning you'll lose some wine, and it's trickier to prepare than Bentonite. Usually wines fall clear with an addition of 0.5 to 1.0 gram per gallon (130 to 260 parts per million), although occasionally you may want to try adding up to 1.5 grams per gallon. Make sure you buy *hot mix* Sparkalloid; cold mix is used to clarify raw juice. Here's how to get it ready for use. (The following formula makes 500 milliliters of solution, enough to run pretreatment tests and to treat up to 10 gallons of wine.)

1. Prepare 500 milliliters of a 2 percent solution of Sparkalloid by heating about 400 milliliters of distilled or deionized water to boiling, and then stirring in 10 grams of Sparkalloid powder (10 milliliters of this solution adds 0.2 gram of Sparkalloid). Keep the mixture simmering, stirring frequently until the lumps vanish and a smooth solution forms, 15 to 20 minutes. Pour the hot solution into a graduated cylinder or beaker, and add distilled or deionized water to bring the total volume to 500 milliliters.

2. Immediately run a bench trial (see the sidebar "How to Set Up a Bench Trial before Fining," page 224) to find the right amount to add to your wine. Set the remaining solution aside until you're ready to use it.

3. Reheat the solution to 180°F. Slowly stir the proper dose of hot Sparkalloid solution into the wine. Allow it to settle for up to two weeks, and then rack.

- Isinglass. A refined and gentle form of gelatin—actually extracted from the buoyancy organs, or swim bladders, of sturgeons—isinglass comes as a liquid, a powder, or a dry sheet (like thin, hardened Jell-O). It's more suitable for white wines than is gelatin, which could require counterfining with tannin. You'll find the liquid and

How to Set Up a Bench Trial before Fining

One danger in using fining agents is adding too much, or overfining, so that the agent may itself someday produce a haze or deposit. That's why it can be important to run a simple test before fining that vintners call a bench trial. Here are the steps.

- Using identical bottles, jars, or beakers, set up a series of four to eight samples, each holding at least 100 milliliters of wine, preferably more.

- Going down the row, add increasing amounts of the fining agent—say 0.1 gram to the first sample, 0.2 to the second, 0.3 to the third, and so on.

- Vigorously shake or stir the mixtures and allow them to stand for 24 hours.

- Note the smallest addition needed to clarify the wine.

- Using a calculator, scale up the milliliters of the sample to the amount of wine you plan to fine, and then multiply the grams of fining agent by the same factor.

- Use the same method to stabilize clear wines that you suspect are high in protein. But instead of checking

(continued)

powdered forms easiest to use—the sheets of isinglass can take days to dissolve. Two common brands are Biofine P19 (liquid and powder) and Drifine (powder). Usually 0.03 to 0.5 gram per gallon (about 10 to 130 parts per million) is enough to clarify the wine, but always check the manufacturer's directions, and run a bench trial.

- Pectinase. Although pectic enzymes are often used before fermentation (above), they may also be added to wines that fail to turn clear after fining with bentonite, Sparkalloid, or isinglass. Check the Web sites of major makers of fermentation supplies to find the suitable variety—there are more than you might imagine—and follow the directions for that product. Run a bench trial before adding the agent to the whole batch of wine.

A white wine can be perfectly clear but still appear browned and oxidized—think of Spanish sherries, for instance. In most whites, even a hint of sherry character is unwelcome, and that's where two other fining agents come in.

- Potassium caseinate. Mainly used to rescue white wines harmed by oxidation, potassium caseinate is made from casein, the principal protein in milk. Dissolved in water, the powder helps reduce or remove brown pigments and oxidized aromas, and can also help clear up light hazes. Potassium caseinate tends to coagulate instantly in the acidic wine, forming curds that sink too fast to do much good, and when overused it can leave wines with a cheesy aroma. So it should be added with care, typically at a level of 0.2 to 1.0 gram per gallon (about 50 to 260 parts per million). But if you're treating a browned wine, sometimes more is warranted. Here are the steps.

clarity, note the thickness of the deposit on the bottom of each sample. The thickness should increase with the amount of fining agent until it levels off—the point at which adding more agent fails to produce more sediment. The smallest of the same-result additions is where the fining agent and protein equal each other, and that's the dose of fining agent to use.

1. Prepare a 1 percent solution by stirring 1 gram of potassium caseinate into enough distilled or deionized water to equal 100 milliliters (10 milliliters of this solution adds 0.1 gram of caseinate). Allow the solution to stand for 2 to 3 hours.

2. Run a bench trial, testing the solution in 2-milliliter increments.

3. While vigorously stirring the wine, add the caseinate solution bit by bit and continue mixing until the solution is thoroughly dispersed. Or better yet, while stirring the wine, slowly inject the solution using a large syringe and large-bore needle; or use a pipette to blow the solution down into the center of a full carboy of wine.

4. Allow the treated wine to settle for about a week, and then rack.

- PVPP. Sold under the brand name Polyclar, PVPP (polyvinylpolypyrrolidone) is a powdered synthetic polymer that is especially handy for removing brown colors from white wines. It also lessens bitterness and can be used to clarify wines, although it will noticeably lighten the color of reds. There are a few varieties of Polyclar, but the best for home use is Polyclar VT. A related product, Polyclar V, is a superfine powder that settles so slowly it requires filtering. Usual doses of Polyclar VT run from 0.5 to 2.5 grams per gallon (about 130 to 650 parts per million).

Reducing the total acidity—for balanced flavors. If the acidity of the finished wine remains too high, try one or more of these postfermentation methods. Always test the wine's total acidity before taking any new steps.

- Inoculate the wine with malolactic bacteria (see page 183), encourage the malolactic fermentation to finish, and then check for completion (see page 161). This approach has the greatest effect in wines with large amounts of malic acid.

- Chill the finished wine to near freezing to precipitate out mildly acidic potassium bitartrate.

- Blend the wine with a compatible low-acid wine.

- Add potassium bicarbonate, available at brew shops. To achieve a 0.1 percent drop in acidity, add 3.4 grams per gallon, and chill the wine to encourage potassium bitartrate to precipitate. Only tartaric acid will be lowered, so wines with high levels of malic acid may not improve, and the pH can also rise markedly. A new product called Acidex Super-K (not the same as plain Acidex, mentioned in chapter 13) contains potassium bicarbonate.

Adding sugar—for balanced flavors. If you've made a white wine that's unlikably tart, it's perfectly fine to bring its flavors into balance by sweetening it with table sugar. In fact, lots of purportedly dry white wines contain enough residual sugar to confirm the wry observation that Americans talk dry but drink sweet. The sugar levels in off-dry table wines typically run around 1 percent to 2 percent, but may go as high as 4 or 5 percent.

Because many things influence tartness—alcohol level, acid content, grape variety, residual sugar—there's no set target. That is, you can't say a Sauvignon Blanc needs this residual sugar and a Chardonnay that. You have to let your taste buds decide. That means doing a controlled tasting, setting up several samples of the newly made wine to which you then add different doses of sugar.

It doesn't take much. One gram of white sugar added to a liter of wine will raise its sugar content by 0.1 percent. In a wine already at 0.5 percent, a 0.1 percent sugar boost can be noticeable. But let's be realistic: You won't want to experiment with several whole liters of wine. Instead, use smaller samples, proportionally scaling down the grams of sugar and liters of wine. Then, when one blend stands out, scale the sugar dose back up.

It's easiest to figure these additions using decimal measures. You'll need a 10- or 20-milliliter pipette for measuring the wine and—no getting around it—an accurate gram scale so you can weigh out tenths of a gram of sugar. Start with three wine samples to which you'll add sugar, plus a fourth sample of the original wine. For simplicity's sake, make each sample exactly 100 milliliters, and add plain white granulated sugar in 0.1-gram increments. Here are the steps.

- Always start with clear, stable, healthy wine.

- Send a sample of the wine to a lab for a free sulfur dioxide test.

- Using a marking pen, label four wineglasses 0, 1, 2, and 3. Pipette 100 milliliters of wine into each.

- Weigh out and add 0.1 gram of sugar to the glass labeled 1. To glass 2 add 0.2 gram, and to glass 3 add 0.3 gram. Swirl the wine in the glasses until the sugar dissolves.

- Taste the 0.1-gram sample, carefully swirling the wine in your mouth. Spit it out—you want to stay sober—and take a sip of water. Now taste the original wine. Go down the row of glasses, trying to choose one over the others.

- If all the samples seem too tart, make new 100-milliliter samples that are sweeter, perhaps one with 0.5 gram of added sugar and another with 1.0 gram. Taste through the whole series. If you feel the sample you might like would fall between 0.5 and 1.0, set up a new series at 0.1-gram increments and taste again until you find the right addition.

- Scale up the sugar addition to grams and liters by multiplying the tenths of grams and the milliliters by 10. An addition of 0.1 gram per 100 milliliters equals 1 gram per liter.

- Multiply the grams of sugar to add per liter by 3.785, the number of liters in 1 gallon, to find the grams of sugar to add per gallon.

- Multiply the grams of sugar to add per gallon by 5, the number of gallons in one full carboy, to find the grams of sugar to add per carboy. Suppose you decided on adding 0.2 gram of sugar per 100 milliliters. Simply weigh out and add 2 grams of sugar for each liter of wine, or 2 times 3.785 for every gallon, or 38 grams per 5-gallon carboy.

- Using a wine thief, withdraw a cup or two of wine from each carboy to be adjusted and add to it the appropriate amount of sugar for the whole carboy. Pour the sweetened wine back into the carboy and stir thoroughly with a racking wand.

- Add enough sulfite to raise the level of molecular sulfur dioxide to 0.8 parts per million (see page 194).

Adding potassium sorbate—to stabilize sweet wines. Wines with upwards of 0.2 percent residual sugar can be unstable after they're bottled, possibly undergoing an unwanted new fermentation. Your wine may look beautifully clear, as if there are no drifting yeasts, but it's possible that some stragglers are in there waiting for a fresh batch of unfermented sugar. That's why it's crucial to use sulfite as prescribed, and to chill and fully clarify the wine. But those steps may not go far enough. To suppress the last yeast cells, many winemakers add a stabilizer, called potassium sorbate, available as a dry powder at brew shops. (If you see products called simply sorbate or possibly sorbic acid, they're probably potassium sorbate, which in wine yields sorbic acid.) Here's how you'd use it.

To stabilize a sweet white, add 250 parts per million (250 milligrams per liter) of potassium sorbate. That level works out to a scant 1 gram per gallon. Keep in mind that sorbate suppresses but doesn't kill yeasts and cannot stop an active fermentation. You should never add potassium sorbate to any wine that has gone through malolactic fermentation: dormant malolactic bacteria may come to life and attack the sorbic acid, producing geraniol, a compound with a disagreeable crushed-geranium odor. And be cautious if you choose to use a product called "wine conditioner," which is essentially sugar water with sorbate added. It's safer to add the sugar and sorbate separately so you control the level of each.

TANKS, PUMPS, FILTERS, AND MORE

You can of course immerse yourself more deeply in winemaking. For instance, you may want to follow the lead of many professional vintners and filter your wines. Or you may decide to start making larger batches. Federal law permits you make up to 200 gallons of wine a year, and at that scale you could end up dealing with 40 full carboys—meaning it's time, perhaps, to start contemplating stainless steel tanks and electric pumps. To move on to a more technical and intensive level of winemaking, begin with the following books; and consult the further reading list (page 237) for other books on various aspects of the subject.

Modern Winemaking, by Philip Jackisch (Ithaca, NY: Cornell University Press, 1985, 289 pages). Aimed at home vintners but highly technical, Jackisch's book covers the whole span of winemaking, from grape genetics to wine-contest judging to the chemistry of fermentation. Jackisch writes, "The main sugars in grapes are glucose and fructose, both reducing sugars; the ratio of the former to the latter at grape maturity is about 1:1 but can range from 0.7 to 1.5:1. Fructose is approximately twice as sweet as glucose and about $1^1/_2$ times as sweet as sucrose (table sugar). Small amounts of sucrose and other sugars are also present in grapes. When sucrose (a nonreducing sugar) is added to sugar-deficient grape musts, it is hydrolyzed to the two simpler sugars, glucose and fructose, aided by acids in the must or enzymes in the yeast."

Techniques in Home Winemaking: A Practical Guide to Making Château-Style Wines, by Daniel Pambianchi (Montreal: Véhicule Press, 2001, 266 pages). If you don't mind converting wine amounts from hectoliters to gallons and temperatures from Celsius to Fahrenheit, this Canadian book can help you reach the next stage. In particular, Pambianchi offers details on large fermenters and tanks and on the intricacies of filtering systems and electric wine pumps. "Pumps are classified into two general categories according to the fluid displacement method and priming requirements," Pambianchi writes. "The categories are positive displacement and centrifugal pumps. Priming refers to the process of filling a pump's cavity with the fluid to be displaced prior to the pumping operation. Pumps can be classified as unprimed or self-priming."

Winery Technology & Operations: A Handbook for Small Wineries, by Yair Margalit (San Francisco: Wine Appreciation Guild, 1990, 224 pages). Margalit, who has a PhD in physical chemistry, clearly reviews many of winemaking's tricky fine points, from divining the chemical attributes of pigments and tannins to the difficulties of must adjustment. "In a case where the TA is high enough, but the pH is too high (high potassium content)," Margalit writes, "one may consider using phosphoric acid in order to lower the pH without adding too much to the total acidity. The use of phosphoric acid is common practice in the food industry, although it is not used in the wine industry. Its use is not recommended (also illegal in the U.S. as a wine additive). It gives the must and the wine a 'watery' or low body feeling."

Suppliers and Laboratories

THE SOURCES OF SUPPLIES AND TESTING SERVICES listed here offer not only equipment, materials, and analyses, but also wide-ranging Web sites loaded with information. To find brew shops around the country, contact the Home Wine & Beer Trade Association, P.O. Box 1373, Valrico, FL 33595, 813-685-4261, or go to www.hwbta.org.

SUPPLIES, EQUIPMENT, AND GRAPES

All World Scientific (lab equipment), 5515 186th Place SW, Lynnwood, WA 98037; 800-289-6753; www.wine-testing-supplies.com.

American Wine Grape Distributors, Inc. (fresh grapes), 152 Beacham St., Everett, MA 02149; 617-387-6107; www.americanwinegrape.com.

Barrel Builders (oak barrels, services), P.O. Box 268, St. Helena, CA 94574, 707-942-4291; http://barrelbuilders.com.

Beverage People (supplies), 840 Piner Rd., #14, Santa Rosa, CA 95403; 800-544-1867; www.thebeveragepeople.com.

Brehm Vineyards (fresh and frozen grapes), P.O. Box 6239, Albany, CA 94706; 510-527-3675; www.brehmvineyards.com.

E. C. Kraus Home Wine & Beer Making Supplies, 733 S. Northern Blvd., P.O. Box 7850, Independence, MO 64054; 800-353-1906; www.eckraus.com.

Gilbert Vineyards (fresh grapes), P.O. Box 9066, Yakima, WA 98907; 509-966-2600; http://gilbertorchardsyakima.com/vineyards.

Grapestompers (supplies), 102 Thistle Meadow, Laurel Springs, NC 28644; 800-233-1505; www.grapestompers.com.

Kelvin Cooperage (oak barrels), 1103 Outer Loop, Louisville, KY 40219; 502-366-5757; www.kelvincooperage.com.

Lallemand Inc. (Lalvin brand yeasts), P.O. Box 5512, Petaluma, CA; 626-798-8747; http://consumer.lallemand.com/danstar-lalvin/lalvin.html.

Lesaffre Yeast Corporation (Red Star brand yeasts), 433 E. Michigan St., Milwaukee, WI 53202; www.lesaffreyeastcorp.com/wineyeast/products.html.

M&M Produce, Inc. (grape juices), 101 Reserve Rd., Hartford, CT 06114; 888-378-4884; www.juicegrape.com.

Napa Fermentation Supplies, 575 Third St., Bldg. A, Napa, CA 94559; 707-255-6372; www.napafermentation.com.

Oak Barrel Winecraft (supplies, grapes), 1443 San Pablo Ave., Berkeley, CA 94702; 510-849-0400; www.oakbarrel.com.

Oak Grove Vineyards (fresh grapes), 7581 W. Kile Rd., Lodi, CA 95242; 866-214-7273; www.ogvineyards.com.

Presque Isle Wine Cellars (supplies, grapes), 9440 W. Main Rd., North East, PA 16428; 814-725-1314; www.piwine.com.

Seguin Moreau (oak barrels), 151 Camino Dorado, Napa, CA 94558; 707-252-3408; www
.seguinmoreaunapa.com.

Valley Vintner (supplies, grapes), 6040 Dougherty Rd., Dublin, CA 94568; 866-812-9463;
www.valleyvintner.com.

White Labs, 7960 Niwot Rd., C-11, Longmont, CO 80503; 888-593-2785; www
.whitelabs.com.

World Cooperage (oak barrels), 2557 Napa Valley Corporate Way, Suite D, Napa, CA
94558; 707-255-5900; www.worldcooperage.com.

Wyeast Laboratories, Inc., P.O. Box 146, Odell, OR 97044; 541-354-1335; www
.wyeastlab.com.

TESTING LABS

Some of these well-respected labs also offer winemaking equipment and cellar supplies, and
their Web sites and catalogs can be enormously valuable sources of information. Always contact the lab before sending juice or wine samples for testing.

ETS Laboratories, 899 Adams St., Suite A, St. Helena, CA 94574; 707-963-4806; www
.etslabs.com. Also: 1819 N.E. Baker St., McMinnville, OR 97128; 503-472-5149; and 3020
Isaacs Ave., Walla Walla, WA 99362; 509-524-5182.

Gusmer Enterprises, 640-D Airpark Rd., Napa, CA 94558; 800-224-7903; www.thewinelab
.com; gusmerenterprises.com. Also: 81 M St., Fresno, CA 93721; 559-485-2692; 1165
Globe Ave., Mountainside, NJ 07092; 908-301-1811; and 1401 Ware St., Waupaca, WI
54981; 715-258-5525.

Lodi Winery Laboratory, 6100 E. Highway 12, Lodi, CA 95240; 209-339-1990; www .lodiwinerylaboratory.com.

New York State Wine Analytical Laboratory, New York State Agricultural and Experiment Station—Food Science Lab, 630 W. North St., Geneva, NY 14456; 315-787-2263; www.nysaes.cornell.edu/fst/faculty/henick/NYSWAL.

Scott Laboratories, Inc., P.O. Box 4559, Petaluma, CA 94955-4559; 800-821-7254; www .scottlaboratories.com.

Vinquiry, 7795 Bell Rd., Windsor, CA 95492; 707-838-6312; www.vinquiry.com. Also: 2025 Redwood Rd., Suite 9, Napa, CA 94558; 707-259-0740; and 2717 Aviation Way, Suite 100, Santa Maria, CA 93455; 805-922-6321.

Further Reading

Although it's easy to turn up home wine sites on the Internet—just type "winemakers," "winemaking," or "home winemaking" into your computer's search engine—you may well find the information in conventional printed works to be more accessible. Beyond the three "next step" references named and quoted at the end of chapter 15, the following volumes are some of the many I've referred to over the years.

American Vintage: The Rise of American Wine, by Paul Lukacs. New York: Houghton Mifflin, 2000.

The Backyard Vintner: An Enthusiast's Guide to Growing Grapes and Making Wine at Home, by Jim Law. Gloucester, MA: Quarry Books, 2005.

The Complete Handbook of Winemaking, edited by the American Wine Society. Ann Arbor: G. W. Kent, 1997.

From Vines to Wines: The Complete Guide to Growing Grapes and Making Your Own Wine, by Jeff Cox. Pownal, VT: Storey Books, 1999.

Grapes into Wine: The Art of Winemaking in America, by Philip M. Wagner. New York: Alfred A. Knopf, 1980.

Growing Wine Grapes, by J. R. McGrew, J. Loenholdt, T. Zabadal, A. Hunt, and H. Amberg. Ann Arbor: The American Wine Society, 1994.

Handmade Table Wines, by Desmond Lundy. Victoria, BC: Fermenthaus, 1986.

Home-Made Wines, by Louise Morgan. London: Hutchison, 1958.

The Home Winemaker's Companion: Secrets, Recipes, and Know-How for Making 115 Great-Tasting Wines, by Gene Spaziani and Ed Halloran. Pownal, VT: Storey Books, 2000.

Home Winemaking Step by Step: A Guide to Fermenting Wine Grapes, by Jon Iverson. Medford, OR: Stonemark Publishing, 2000.

Making Table Wine at Home, by George M. Cooke and James T. Lapsley. Davis: University of California Division of Agriculture and Natural Resources, 1988.

Northern Winework: Growing Grapes and Making Wine in Cold Climates, by Thomas A. Plocher and Robert J. Parke. San Francisco: Wine Appreciation Guild, 2003.

The Oxford Companion to Wine, edited by Jancis Robinson. 2nd ed. Oxford and New York: Oxford University Press, 1999.

Principles and Practices of Winemaking, by Roger B. Boulton, Vernon L. Singleton, Linda F. Bisson, and Ralph E. Kunkee. New York: Kluwer Academic/Plenum Publishers, 1998.

A Short History of Wine, by Rod Phillips. New York: HarperCollins, 2001.

Techniques for Chemical Analysis and Quality Monitoring during Winemaking, by Patrick Iland, Andrew Ewart, John Sitters, Andrew Markides, and Nick Bruer. Campbelltown, South Australia: Patrick Iland Wine Promotions, 2000.

Understanding Wine Technology: The Science of Wine Explained, by David Bird. San Francisco: Wine Appreciation Guild, 2001.

The Vintner's Art: How Great Wines Are Made, by Hugh Johnson and James Halliday. New York: Simon & Schuster, 1992.

The Winemaker's Guide: Essential Information for Winemaking from Grapes or Other Fruits, by F. S. Nury and K. C. Fugelsang. Fresno: Valley Publishers, 1978.

Wine Making at Home, by Maynard A. Amerine and George L. Marsh. Berkeley: Wine Publications, 1969.

Index

Italicized page numbers refer to illustrations, tables, and sidebars.

cleanliness, 24, 25
    crushing and, 40–41
    pressing and, 66–67
    sanitization, 32–34
    stirring the must and, 51
    storage of cleansers, 33, 34
    See also potassium metabisulfite
Clinitest, 166
cloudiness
    after racking, 83, 85–86, 117–18, 129
    clarification and, 118–21
    final racking and, 94
    overfining and, 213
    in white wine, 116, 133, 219
    See also clarification; fining
cofactors, 210
cofermentation, 209–11
cold soaking, 205–7, *208–9*
color
    after racking, 83, 87, 129
    cofermentation and, 209–11
    powdered tannins and, 208–9
    red wine grapes and, 139
    of red wines, 15, 204–7, 208–10
    white wine grapes and, 104, 139
    See also cloudiness
complexity, increasing, 207–8
compressed gas, 208–9

Concord grapes, *145–46*
"contract" growers, 145
corkers, 35, 97–98
corks, 97, 98, 99, 100, 130
crusher-stemmers, 4, *36*
    cleaning, 40, 125
    rental of, 35, 39–40, 107, 125
    use of, 39–40
    white wines and, 107
crushing, 37–47, 125–26
    cofermentation and, 209–11
    cold soaking and, 205–7
    pectic enzyme and, 220
    traditional methods, 3–4, 38
    white wine and, 131
    See also crusher-stemmers
crystals
    See tartrate crystals
Cynthiana grapes, *145*

Dashe Cellars, 2
Delaware grapes, *145–46*
detergents, 33
Dextrocheck, 166
diacetyl, 185, 221
diammonium phosphate (DAP), 181–83
dirty-socks odor, 75
disposable pipettes, 29

gleaning, 148–49

"going dry," 60

Grahm, Randall, 89

gram scale, 20–21, *168*

grapes

    buying, *140–42*, 143, 144–49

    cleaning before crushing, 40

    cofermentation and, 209–11

    complimentary blends of, 218

    frozen, 15–16, 211

    gauging ripeness of, 138–43

    hang-time dilemma and, 140–41

    high sugar levels in, 45, 46–47, 170–72

    hybrid varieties of, 145

    low acid levels in, 46–47

    maturity of, *136*, 138, 139–40

    quantities of, *16*

    sources of, 2, 13, 14–16, 145–49, 233–35

    target standards for, 170

    varieties of, 15, 144–45, *145–47*

    for white wine, 47, 104

    wine yield and, 148, 171

    See also specific varietals; musts

grape seeds, 139, 205

Grapes into Wine (Wagner), 119

grape-skin cap

    See cap of grape skins

gravity, 28–29, 70, 74, 85–86

green apple flavor, 70–71

gross lees, 81

    See also lees

hang-time dilemma, 140–41

haziness

    See cloudiness

home lab tests, 151–67

    for free sulfur dioxide, 200–1

    for malolactic completion, 160–65

    for pH, 159–60

    for residual sugar, 165–67

    for sugar level, 152–54, *154*

    for total acidity, 154–59

Home Wine & Beer Trade Association, 233

home winemaking

    calendar checklist, *8–9*

    containers and, 24–28

    legal concerns about, 6–7

    quantity and, *16*

    questions about, 2–4

    reasons for, 5–6

    reputation of, 1–2

    steps in, 125–33

    universality of methods, 11

    winery location and, 23–24

hydrogen sulfide, 54, 75–76, 86, 179

hydrometer, 31
    calibration of, *154*
    pressing and, 59–60
    use of, 42–43, 152–54
    See also sugar level

isinglass, 223–24

Jackisch, Philip, 230
Jefferson, Thomas, 6, 144

labels, 101, 130
laboratories, 235–36
lab testing
    for free sulfur dioxide, 198–200
    home lab tests, 151–51, 161–62
    for YAN, 181
    See also chemical tests; home lab
        tests
Lallemand (Lalvin), 178, 181, 184, 220
lees
    red wine and, 70
    white wine and, 116
    wine volume and, 75, 171
legs, 69, 84
Lukacs, Paul, 6
lysozyme, 187, 221–22

maceration
    carbonic, 211
    extended, 207–8
magnetism, 120
Making Table Wine at Home (Cooke and
    Lapsley), 175–76
malate level, 161–62
malolactic bacteria, 19, 161
    addition of, 55–56, 57, 113, 127, 132
    cultured forms of, 19, 57, 183–84
    effects of, 161–62, 183–84
    freelance, 105, 116
    lees and, 70
    total acidity and, 226
malolactic fermentation, 70–72, 117, 128
    benefits of, 184–85
    discouraging, 187
    halting, 220–22
    pinprick bubbles and, 83, 85
    red wine and, 184–85
    sensory signals of end of, 161
    split-batch approach and, 104, 220–21
    stuck fermentation, 78–79
    testing for completion of, 71–72, 160–65
    timing of inoculations and, 185–87
    white wine and, 104–5, 113, 116, 117, 133,
        220–22

pH meter, 150, 155–59, 174

pink wine, 108

Pinot Grigio, 105

Pinot Gris, 179

Pinot Noir, 206, 218

plastic containers, 25, 26, 28

Polyclar (PVPP), 226

polymerization, 204–5

polyphenols

    See tannins

potassium bicarbonate, 226–27

potassium bitartrate

    See tartrate crystals

potassium caseinate, 225–26

potassium metabisulfite, 4, 19–21

    bottling and, 94

    Campden tablets, 21

    cleanliness and, 33, 40–41

    guidelines for addition of, 20, 41, 108

    pH and, 159–60, 192–96

    red wine crushing and, 40–41, 126, 131

    red wine racking and, 72–74, 76, 86–87, 88, 128, 129

    in sulfite solution, 74, 197–98

    white wine finishing and, 121–22, 132, 133

    white wine pressing and, 107–8

    white wine racking and, 116–17

    See also sulfur dioxide

potassium sorbate, 229

pouring, 100–1

pressing, 59–67, 127–28, 131

    equipment for, 61–63

    pectic enzyme and, 220

    process of, 61–65

    red wines and, 59–67

    second, 64–65

    tannins and, 205

    when to start, 59–60

    white wines and, 108–9

press wine vs. free-run wine, 127

primary fermentation, 49–57, 126–27

    container for, 25

    duration of, 56

    end of, 59–60, 115

    foam and, 51–52

    malolactic bacteria and, 55–56

    punching down and, 9, 48, 52–54

    slowing of, 127

    starting, 51–52

    stuck fermentation, 76–78

    sweetness and, 77, 105–6

    temperature during, 53–54, 55–56, 111–12, 113, 127

    white wine and, 111–12, 113, 130–32

    yeast feeding during, 54–55

    See also musts; yeasts

containers for, 25–28
of sodium hydroxide, 155
of sulfite solution, 197
of yeasts, 179
See also bottling
stuck fermentation, 56, 76–78
sugar level
addition of sugar, 121, 174–76, 227–29
correction guidelines, 44–45, *45*, 170–72
dilution and, 45
formulas for sugar addition, 175–76
grape ripeness and, 138
hang-time dilemma and, 140–41
measurement of, 31, 42–43, *54, 114*, 126,
127, 131, 132, 152–54, *154*
residual sweetness, 105–6, 110, 227–29
stuck fermentation and, 77
white wine and, 109–10, 116, 132, 133–34
See also hydrometer; residual sugar
"sulfide stink," 54, 191
sulfite
See potassium metabisulfite; sulfur
dioxide
sulfite solution, 74, 197–98
sulfur dioxide, 19–21, 87
adjustment of, 193–96
benefits of, 190
cold soaking and, 206
forms of, 190–92
sulfite solution, 73, 197–98
testing for, 198–201
tips for minimizing, *198–99*
See also potassium metabisulfite
Superfood, 55, 112–13, 181–82
suppliers, 233–35
swirl-and-sniff test
See sniff test

TA
See total acidity
tannins
adjustments and, 87, 205–7, 208–10
grape ripeness and, 140
maceration and, 207
powdered, 208–9
pressing and, 64
tartaric acid, *18, 87*, 173–74
tartrate crystals
buildup of, 87–88
precipitation of, 118, 129, 133, 226
tasting, 139
extended maceration and, 208
malolactic fermentation and, 71–72
oak flavor, 129
at pressing, 63
at racking, 82–85

DESIGNER: *Victoria Kuskowski*   ILLUSTRATOR: *Mary Sievert*   INDEXER: *Marcia Carlson*

TEXT: *10.5/17 Chaparral MM Regular*   DISPLAY: *Chaparral, Gothic*

COMPOSITOR: *Integrated Composition Systems*   PRINTER AND BINDER: *Friesens Corporation*